Contents

Part Four

Group Dynamics

Part Five

Programs and Special Events

Part Six

Programs Designed for Outreach

Part Seven

Hurdles and Hindrances

Part Eight

Growing Pains

Welcome to
the Construction Site!

In my work as a writer and speaker, I have had the privilege of traveling from coast to coast participating in various ministry events. Over the years I have seen a variety of women's ministries, from thriving organizations that run like well-oiled machines to fledgling groups groping around in the dark trying to figure out what in the world to do to a huddle of five weary women who have determined to reach out to the women in their church despite little direction or support. Many, by the time they figure out what works and what doesn't, are too exhausted to do the ministry their hearts longed to do in the first place.

For those who have a thriving women's ministry in place, this manual will be like walking through a tour of homes. I hope you will see something you can incorporate into your "home" that will spruce things up a bit and bring new life to an already lovely structure.

For those who are just beginning the journey of building a women's ministry, this manual will serve as a generic blueprint. Feel free to pick and choose what will work for your church family and community. My hope is that this manual will alleviate the stress of trying to discover where to begin and help you get your creative juices flowing.

For those who have a struggling women's ministry, you may need to knock down a few walls, clean out some closets, apply a fresh coat of paint, and do some intense remodeling. Don't let change make you fearful. Our God is all about change! Take a deep breath and pray that He will show you what needs to go and what needs to stay the same.

For those who have inherited a women's ministry that is simply not meeting the needs of your church and community, you may have to begin at ground zero. My prayer is that this manual will help you avoid common pitfalls of demolition and help make reconstruction as painless as possible.

Let's grab our hard hats and get to the business of building an effective women's ministry.

PART ONE
Understanding *the Need*

*W*hen a builder constructs a house, he has two options—a "spec" house or a custom home. A "spec" (speculative) house is one in which the *builder* selects the plan, chooses the materials, and designs the interior to his liking. When the project is complete, he puts up a For Sale sign in the hope that someone will fall in love with the house, put their name on the mailbox, and take over the mortgage payments. On the other hand, a custom home is one built especially for the person or persons who will be living there. The *family* chooses a plan that will suit their specific needs, selects the materials that fit within their budget, and designs the interior with each family member in mind.

There is little to no risk in building a custom home because the family who will be living there has been involved in the process all along. However, there is great risk in a spec house. Just because the builder thinks his plan is a good one does not mean that it is. I have known builders who have gone bankrupt because they did not do the proper research to build according to a community's need, but plowed ahead with what they thought would sell.

Likewise we have two options when building a women's ministry—a spec ministry or a custom ministry. The first option is very risky and may leave women spiritually bankrupt, but the second option promises a ministry that women will be glad to call "home." Before we begin, let's answer two important questions: Why do we need women's ministry? What is the purpose of women's ministry?

∼ ∼ ∼

Why Do We Need Women's Ministry?

I was flipping through my local newspaper one day and noticed a calendar of events for the week. For the first time I perused the list to see what was happening in my fair city. Then a stark reality hit me and I began to count. In that one week, there were 146 support group meetings scheduled. There was everything from Alcoholics Anonymous to Codependents Anonymous to Recovery from Food Addiction. Then over to the side a note read, "If you're looking for a support group not listed here, call…" Once again I was struck with how desperately people need encouragement and support, and how they will go just about anywhere to get it.

Women need encouragement as never before. Because of the trends in our society, women feel isolated, disconnected, and stressed. They no longer have the family support and sense of community support prevalent just a few generations ago. Each year, 44 million people relocate. That's 20 percent of the population. We once sang, "Over the river and through the woods to Grandmother's house we go." But because we live in such a transient and mobile society, Grandmother's house, in many incidences, is no longer *over the river and through the woods*, but across several state lines. And when you get to Grandma's house, she's probably not at home, but out with her Rollerblading club, on an Alaskan cruise, or at a water aerobics class. Grandmothers today live very busy and active lives of their own.

Not only do women not have the support of family readily available as in times past, they many times do not have the support of neighbors, nor do they feel a sense of community where they live. Where we once had a welcome mat at our front door, we now have a warning sticker alerting those who approach that we have an alarm system. We've moved from welcome to warning, and many of us don't even know our neighbors right next door.

In his book *Come Before Winter and Share My Hope*, Chuck Swindoll tells of a time in America's history when men and women discovered the necessity of joining together.

> It occurred when "Go west, young man!" was the challenge of America…when squatter's rights seemed the most advantageous way to pry families loose and dare them to brave the elements via the covered wagon.
>
> So out they came, exchanging the crowded, soot-choked industrial cities back East for the open plains, clear skies, and fertile, albeit rugged, farmland of the West. Predictably, those early settlers built their cabins or sod huts smack dab in the middle of their homestead, acres (often miles) from the nearest family. Strong, sturdy fences marked property lines as pride of ownership became the badge of courage. Words, like independence and private property, were common table talk as the young were taught how to fight for survival.
>
> But as time passed all that began to change. When photographers returned from those lonely houses, they showed pictures of wild-eyed women, stooped, gaunt, prematurely old men, and haunted-looking children. Life was hard making it on their own, especially through the bitter winters, fighting off disease and starvation.
>
> More and more settlers learned that they had a better chance of making it if they would build their houses near

each other, in the corner of their property rather than in the center. Four families could survive much easier if they loosened their grip on independence, built a gate in their fence, and relinquished their overstated emphasis on privacy. Enduring winter's blast or a lengthy illness wasn't nearly so frightful if you had three other families within walking distance. It proved to be much more fun coming together instead of living lonely, separate, touch-me-not lives of isolation...

Those old settlers learned what we seem to have forgotten today: pulling closer together is better than existing so far apart. Sharing is still to be preferred to staying aloof. The risks and periodic hassles notwithstanding, four in the corner are better than one in the middle.[1]

Never before in the history of man do people have such ready access to others. We have e-mail, instant messaging, call-waiting, call forwarding, caller ID, and call return. We clip on beepers, tote cell phones, and even wear headphones so as not to miss a single call while driving or working. And yet women feel more isolated and alone than ever before. It seems we've forgotten to put the gates in the fences around our hearts and opted for independence over community. The result has been devastating.

I think this inborn need to know others and be known is the pull of such TV programs as *The Oprah Winfrey Show.* Many people spend five hours a week with Oprah when they may not spend five minutes getting to know the person right next door. The person next door may be more interesting, but getting to know your neighbor is a lot of work, and TV is easy.

Women today lead very different lives from the homemakers of the '60s. Almost 70 percent of Christian women work outside the home, either full-time or part-time. Forty percent of those have preschoolers, and 36 percent are single.[2] Today's woman is being pulled in several directions at the same time and typically feels guilty that she is letting someone down—that someone or something is not getting the proper amount of her attention.

At the dawn of the feminist movement, Helen Reddy sang, "I am woman, hear me roar in numbers too big to ignore." However, today's woman would be more likely to resonate with the bumper sticker that reads "I am woman. I am invincible. I am tired."

This cultural pull on women to do it all and have it all—all at the same time—is causing insurmountable stress. We can all agree that stress haunts every woman to some degree. Yet how she deals with that stress varies. "It is estimated that seventy percent of all physician office visits are for stress-related illnesses."[3] "It is not the stress in itself that damages us, but unrelenting stress...It is our failure to regularly retreat from the front lines that creates trouble."[4]

Throughout Scripture we see how God placed women together in relationships to encourage one another and provide a place of retreat. Just as God sent Mary to Elizabeth and Ruth to Naomi, He continues to place women together for mutual support, accountability, and friendship. That's why we need women's ministry in our churches today. Women are the very heartbeat of the home, community, and church, and many are in desperate need of resuscitation!

I remember what I read once about the draw of the local bar:

> The neighborhood bar is possibly the best counterfeit there is to the fellowship Christ wants to give His church. It's an imitation, dispensing liquor instead of grace, escape rather than reality, but it is a permissive, accepting, and inclusive fellowship. It is unshockable. It is democratic. You can tell people secrets and they usually don't tell others or even want to. The bar flourished not because most people are alcoholics, but because God has put into the human heart the desire to know and be known, to love and be loved, and so many seek a counterfeit at the price of a few beers.[5]

We can do better than the neighborhood bar! Jesus has what people are truly longing for. Many can't define the longing or who put it there. We know—and we have a privilege of telling them!

Bill Hybels, author of *Courageous Leadership*, notes:

> There is nothing like the local church when it's working right. Its beauty is indescribable. Its power is breathtaking. Its potential is unlimited. It comforts the grieving and heals the broken in the context of community. It builds bridges to seekers and offers truth to the confused. It provides resources for those in need and opens its arms to the forgotten, the downtrodden, the disillusioned. It breaks the chains of addictions, frees the oppressed, and offers belonging to the marginalized of this world. Whatever the capacity for human suffering, the church has a greater capacity for healing and wholeness.[6]

As women ministering to other women, we offer an "indescribable beauty" of our own. To borrow from Hybels' words, God's power working through us is breathtaking, God's potential working in us is unlimited, and God's love spilling over from us knows no bounds.

What Is the Purpose of Women's Ministry?

*I*n Hebrews 12:1 Paul encourages us, "Let us run with perseverance the race marked out for us." We, as Christian women, are running the great race of life. As a mother, I have watched the power of encouragement at sporting events of every sort. I've watched runners quicken their pace when they heard a word of cheer. I've seen a fallen youngster rise up and continue toward the goal when coaxed by the crowd. I've witnessed runners slacken when opposing teams' fans hurled insults.

Let me share a story from my book *Being a Great Mom, Raising Great Kids:*

> My nephew Stu began running on his school cross-country team when he was in the eighth grade. Since we lived 200 miles from his home, I didn't get to watch him run at his meets. However, I heard that the main attraction at Stu's races was not the runners, but his enthusiastic mother.
>
> Finally, when Stu was a senior in high school, his team came to my hometown for a state competition. I don't know if you have ever been to a cross-country race, but it is not exactly a spectator sport. Runners line up on the starting mark. Someone fires a gun for the race to begin. The participants disappear

down a trail in the woods, and then they reappear some 16 minutes later.

Before the race my family stood on the sidelines, watching legs stretch, backs bend, and arms swing in an effort to warm up. Seventy anxious young men clustered around the starting line in ready position. The shot was fired into the air and the herd of boys began their 3.1 mile jaunt through the woods. As soon as Stu's foot left the starting position, his mother, Pat, picked up her 36-inch megaphone and began to yell louder than any woman I have ever heard.

"GO, STU!" she cheered, not once but at ten-second intervals. When he was out of sight, she ran to another strategic spot along the winding trail where the runners would eventually pass by. And even though the boys were nowhere in sight, Pat continued to cheer, "GO, STU!"

"Pat, do you have to yell so loud?" my husband asked.

"Yep," she answered. "GO, STU!"

Steve inched his way a few paces behind us and pretended as though he had no idea who we were.

"GO, STU!"

I'll admit, it was a little embarrassing. She had no shame.

At one point she yelled, "GO, STU!" and a man from across the park yelled, "HE CAN'T HEEEAAARRR YOOOUUU!"

"Pat, Stu can't hear you when he's deep in the woods. Why don't you let up a bit?" I asked.

"I don't know whether he can hear me or not, but if there's a chance that he can, I want him to hear my voice cheering him on," she answered. So for 16 minutes this little dynamo continued to pump confidence and inspiration into her son's heart.

Later, I asked my nephew, "Stu, when you are running on a trail in the woods, can you hear your mother cheering for you?"

"Oh, yes," he answered. "I can hear her the whole way."

"And what does that do for you?"

"It makes me not want to quit. When my legs and lungs ache, when I feel like I'm going to throw up, I hear my mom's voice cheering for me and it makes me not want to stop."

A few years later, my son became a cross-country runner and I learned a few facts about a foot race. As you near the end of a race, your throat burns, your legs ache, and your whole body cries out for you to stop. That's when friends and fans are the most valuable. Their encouragement helps you push through the pain to the finish.[1]

As women in women's ministry, that's what we can do for each other. We can help each other run the race of life with endurance by offering a word of cheer, a cool drink to a thirsty soul, coaching tips for running well, and stretching exercises for those who are just getting started.

A Pastor's Thoughts on Women's Ministry

Why do we need women's ministry and what is its purpose? My pastor, John Sittema, wrote the following to our congregation:

Women's ministry in any Bible-believing church is increasingly important in today's world. That's true not only to provide connection points, Bible studies, and service opportunities, but especially because ministry by women to women is one of the most critical ways in which the Lord's church can break into the lives of unsaved people in our culture. My own recent history as a senior pastor convinced me that a dynamic, outward-looking, and fresh women's ministry is absolutely essential to the broader kingdom impact of the church's life. Those years of my experience also convinced me, to my shame, that I had spent far too little time encouraging and empowering women for just that sort of ministry.

Allow me to tell you of a single week I had in ministry about a year and a half ago. It began on a Monday, usually my day off.

I received a call from a woman in the church. She asked for an appointment to discuss with me the years of physical abuse she had endured from her husband, and to ask my counsel on what to do. When I asked her why she waited so long to talk with me, she looked at me with a blank stare and said, "You're a man."

That evening, in a separate pastoral visit, another woman admitted that she had been sexually abused throughout her childhood, but she had never been free to discuss it with anyone because "everyone who could have done anything about it was a man, and I don't trust men."

Then, on Tuesday, a 19-year-old woman walked into the office, and in the space of ten minutes told my receptionist/secretary (a young Christian) that:

1. She had "an exotic dancer" for three years but had recently been under conviction that stripping was sinful.

2. She wanted "out" of the life, but she didn't know how to break free physically, emotionally, or sexually.

3. She needed a place to stay for a few months with a female roommate.

4. She had "been in a church once," and felt good there, and wondered if anything in the Bible was about women.

5. She wanted to talk to somebody about some horrible things she had done, but she didn't want to talk to a man.

My secretary took her into her home (for a year!). During that year the elders and I realized again and again how woefully unprepared we were for such ministry, both because we did not understand the grip of the evil one on many young women in our culture, and because we were men, and young women in our culture couldn't trust us because they had never known a man they could trust.

Fact is, we had a women's ministry. But it was the ministry model that had been developed many decades earlier in the denomination in which I was then serving, a model that presupposed healthy families and stay-at-home moms. And that model for ministry really was unprepared, as well, for the needs of women God was bringing into our church. Almost all of them worked full-time. Most of them came from broken homes or had been raised in broken families. A large percentage of them had a history of some sort of abuse in their backgrounds.

Our church, by God's wonderful providence, has reached many of "today's women" in recent years. Fully one half of the women in the congregation now work outside the home. A growing number have unique spiritual needs brought about by backgrounds of abuse, family breakdown, or marital failure. And many are very young in the faith...[2]

Dr. Sittema went on to explain a new initiative to build a dynamic women's ministry. What a wise man to see that women have specific needs that are best understood and addressed by other women.

Women love beautiful jewels. Rubies, diamonds, and emeralds are precious and hard to find. But I propose that a true encourager is much more valuable, sought after, and beautiful than these. Do you desire to be a treasure? Invest in someone's life. Do you desire to be remembered? Do something memorable to build up another person. Do you desire to have fulfilled dreams? Help others fulfill their dreams. Do you desire to have blazing passion for Christ in your life? Fan the smoldering embers of someone's spiritual life and watch the flames ignite.

Is it easy? Does building a women's ministry happen without hard work and sacrifice? Not on your life. Chuck Swindoll said it well,

It takes courage, tough-minded courage, to trust God, to believe in ourselves, and to reach a hand to others. But what a beautiful way to live. I know of no one more needed, more valuable, more Christlike than the person who is committed to encouragement. In spite of others' actions. Regardless of others' attitudes. It is the musical watchword that takes the grind out of living—encouragement.[3]

What is the purpose of women's ministry? In my own life, I have adopted Colossians 2:2-3 as my personal purpose statement, and I believe it is the purpose for women's ministry as well: "My purpose is that they may be encouraged in heart and united in love, so that they may have the full riches of complete understanding, in order that they may know the mystery of God, namely, Christ, in whom are hidden all the treasures of wisdom and knowledge."

—— PART TWO ——
Where Do We Begin?

*W*hether you are building a cozy bungalow or a stately mansion, the preliminary steps remain the same. Likewise, whether you are building a women's ministry for a church of 100 members or for a church of 10,000 members, the preliminary steps remain the same. Before we pick up the hammer and nails and begin construction, let's take a look at a few of the essentials that apply to building a women's ministry of any size, shape, or dimension.

Prayer

Paving the Way

One of the first building blocks of an effective women's ministry is prayer. Wise King David reminds us: "Unless the LORD builds the house, its builders labor in vain" (Psalm 127:1). Pastor David Ruff once said, "Efficiency is doing things right. Effectiveness is doing the right things." When we begin with prayer, we are asking God to show us "right things" to do.

As women, we can prepare perfect plans, dish out delicious dinners, and roll out radical retreats—all with balanced budgets and divine decorations. In a word, we can be efficient and have teams working like well-oiled machines. Yet, while there is nothing wrong with efficiency, it is not the ultimate goal. The ultimate goal is effectiveness—impacting the women in our churches to take the next step toward the heart of God. The only way we can be effective is to join God where He is working, rather than depending on our own abilities.

I am often reminded of Peter and Andrew, who fished all night but caught nothing. Then Jesus came by the next morning and said to them, "Put out into deep water, and let down the nets for a catch." Peter answered that they had worked hard all night and hadn't caught anything. "But because you say so, I will let down the nets" (Luke 5:4-5). When Peter listened and followed Jesus' instructions, he caught so many fish the nets began to break. We can work very hard and still be ineffective. However, when we pray and ask Jesus where to throw the nets, where to place our energy, our nets will be full.

Nehemiah was a man who knew the importance of prayer—not in building a ministry, but in rebuilding a wall. He was called to a seemingly impossible task—to rebuild the walls of Jerusalem, which had been shattered by brutal enemies. In a war against Israel, the walls of Jerusalem had been broken down and destroyed, leaving the Israelites defenseless against further attack. The city stood naked and vulnerable to wild animals, relentless foes, and jeering nations. When Nehemiah heard about the condition of his homeland, he wept, mourned, fasted, and prayed (Nehemiah 1:4). He felt called to return to Jerusalem and head up the rebuilding of the wall.

This daunting job had seemed so big that no one was even willing to begin...until Nehemiah. Under his guidance the walls were restored in a mere 52 days. How did he do it? He began with prayer (Nehemiah 1:5-11), continued with prayer (Nehemiah 2:4; 4:9; 6:9), and ended with prayer (Nehemiah 9:5-38). In between, he presented his plan to the correct authorities, surveyed what needed to be done, collected his supplies, rallied the volunteers, and kept the workers motivated. Come to think of it, Nehemiah gives us a wonderful example of not only how to build a wall, but how to build a ministry.

You may already have a group of women who have a passion for women's ministry. If not, pray that God will stir the hearts of women to get involved. Once you have a core group for the "construction crew," begin by setting apart time to pray for direction.

Can you imagine a brick house built without mortar? Think what would happen if a builder began stacking bricks one on top of another but omitted the mortar that holds them together. It would quickly fall apart.

As you begin to see the foundation laid, the walls go up, and the windows set in place, remember that it is the mortar that holds it all together. Likewise, prayer will be the mortar that holds your women's ministry together.

> *Dear Lord, thank You that You have called me to join You in ministering to women. I know that I cannot do this on my own. Just as Moses prayed, Lord, if You do not go with me, then I do not want to go (Exodus 33:15). I commit to wait on You. Help me to not run ahead nor lag behind, but walk in tandem with You. Help me to see clearly, to love deeply, and to choose wisely.*
>
> *As we begin, help us to be more concerned with people than with programs, more concerned with effectiveness than with efficiency, and more concerned with loving rather than learning.*
>
> *I am available to You. My desire is to bring honor and glory to Your name and not to my own. Please remove any selfish ambition or personal agendas, and help me to keep my ear pressed to Your heart. Lord, I want to accomplish Your goals. I want to have Your vision for ministry. Help me be a woman who listens to You and radically obeys. In Jesus' name, amen.*

Mission Statement
Defining Your Purpose

*W*henever I walk into a lumberyard, my mind races back to my childhood days of playing in the warehouse of my daddy's lumber company in Rocky Mount, North Carolina. I can still smell the freshly cut timbers in the millwork shop and see the mounds of saw-dust piled under imposing band saws.

On Saturdays I'd ride around town with my dad while he inspected various construction sites. I loved to run up and down skeletal stairwells in partially built homes, but I disliked it when he spent what seemed like hours inspecting new construction where only the foundation was complete.

"Sharon," he would say, "the foundation is the most important part of a house. If the foundation isn't built just right, the walls can shift later, jeopardizing the integrity of the entire structure."

Defining your purpose statement or mission statement is the foundation to beginning a women's ministry or remodeling an exist-ing ministry. What are you trying to accomplish? What do you hope to achieve? What is the bull's-eye of your target? Beginning a women's ministry without a purpose statement would be like a builder placing piles of cement, bricks, lumber, shingles, nails, floor-ing, insulation, wiring, and various hardware in a yard and telling the workers to get busy building a house. All the right materials might be there, but the workers would not know what to do. Some would start building a ranch house while others might begin on a Tudor home. Then before you know it, everyone is arguing.

If you've ever built a house or had a house built, you know the importance of a blueprint. So let's begin by marking out those first lines.

Mission Statement

A mission statement encapsulates in a few words or sentences the purpose of your women's ministry. It answers the question: "Why are we doing what we are doing?" A mission statement will be different for different churches, depending on your denomination and your church's individual focus. However, it should always clearly define your goals, purpose, and direction. It is a short, concise, compact declaration of what you hope to accomplish.

A mission statement should be an extension of your church's mission statement and not appear as a separate "mini church" within the church. The question to ask is, How can we, as women, uniquely fulfill our church's mission statement and help fulfill its purpose?

Jesus has a mission statement: "I have come that [you] might have life to the full" (John 10:10). Even Satan has a mission statement: "The thief comes only to kill and steal and destroy" (John 10:10). The disciple John wrote of another mission statement of Christ: "The reason the Son of God appeared was to destroy the devil's work" (1 John 3:8). Jesus gave Paul a mission statement: "I am sending you to them [the Gentiles] to open their eyes and turn them from darkness to light, and from the power of Satan to God, so that they may receive forgiveness of sins and a place among those who are sanctified by faith in me" (Acts 26:17-18).

A mission statement is something that can be repeated and memorized easily. It should state clearly and succinctly who you are and what you do. For example, the Disney World "mission statement" is "Fun, Family, Entertainment." Nike's "mission statement" is "Authentic Athletic Performance." Borrowing from the corporate world, our mission statement should describe our purpose in a manner easily repeatable and understandable.

A women's ministry cannot be all things to all people. A mission statement helps you set up goals for what you can do just as much as it may set boundaries for what you cannot do. Bill Hybels, pastor of Willow Creek in Chicago, once said, "Nothing neutralizes the redemptive potential of a church faster than trying to be all things to all people."[1]

While a mission statement or purpose statement is the compass for the women's ministry, it should be reevaluated from time to time and revised as the needs and direction of the ministry changes. For example, for many years Proverbs 31 Ministries' mission statement was "touching women's hearts, building godly homes." However, in 2004 we looked at our mission statement again and decided that the ministry had outgrown it. Therefore, we adopted a new mission statement: "Bringing God's peace, perspective, and purpose to today's busy woman."

Here are some examples of mission statements from various women's ministries:

- ∾ The purpose of our women's ministry is to provide opportunities, equipping, and encouragement for all the women of Perimeter Church to grow toward maturity in Christ through worship, study, service, fellowship, and evangelism.

- ∾ Women's ministries is committed to equipping women to know God and to glorify Him in our home, church, community, and the world.

- ∾ Our women's ministry exists to extend the transforming presence of Jesus Christ to women in all life seasons and is committed to their growth through prayer, Bible study, discipleship, and outreach.

- ∾ Our mission is to provide a safe place for women to meet God and make friends.

- ❧ Our focus is to create opportunities for women to come to know Jesus Christ, to be mentored in their Christian life, and to provide a place for women to connect and cultivate Christian friendships.

- ❧ We are a community of women, grounded in God's Word and living out the teachings of Jesus by reaching out to unchurched women, by influencing the next generation of young women, and by serving those in need with hearts of compassion.

The following is an example of an ineffective mission statement:

- ❧ Keeping Christ above all things, the ministry to women at First Church seeks to draw women to God through solid biblical teaching from Scripture in order to grow women to maturity. The overflow of this will result in our exaltation of Jesus Christ as we worship together, our deep and sincere abiding love for one another as we live in community, our desire to reach out to the lost as we extend our hands to those in our sphere of influence, and our effective use of spiritual gifts as we edify the entire body of Christ.

Is it clear?

Can it be memorized easily?

Does it explain the purpose succinctly?

Can it be conveyed to others easily?

Dan Southerland, author of *Transitioning: Leading Your Church Through Change* and founder of Church Transitions, Inc., helps churches make changes that will enable them to reach their communities for Christ. One of the most important changes is establishing their mission statement. While teaching a transitions conference, Dan was approached by one of the attending pastors who wanted Dan to approve the page-long mission statement of his church. Dan took one glance and handed it back to the man.

"It's not any good."

"You didn't even read it!" the man exclaimed.

"Nope. That's the point. Neither will anyone else."

Dan went on to explain that the mission statement was much too long, and he showed the man how to make it more concise and succinct.

Brainstorming Exercise for Developing a Mission Statement

Brainstorming is a wonderful exercise for developing a mission statement. In this section we will look at how to conduct a brainstorming session, and this process can be used for many other decisions you will make along the way. Brainstorming provides a safe environment in which everyone is encouraged to participate and share their ideas. Every idea is viable because even a mediocre idea can be the fuel to ignite a brilliant idea! Thomas Edison said, "In order to have a good idea, have lots of them." Let's walk through the process step-by-step.

Dear God

1. Begin with prayer.

> *Dear Lord, we come humbly before You today asking that You give us wisdom and discernment. We put all of our agendas aside and pray for Your direction. We pray that the words that come out of our mouths will not be an overflow of past disappointment but an overflow of future joy. Lord, help us to see how we can effectively fulfill the purpose of our church, creating a new spoke for the wheel rather than another wheel.*
>
> *Anoint us with grace, love, and unity of spirit. Help us to add value to the church and to the women who worship here.*
>
> *In Jesus' name, amen.*

2. Select a facilitator to lead the discussion, record ideas, and keep the group on track.

3. Record ideas on a whiteboard or large flip chart.

4. Involve as many participants as possible.

5. State the rules of the exercise.

   ◦ No idea is a bad idea.

   ◦ All ideas will be recorded and accepted.

   ◦ There will be no negative comments about anyone's ideas.

   ◦ Accept repeated ideas.

   ◦ Think outside the "church" box.

   ◦ Understand that one idea spurs another.

6. Write the following question at the top of the board or page: "What are the needs of the women in our church and community?" Then begin recording the women's answers. This is what you might see:

encouragement	maturing	fellowship
mentoring	Bible study	a place to use their gift
equipping	in-depth teaching	leadership development
fun	beginner Bible study	prayer
relaxation	discipleship	recreation
community	connectedness	a place to serve
friends	working women	widows
mothers	support	a place to be loved

7. The facilitator should offer encouraging words such as "great idea," "wonderful," "you're on to something."

8. As you can see, some ideas will be very similar. That's fine. Record them anyway. Now look and see if you see any "categories" or grouping of needs. Go back and place markings by ones that are similar.

*encouragement	!maturing	*fellowship
!mentoring	+Bible study	!a place to use their gift
!equipping	+in-depth teaching	!leadership development
*fun	+beginner Bible study	+prayer
*relaxation	+discipleship	*recreation
*community	*connectedness	a place to serve
*friends	working women	widows
mothers	*support	*a place to be loved

9. Look to see if there are common themes. In this scenario, there seems to be a need for encouragement, equipping, Bible study, and fun. Do not exclude the need for recreation among the women of your church and community just because it doesn't sound spiritual. God created us body, soul (mind, will, emotions), and spirit. Our ministry may be aimed at providing refreshment for all three.

10. Now you are ready to come up with your mission statement. Think big picture when you decide on a mission statement. Later, as various programs are developed, they will have purpose statements of their own. For example, a women's ministry mission statement may be to "Encourage and Equip Women with Biblical Principles." Under this large umbrella, a ministry for young mothers may be more specific: "To give mothers a place of refreshment, rest, rejuvenation, and renewal by equipping them with motherhood skills and embracing their need for support from other mothers."

11. While developing a mission statement can be very exciting, make it a policy to evaluate it every year. State from the very beginning that the mission statement is not set in stone but malleable to the changing needs of the women you seek to serve.

12. Finally, take the mission statement before the leadership of the church (the pastor or the elder or deacon who is over women's ministries) for final approval.

Conducting a Survey

Another way to determine the needs of the women in your church is to do a survey. In order to ensure maximum participation, the survey must be simple to complete and easy to return. If you require the women to find an envelope, address an envelope, place a stamp on the envelope, and mail the envelope, you will see very few envelopes in your mailbox. The following are some survey tips:

1. Create a survey that has simple questions that can be answered with a check mark.

2. Make it attractive and eye-catching.

3. Have lists of options to choose from instead of having to think up answers to open-ended questions. (Would you prefer to meet at night or morning? Would you like to see in-depth Bible studies such as Precepts or Beth Moore, or Bible studies that require approximately one hour of homework a week? Would you go on a retreat for the weekend if one was offered? On which of the following committees would you be willing to serve: (have a list of needs).

4. Make survey retrieval easy:

    ∾ Place surveys in the bulletin and have a drop box in the lobby.

- ∾ Place surveys in the women's bathrooms and note where the drop box is located.

- ∾ Place a survey on the weekly e-mail, if your church has one.

- ∾ Pass surveys out in Sunday school, to the choir, and to nursery workers and give them a few minutes to complete them. Then collect them before you leave.

5. People, in general, don't jump at the chance to complete a survey. Consider giving women a small gift for filling out and returning the survey.

Sample Survey

Thank you for taking the time to complete this survey. Your opinions and needs are very important to us. The women's ministry team desires to custom build a women's ministry that encourages and equips you to be all that God has created you to be!

My greatest need right now is
- ❏ Fellowship with people in my own life stage
- ❏ Introductory Bible study
- ❏ Fellowship with people of all ages
- ❏ In-depth Bible study

I would like to see the following programs offered
- ❏ Daytime Bible studies
- ❏ Short Bible studies
- ❏ In-depth Bible studies
- ❏ Studies on marriage
- ❏ Studies on raising children
- ❏ Classes on home organization
- ❏ Classes on how to study the Bible
- ❏ Classes on financial management
- ❏ Classes on balance and priorities
- ❏ Classes on prayer
- ❏ Other_____
  _____

The best time for me to attend a weekly class is
- ❏ Weekday morning
- ❏ Weekday evening
- ❏ Saturday morning
- ❏ Sunday evening

I am interested in reaching out to the community by
- ❏ Volunteering on a regular basis for a few hours a week
- ❏ Volunteering for a one-time project

I have the following skills and would like to offer my services to teach or assist the women's ministry
- ❏ Speaking
- ❏ Teaching
- ❏ Decorating
- ❏ Drama
- ❏ Scrapbooking
- ❏ Graphic design
- ❏ Other _____
- ❏ Gardening
- ❏ Painting
- ❏ Time management
- ❏ Creative writing
- ❏ Parenting
- ❏ Photography
- ❏ Marriage
- ❏ Self-defense
- ❏ Depression
- ❏ Health issues
- ❏ Computer skills
- ❏ Newsletter development

I work outside the home and would like to know more about
- ❏ Witnessing at work
- ❏ Leading a Bible study for working women
- ❏ Balancing home and career
- ❏ Other_____

I am interested in teaching or leading
- ❏ A morning Bible study
- ❏ An evening Bible study
- ❏ Sunday school
- ❏ A special event
- ❏ Working with preschoolers
- ❏ Working with elementary-age children
- ❏ Working with teens
- ❏ Mentoring young mothers
- ❏ Working with senior citizens

Marital status
- ❏ Single
- ❏ Married
- ❏ Divorced
- ❏ Widowed

Age of children_____

I currently attend
- ❏ A Bible study (which one) _____
- ❏ Church regularly (which service)_____
- ❏ Sunday school regularly (which one)_____

I work outside the home
- ❏ Part-time
- ❏ Full-time

Would you participate in a women's retreat weekend?
- ❏ Yes
- ❏ No

  If no, why not?_____

Were you active in women's ministry this past year?
- ❏ Yes
- ❏ No

  If no, why not?_____

Name: _____Age_____
Address:_____
City/State/Zip code_____
Phone Number: Home_____Cell_____
E-mail address_____

5

℘rogram Options
Devising Your Plan

$\mathcal{A}$fter the mission statement (the foundation) has been developed, you are ready to start framing the house. But first, let's take a look at the floor plan. Let's suppose a builder decides he wants to build a home just like the one he grew up in 50 years ago. He liked the A-frame structure, the shag carpet, and the avocado-colored appliances in the kitchen lined with rust-colored counter tops—so that is what he decides to build.

"Hey, Bob," a fellow builder calls out. "What project are you getting ready to start?"

"Hi, Bud," Bob replies as he pulls out the worn dog-eared blueprint from the compartment of his truck. "This is my new project. This is what I'm getting ready to build."

Bud looks at the blueprint and doesn't quite know what to say. Finally, he clears his throat. "Did someone ask you to build this house, or is this a spec house you're going to build and hope someone will buy."

"This is a spec house," Bob replies. "I'm going to invest my own time and money, and I'm sure someone will snatch it up."

"Bob, this looks like something from the '60s. No one's going to buy this house."

"But I like it. This is what my mom had and what I feel comfortable with."

"What do you want?" Bud argues. "Do you want to build what you want or do you want to build a house someone will actually want to invest in and call a home?"

Programs Are for People vs. People Are for Programs

I think we can all agree that women and their needs have changed over the past 50 years. Therefore, in order to have an effective women's ministry, we cannot simply duplicate what has gone before. Fifty years ago, the church was a center for social and spiritual activity. When the church had a program, the women simply showed up...because that's just what church ladies did.

In the new model, women need a good reason to attend. The days of "if you build it, they will come" are gone. The women of the new millennium are extremely busy with a plethora of choices and decisions facing them every day. This new woman weighs all the opportunities available to her very carefully. She can get her perceived need for community and fellowship met at any number of places: the gym, book clubs, school activities, children's extracurricular events, tennis clubs, golf clubs, community service projects, and so on.

Another consideration is women in the workplace. In 1980, about 50 percent of married women with children worked outside the home. That number rose to 70 percent in 1999. Single mothers followed a similar trend with 52 percent working outside the home in 1980 and 73 percent working outside the home in 1999.[1] The U.S. Department of Labor shows that 77.9 percent of those women care for 6- to 17-year-olds and 64.8 percent care for children younger than six years old.[2] These numbers cannot be ignored when planning programs to meet the needs of the women in your church and community.

Today's busy woman asks several questions before committing to an activity. "Is this going to be worth my while?" "Is this going to meet my need for…?" "Is this going to change my life or add to the quality of my life?" "Is this activity going to be a place where I can have an impact or make an eternal difference, or is it simply a program to pass the time?"

In the old model, very little attention was given to being culturally relevant. While the old model boasted of reaching out to nonbelievers in the community in a hope to bring them to Christ, it did very little to pay attention to what would draw them. In the new model, the leaders listen, learn, and adapt. The new model reaches out in words and ways that women understand, loving unconditionally without wanting something in return, welcoming women rather than keeping a record of attendees, and offering a safe place for friendship and authenticity. While we are going to take a look at programs, please keep in mind that an effective women's ministry is people focused, not program focused. Know your women and understand their needs.

Take a moment to consider the following questions:

- What is the makeup of the women in our church?
- Whom are we trying to reach?
- What are their needs?
- Are our current programs meeting the needs of the women in our church?
- What is a program I would want to attend?
- When are the women available?
- Do they work outside the home?
- Who is not attending women's events and why?
- What are our women's greatest needs?
- What have we done in the past that is no longer effective?
- What are needs in the community in general and how can the church help meet them?

Small Groups, Big Rewards

Women love meeting in small groups. Years ago it was quilting bees and canning sessions. Today it is book clubs and exercise groups. As you consider the smorgasbord of program possibilities, keep in mind that while large events spawn life change, small groups *nurture* life change.

Jesus is pictured in the New Testament as the founder and leader of one of the most effective small groups of all time. He chose 12 men with whom He became intimately involved as a teacher and friend. When Jesus began His public ministry, one of the first things He did was establish a small group. It wasn't that He needed assistance or companionship. However, He chose to minister in the framework of interpersonal relationships to model effective ministry. Jesus could have easily remained aloof from any human relationships. Yet He chose to spend time caring for, healing, listening, teaching, discipling, and encouraging people. Jesus chose ordinary, uneducated men and trained them to become the leaders who would be responsible for spreading the gospel to the entire world (John 17:20).

Small groups provide an atmosphere of acceptance and accountability. I love how Luke described the first century church: "Every day they continued to meet together in the temple courts. They broke bread in their homes and ate together with glad and sincere hearts, praising God and enjoying the favor of all the people. And the Lord added to their number daily those who were being saved" (Acts 3:46-47).

Later in the book you will read about Bible studies and various other small groups. You will also learn about group dynamics for the leaders and coleaders.

Types of Programs

Just as the kitchen serves a different purpose than the family room, and the bathroom serves a different purpose than the bedroom, each program will serve a different purpose for accomplishing your mission. As you develop programs, continually ask the question: "Does this program fit within our ministry mission statement?"

Below is a partial list of program possibilities:

Programs That Bring Spiritual Growth

- ∾ Bible studies for beginners
- ∾ In-depth Bible studies
- ∾ Working women's lunchtime Bible studies
- ∾ Neighborhood Bible studies
- ∾ Short-term Bible studies
- ∾ Topical seminars (how to study the Bible, how to pray, etc.)
- ∾ Prayer groups

Programs That Nurture

- ∾ Mentoring programs
- ∾ Widows support group
- ∾ MOPS
- ∾ Mornings for Mothers Bible studies
- ∾ Divorce recovery
- ∾ Working women's evening breaks
- ∾ Unpacking the boxes for newcomers
- ∾ Weight-loss programs
- ∾ Exercise groups
- ∾ Infertility groups
- ∾ Circles
- ∾ Prayer

Programs That Reach Out

- ∾ Teatime with cooking, decorating, fashion show, brief devotional speaker
- ∾ Christmas dinner
- ∾ Spring tea
- ∾ Supper seminar
- ∾ Home improvement seminar
- ∾ Home management or home organization
- ∾ Dinner/speaker events
- ∾ Neighborhood Christmas tea
- ∾ Scrapbooking night
- ∾ Twentysomething event
- ∾ Twentysomething Bible study
- ∾ Prison ministry
- ∾ Missions projects
- ∾ Unwed mothers outreach

Programs That Revive

- ∾ Women's retreat
- ∾ Quarterly outreach dinner with a guest speaker
- ∾ Monthly outreach dinner with a guest speaker
- ∾ Leadership training seminar
- ∾ Girls' night out (movie in the gym with popcorn, bowling party, board game night, etc.)*

---

* Further in the manual, we will take a closer look at some of these programs and how they work.

After you have considered various program possibilities, begin praying for a program/ministry chair and a program/ministry cochair. These need to be women who have a passion for the particular mission and target audience of the program. For example, there might be a woman who feels called by God to minister to young mothers. There might be a woman who feels called to community outreach through dinners. There might be a woman in the workplace who feels called to provide a Bible study to women who work outside the home.

Programs are much like flowers. Some are annuals and some are perennials. Each summer I plant annuals such as periwinkle, impatiens, and begonias. They are beautiful and serve their purpose...for a season. But also in my garden are perennials that come back year after year. These perennials have deep roots and are strong enough to resist the cold of winter. Each year I love to watch them burst through the soil and grow into a beautiful display. After several years, the perennials grow so large they must be separated so they can continue to expand. What began as one plant multiplies into three.

Some programs will be like annuals. They are for a specific time to serve a specific purpose. When the program has accomplished its purpose, don't be afraid to bring it to an end. Celebrate all that God has done and move on.

Then there are programs that will be more like perennials. Year after year they seem to grow and flourish. These programs have staying power for many reasons, one of which is that they are meeting an ongoing need in the church and community.

Reevaluate your programs each year and see which ones have completed their mission and which ones will continue on.

6

$\mathcal{B}$udget $\mathcal{P}$reparation
Counting the Cost

$\mathcal{E}$very good builder counts the costs before beginning a project. Likewise, before you begin to build your women's ministry, you need to set up a budget and make sure the church has sufficient funds to complete the project. Not all programs will have a dollar amount attached to them. For example, Bible studies may incur no cost to the church, unless the church provides child care and Bible study materials. Retreats, quarterly dinners, and other special events will have a cost attached to them. It is best to set up a budget and projected costs for such events. This will help the women's ministry team determine if a certain project is feasible. Below are some sample budgets:

Sample Women's Ministry Budget

Women's dinners (three per year)

Speaker honorarium	$500 x 3	$1500
Gifts for door prizes	$100 x 3	$ 300
Table decorations	$700 x 3	$2100
Linens	$500 x 3	$1500
Sound and lights	$240 x 3	$ 720
Appreciation gifts		$ 340
Meals for servers	$5 x 20 x 3	$ 300
Total		**$6760**

Retreat

Publicity (including postage)	$ 350
Retreat materials (handouts, speaker packets)	$ 500
Coffeehouse and free time activities	$ 250
Registration expenses (name tags, phone calls)	$ 250
Deposit for next year's retreat	$ 500
Speaker fee	$1500
Creative (music dramas, sound, photos, videos)	$ 150
Speaker's room, food, travel	$ 500
Planning retreat and team meeting costs	$ 100
Total	**$4100**

Women's Ministry Kick-off Dinner

Linens	$300
Table decorations	$200
Communications	$100
Speaker gift	$100
Total	**$700**

Small Group Bible Studies

Miscellaneous needs	$1200
Total	**$1200**

Women's Ministry Expenses

AOL, phone line, lunches, etc.	$1000
Total	**$1000**

Appreciation

End of the year dinner	$1000
Gifts for ministry leaders	$1000
Total	**$2000**

Travel/Conferences/Training

Leadership conference (two team members)	$2500
Leadership retreat	$1000
Leadership network	$1500
Seminars for leaders	$2000
Material for training	$1000
Total	**$8000**

Total Women's Ministry Budget Request	**$23,760**

Child Care Considerations
Remembering Little People

One of the best ways to encourage a mother of young children is to give her a break from mothering. However, a mother will not be able to feel relaxed enough to enjoy fellowship unless she knows her children are cared for. Child care is often the biggest challenge for any women's ministry. The reason I have included it in this section is because your child care decisions may affect your budget. Below are some suggestions that have been useful in other small groups:

- The best-case scenario is for the church to cover the cost of child care. However, this may be cost prohibitive in many churches.

- Present child care as a missions opportunity to the church leaders.

- Take up an offering at the end of a women's event to help cover the cost of child care. There may be some older women who remember the strains of motherhood who would like to give as an encouragement to young moms.

- Hire child care workers and pay them out of a special offering that is taken up each week. Consider $3.50 for the first child and $1.50 for the second to be collected at the beginning of each month.

- ❧ Some churches require child care workers to go through a training program before taking care of children. This ensures the safety of the child. You may want to ask the church if there is such a class and gather your child care workers from there. You could advertise for helpers in the church bulletin.

- ❧ Consider posting the need for babysitters on a college bulletin board.

- ❧ One rule of thumb: Never leave children with one adult. Always have at least two present. This ensures the safety of the children if one has to leave for an emergency and reduces liability risks.

- ❧ Consider rotating one mother with one paid child care worker.

- ❧ If there are two or more small groups meeting in your church at the same time, consider trading child care duties with them on alternate weeks.

- ❧ Rotate child care duties with the mothers in the group. Have two mothers take care of the children each week. It is best if a mother has to serve only once a quarter.

- ❧ Invite grandmothers in your church to participate in encouraging young mothers by taking care of the children during the meeting time. Perhaps your group could host a Christmas party for the grandmothers and mothers to enjoy some time together.

- ❧ Inquire about homeschooling families in your area. Older homeschool children would love to earn some extra money, volunteer in a ministry, or even earn some "home economics" school credits. Many areas have homeschool newsletters in which you could advertise.

- ❧ It is very important that each member with children call ahead of time if they will not be attending. The babysitters expect to be paid whether children are there or not. You would not want to waste money on a sitter who is not needed.

- Recruit fathers to work with the children during special nighttime events.
- To ensure that you have quality sitters, you should always check at least two references.

Child Care Guidelines

To ensure against misunderstanding, present each parent with child care guidelines. The following are some suggested guidelines:

- Please do not bring a child who has a contagious illness such as chicken pox, measles, pinkeye, or the flu.
- Please do not bring a child who has a fever or a runny nose that is not clear mucus.
- Please do not bring a child who has fever, diarrhea, vomiting, a cold, or flu symptoms.
- Please do bring extra diapers, wipes, and a change of clothes.
- Please do bring a prepared bottle, if needed.
- Each child must be picked up by _____ (time).
- Each child must be picked up by the person who brought him or her unless previous arrangements have been made.

₱roposal ₱resentation

Obtaining Approval from Church Leadership

*O*nce you have developed your mission statement, sketched out proposed programs, and calculated a proposed budget, the next step is to present your women's ministry initiative to your church's decision makers. This may be a pastor, church council, a group of elders, a budget committee, the deacons, etc. Just as the mission statement is the foundation, prayer is the mortar that holds the structure together, and the programs are the various rooms, the church leadership is the roof or covering of the house. Everything you do will be under their authority, leadership, and protection.

All through the Bible we see that God's plan for human interaction involves leadership and submission to that leadership.

> Everyone must submit himself to the governing authorities, for there is no authority except that which God has established. The authorities that exist have been established by God. Consequently, he who rebels against the authority is rebelling against what God has instituted, and those who do so will bring judgment on themselves (Romans 13:1-2).

> Obey your leaders and submit to their authority. They keep watch over you as men who must give an account. Obey

them so that their work will be a joy, not a burden, for that would be of no advantage to you (Hebrews 13:17).

God is a God of order, and when we step out from under His protective umbrella of that order, we may jeopardize the ministry that He has entrusted to us.

Presentation to Male Leadership

If you are working with male leadership, Diane Passno, executive vice president of Focus on the Family, reminds us that "men just relate better to a feminine woman than a woman who is trying to act like a man in order to be accepted."[1] We, as women, bring many assets to the table.

> A woman in leadership needs to rely on those traits that God built into the genetic code of our gender. We have wonderful verbal abilities—use those to garner enthusiasm for what the Lord has called you to do. We were created as "helpmates"—use that ability to come alongside the men in your congregation to help make your church a fantastic place to be. We are able to put feet to vision—use that to carry out the vision of your pastoral staff.[2]

In my book *Becoming the Woman of His Dreams,* I discuss the difference in communication styles between men and women. Talking is something that just comes natural to us girls. Research makes it clear that little girls are more verbal than little boys. Dr. James Dobson notes, "God may have given her [the wife] fifty thousand words per day and her husband only twenty-five thousand. He comes home from work with 24,975 used up and merely grunts his way through the evening. He may descend into Monday-night football while his wife is dying to expend her remaining twenty-five thousand words. That means, when your husband comes home from work, he is most likely running low in the words department."[3]

When it comes to understanding how a man's mind works in the words department, reading the newspaper is an effective exercise. A trained newspaper reporter will give the article a catchy title, and then he or she will list the important facts of the article in the first few sentences. If you are intrigued, you'll read more. If not, you've got the gist of the situation in the first paragraph and that may be enough. Bingo. That's how the male mind wants to receive information. First get his attention...Give him a title. (I need to talk to you about our son's wrecking the car last night.) Give him the main points. (He drove your car, exceeded the speed limit by 20 miles per hour, and hit a fence.) Then, move along to the other paragraphs of interest, such as ramifications and emotions. (I am furious and think we should take the keys away from him for a month, make him pay for the damages, and insist he take the driver's safety class for the next four Saturdays.)

The same communication method applies when working with men in ministry. Give the main idea first, elaborate where needed, and address the emotional ramifications at the end.

Author Pam Farrel explains that men are like waffles and women are like spaghetti. Men process life in boxes, one issue at a time. Women process life as though it were a big plate of spaghetti. "Every thought and issue is connected to every other thought and issue in some way...If you attempted to follow one noodle around the plate, you would intersect a lot of other noodles, and you might even switch to another noodle seamlessly."[4]

Because men tend to compartmentalize, or deal with one issue at a time, it is important that we stick to the issue at hand and verbalize the presentation in an orderly and concise manner.

Presentation to Female Leadership

What if you are presenting your women's ministry proposal to women in leadership or to a female pastor? There are many churches with female pastors or directors, and while it may be easier to relate woman to woman, we must remember to respect their leadership role and not simply come to them as a peer. One danger is to forget that the women serving in leadership are in leadership over the church body—and over you. While it is easy to see a female leader as a sister in Christ, remember to give her the respect that is due someone serving the church in a leadership position.

Presentation Protocol

Below are some points to remember when presenting a proposed women's ministry plan to church leadership:

1. Make an appointment with the appropriate decision makers.

2. Know and follow the proper protocol for such meetings.

3. Present the need in a concise manner and avoid unnecessary details.

4. Show how the mission statement of the women's ministry works in tandem with the mission statement of the church.

5. Avoid becoming overly emotional if you are presenting the proposal to men. Remain on the point.

6. Present a female point of view. You may want to use Pastor's Sittema's letter found in chapter 2.

7. Present the committee's plan for meeting those needs and the hoped-for outcome.

8. Be brief and to the point.

9. Avoid bringing up failures of past attempts.

10. Avoid criticism of current policies or programs.

11. Show the trickle-down effect of how well-equipped women will be more effective at ministering in other areas of the church body.

12. Explain that the young women the church invests in today will become the church leaders and workers of tomorrow.

13. Listen respectfully to their comments.

14. Be prepared to answer questions.

15. Select a designated spokesperson to represent a unified women's ministry committee.

16. Explain the goals for the coming year and how you plan to measure success.

After the presentation, thank the church leadership for their time and let them know that you are excited about working with them to accomplish the church's mission statement…to impact the world for Christ.

PART THREE

Leadership Development

*H*ave you ever considered that Jesus did not put out a sign-up sheet when it came to choosing His leadership team? Rather, He spent a night in prayer (Luke 6:12) before He carefully invited 12 of His disciples to join Him in ministry. After the team was assembled, He spent the next three years modeling servant leadership, teaching spiritual principles, and equipping the team for service. He encouraged them when they were down, corrected them when they failed, and cheered for them when they did well. While Jesus invited, inspired, instructed, invested, interceded, and imparted responsibility, He also called the team away for times of quiet and rest. I am sure one of His greatest joys was to pass the final baton at His ascension and watch His disciples change the world.

There are many wonderful books available on the topic of leadership. In *Leaders: Strategies for Taking Charge*, Warren Bennis and Burt Nanus report that they discovered over 850 different definitions of leadership.[1] However, my favorite definition was penned by Henry and Richard Blackaby: "Spiritual leadership is moving people on to God's agenda."[2] That is my heart's cry, and I pray that it is yours as well.

In this section we will focus on the most amazing, extraordinarily effective leader of all time—Jesus Christ.

❧   ❧   ❧

Servant Leadership
Understanding the Model

*I*f you had to choose the type of leadership Jesus exemplified, would you say He was a boss, army general, team captain, law enforcement officer, or shepherd? Throughout Scripture, Jesus is referred to as our Shepherd. This is not a flashy position, but one of humble service. This is the type of leadership style we want to convey to those on our team. Someone once said, "You teach what you know, but you reproduce what you are." As we gather women to serve in women's ministry, they will be watching more *how* we lead than listening to *what* we teach. Paul wrote to young Timothy, "Let no one look down on your youthfulness, but rather in speech, conduct, love, faith and purity, show yourself an *example* to those who believe" (1 Timothy 4:12, emphasis added).

The apostle Peter gives us some insightful directives on how we are to lead:

> Be shepherds of God's flock that is under your care, serving as overseers—not because you must, but because you are willing, as God wants you to be; not greedy for money, but eager to serve; not lording it over those entrusted to you, but being examples to the flock (1 Peter 5:2-3).

A women's ministry leader is one who desires to serve Christ for the purpose of equipping and encouraging women. She is a servant leader who strives to guide and not drive her team members. Jesus set an example of how we are to serve:

> The evening meal was being served, and the devil had already prompted Judas Iscariot, son of Simon, to betray Jesus. Jesus knew that the Father had put all things under his power, and that he had come from God and was returning to God; so he got up from the meal, took off his outer clothing, and wrapped a towel around his waist. After that, he poured water into a basin and began to wash his disciples' feet, drying them with the towel that was wrapped around him.
>
> He came to Simon Peter, who said to him, "Lord, are you going to wash my feet?"
>
> Jesus replied, "You do not realize now what I am doing, but later you will understand."
>
> "No," said Peter, "you shall never wash my feet."
>
> Jesus answered, "Unless I wash you, you have no part with me."
>
> "Then, Lord," Simon Peter replied, "not just my feet but my hands and my head as well!"
>
> Jesus answered, "A person who has had a bath needs only to wash his feet; his whole body is clean. And you are clean, though not every one of you." For he knew who was going to betray him, and that was why he said not every one was clean.
>
> When he had finished washing their feet, he put on his clothes and returned to his place. "Do you understand what I have done for you?" he asked them. "You call me 'Teacher' and 'Lord,' and rightly so, for that is what I am. Now that I, your Lord and Teacher, have washed your feet, you also should wash one another's feet. I have set you an example that you should do as I have done for you. I tell you the truth, no servant is greater than his master, nor is a messenger greater than the one who sent him. Now that

you know these things, you will be blessed if you do them" (John 13:2-17).

Paul taught about the humility of Jesus in Philippians 2:5-7:

Your attitude should be the same as that of Christ Jesus: Who being in very nature God, did not consider equality with God something to be grasped, but made himself nothing, taking the very nature of a servant, being made in human likeness.

An effective women's ministry leader is one who is not ashamed to put the towel of servanthood around her waist and serve the ladies on her team. Whenever God did a mighty work in the Bible, He inaugurated a leader to join Him. He chose people like Moses, Esther, Abraham, Nehemiah, and David. And now He may be choosing you! Below are some evidences of a servant leader:

- ∾ Serves at an event rather than being served

- ∾ Enjoys giving other people credit for a job well done

- ∾ Promotes others

- ∾ Fills in at events when there is a gap

- ∾ Does what needs to be done at the last minute

- ∾ Is God-centered vs. self-centered
  (One of the distinguishing characteristics of a servant leader is that she is God-centered and others-centered rather than self-centered. She seeks to promote the group as a whole and not just her area of the ministry. She guides rather than drives others, and she has a servant leadership style, which is influential in nature, rather than authoritative.)

A servant leader understands we are serving God and those within our sphere of influence. Paul wrote, "Serve wholeheartedly, as if you were serving the Lord, not men, because you know that the

Lord will reward everyone for whatever good he does" (Ephesians 6:7-8).

My dictionary defines the word "lead" as "to show [someone] the way to go by accompanying him." A servant leader doesn't simply point the way; she takes her charge by the hand and walks along life's path side by side.

Spiritual Gifts

Utilizing God-Given Abilities

*O*nce upon a time, a group of animals decided they should do something meaningful to meet the problems of the new world. So they organized a school.

They adopted an activity curriculum of running, climbing, swimming, and flying. To make it easier to administer the curriculum, all the animals took all the subjects.

The duck was excellent in swimming; in fact, better than his instructor, but he made only passing grades in flying, and was very poor in running. Since he was slow in running, he had to drop swimming and stay after school to practice running. This caused his web feet to be badly worn, so that he was only average in swimming. But average was quite acceptable, so nobody worried about that—except the duck.

The rabbit started at the top of his class in running, but developed a nervous twitch in his leg muscles because of so much makeup work in swimming.

The squirrel was excellent in climbing, but he encountered constant frustration in flying class because his teacher made him start from the ground up instead of from the treetop down. He developed charley horses from overexertion, and so he only got a C in climbing and a D in running.

The eagle was a problem child and was severely disciplined for being a nonconformist. In climbing classes he beat all the others to the top of the tree, but insisted on using his own way to get there...[1]

Of course, this is just a make-believe tale, but it is also a great example of the fact that God has created each of us with unique gifts, talents, and abilities. When we, like the animals, spend time focusing on what we are not, instead of what we are, we will be wasting valuable time and resources. Rabbits don't fly. Eagles don't climb. Ducks don't run...at least, not very well.

Paul wrote to the church in Rome, "Just as each of us has one body with many members, and these members do not all have the same function, so in Christ we who are many form one body, and each member belongs to all the others. We have different gifts, according to the grace given us" (Romans 12:4-6). When each person on the women's ministry team operates in her spiritual gift, the body of Christ moves as one in effectiveness, as well as efficiency.

There are three major passages in the Bible that describe spiritual gifts: Romans 12:6-8; 1 Corinthians 12:4-31; and Ephesians 4:11-13. The following list is a summary of the gifts and a brief description:

Preaching (Prophecy): The ability to publicly communicate God's Word in an inspired way that convinces unbelievers and both challenges and comforts believers.

Evangelism: The ability to communicate the Good News of Jesus Christ to unbelievers in a positive, nonthreatening way. The ability to sense opportunities to share Christ and lead people to respond with faith.

Missions: The ability to adapt to a culture in order to reach unbelievers and help believers from that culture.

Apostles: The ability to start new churches and oversee their development.

Teaching: The ability to educate God's people by clearly explaining and applying the Bible in a way that causes them to learn. The ability to equip and train other believers for ministry.

Encouragement (Exhortation): The ability to motivate God's people to apply and act on biblical principles, especially when they are discouraged or wavering in their faith. The ability to bring out the best in others and challenge them to develop their potential.

Wisdom: The ability to distinguish right from wrong, truth from error, and to give an immediate evaluation based on God's Word. The ability to discern whether the source of an experience is Satan, self, or God's Spirit.

Knowledge: The ability to discover, collect, analyze, and organize information vital to individual believers or the entire church family. The ability to comprehend a large amount of information and provide it when needed for effective decision making.

Service: The ability to recognize unmet needs in the church family and take the initiative to provide practical assistance quickly, cheerfully, and without a need for recognition.

Hospitality: The ability to make others, especially strangers, feel warmly welcome, accepted, and comfortable in the church family. The ability to coordinate factors that promote fellowship.

Pastoring (Shepherding): The ability to care for the spiritual needs of a group of believers and equip them for ministry. The ability to nurture a small group in spiritual growth and assume responsibility for their welfare.

Giving: The ability to generously contribute material resources or money beyond the ten percent tithe so that the body of Christ may grow and be strengthened. The ability to earn and manage money so it may be given to support the ministry of others.

Music: The ability to celebrate God's presence through music, either vocal or instrumental, and lead the church family in worship.

Intercession: The ability to pray for the needs of others in the church family over extended periods of time on a regular basis. The ability to persist in prayer and not be discouraged until the answer arrives.

Healing: The ability to pray in faith specifically for people who need physical, emotional, or spiritual healing and see God answer. The ability to sense when God is prompting you to pray this kind of prayer.

Miracles: The ability to pray in faith specifically for God's supernatural intervention into an impossible situation and see God answer. The ability to sense when God is prompting you to pray this kind of prayer.

Praying with My Spirit (Tongues/Interpretation): The ability to pray in a language understood only by God or one who is given the gift of interpretation at that time.

Leadership: The ability to clarify and communicate the purpose and direction (vision) of a ministry in a way that attracts others to get involved. The ability to motivate others by example to work together in accomplishing a ministry goal.

Administration (Organization): The ability to recognize the gifts of others and recruit them to a ministry. The ability to organize and manage people, resources, and time for effective ministry. The ability to coordinate many details and execute the plans of leadership.

Faith: The ability to trust God for what cannot be seen and to act on His promise, regardless of what the circumstances indicate. The willingness to risk failure in pursuit of a God-given vision, expecting God to handle the obstacles.

Mercy: The ability to detect hurt and empathize with those who are suffering in the church family. The ability to provide compassionate and cheerful support to those experiencing distress, crisis, or pain.[2]

God has given each one of His children spiritual gifts to edify or build up the body of Christ—the church. "There are different kinds of gifts, but the same Spirit. There are different kinds of service, but the same Lord. There are different kinds of working, but the same God works all of them in all men" (1 Corinthians 12:4-6). Consider the spiritual gifts of each woman involved in women's ministry. They will be happier and more fulfilled when they work in an area that fits how God has wired them to function in the body of Christ.

In the appendix you will find resources available for discovering spiritual gifts. Once someone has discovered her particular spiritual gift or gifts, it will help her understand how God has created her for service and the most effective area in which she can serve.

Before we leave this section on spiritual gifts, let me share one more story...

> Someone has imagined the carpenter's tools holding a conference. Brother Hammer presided. Several suggested he leave the meeting because he was too noisy. Replied the Hammer, "If I have to leave this shop, Brother Screw must go also. You have to turn him around again and again to get him to accomplish anything."
>
> Brother Screw then spoke up. "If you wish, I will leave. But Brother Plane must leave too. All his work is on the surface. His efforts have no depth."

To this Brother Plane responded, "Brother Rule will also have to withdraw, for he is always measuring folks as though he were the only one who is right."

Brother Rule then complained against Brother Sandpaper, "You ought to leave too because you're so rough and always rubbing people the wrong way."

In the midst of all this discussion, in walked the Carpenter of Nazareth. He had arrived to start His day's work. Putting on His apron, He went to the bench to make a pulpit from which to proclaim the gospel. He employed the hammer, screw, plane, rule, sandpaper, and all the other tools. After the day's work when the pulpit was finished, Brother Saw arose and remarked, "Brethren, I observe that all of us are workers together with the Lord."

God is a God of variety. In nature, what a diversity of animals! Every snowflake is different, every fingerprint, every face. Likewise, God is a God of variety in His church. What a diversity of gifts He has bestowed on believers to equip them for service![3]

The Call to Leadership
Developing the Team

*A*fter the church leadership has given the approval to begin your women's ministry, it is time to begin putting your team together. Just as a thermostat sets the temperature of a home, the leadership team sets the tone for women's ministry. Rest assured—most team leaders feel somewhat inadequate for the job. The apostle Paul felt inadequate for the job set before him. However, he learned a great truth: "When I am weak, then I am strong" (2 Corinthians 12:10). He also said, "I can do everything through [Christ] who gives me strength" (Philippians 4:13). If we begin to think we are qualified to serve God on our own power, abilities, and strengths, we are setting ourselves up for failure.

It might be a good exercise to look back at the reign of King Saul recorded in 1 Samuel 8–15. God allowed the people of Israel to have a king. They chose Saul because he was tall, dark, and handsome...a head taller than the rest. In the beginning, Saul was totally dependent on God. Then one day he decided that being a king wasn't so difficult after all. He took his reign into his own hands and began serving as king on his own terms, in his own way, in his own strength. That was the beginning of the end for King Saul's reign.

God used men like Gideon (Judges 6:11-40), Moses (Exodus 3–4), and Paul (2 Corinthians 12:9), who felt fearful and inferior in

73

their own abilities, to change the world. For these men, the secret to their "success" was total dependence on God. That can be the secret to your success as well. Paul said, "But we have this treasure in jars of clay to show that this all-surpassing power is from God and not from us" (2 Corinthians 4:7).

The disciples were a group of very ordinary men whom God used to change the course of history. And yet they were so terrified at Jesus' arrest and crucifixion that they ran in all directions and went into hiding. However, something happened to them after Jesus' resurrection. Those cowards became courageous. What made the difference in the Peter we see in Mark 14, who denied he even knew Jesus three times, and the Peter we see in Acts 2, who preached such a powerful sermon that 3000 came to faith? He had received the power of the Holy Spirit—the same Holy Spirit that is given to every believer the moment they say "I believe."

Listen to this boldness when Peter was confronted by the rulers who had put him in jail:

> Then Peter, filled with the Holy Spirit, said to them: "Rulers and elders of the people! If we are being called to account today for an act of kindness shown to a cripple and are asked how he was healed, then know this, you and all the people of Israel: It is by the name of Jesus Christ of Nazareth, whom you crucified but whom God raised from the dead, that this man stands before you healed. He is 'the stone you builders rejected, which has become the capstone.' Salvation is found in no one else, for there is no other name under heaven given to men by which we must be saved" (Acts 4:8-12).

Pretty bold, I'd say. How did those who heard Peter respond?

> When they saw the courage of Peter and John and realized that they were *unschooled, ordinary men,* they were astonished and they took note that *these men had been with Jesus* (Acts 4:13, emphasis added).

I don't know about you, but that gives me goose bumps! This verse echoes a desire in my heart, that others will see me and realize that I am an unschooled, ordinary woman…but then take note that I have been with Jesus.

A women's ministry leader is a woman who desires to be all God has created her to be and realizes that she can only do that by the power of the Holy Spirit working in and through her. She is not a woman who knows all the answers, but she knows the One who does and is willing to lead others to Him. The following are qualities to look for in developing a leadership team member:

- Has a personal and intimate relationship with Jesus Christ

- Is a member of the church

- Works well with other people

- Shows a team spirit

- Is sensitive to the thoughts and feelings of others

- Is able to handle quirks and idiosyncrasies of others

- Is innovative and not afraid to think outside the box

- Finishes what she begins

- Serves as salt and light in the world

- Puts the needs of others before those of herself

- Listens well

- Depends on prayer

- Is organized

- Knows when to delegate

- Is not afraid to reveal her weakness and personal struggles to others

- Practices servant leadership

- Is more interested in people than programs

- ∾ Is faithful, available, and teachable

- ∾ Takes great comfort in knowing that God doesn't call the qualified—He qualifies the called

- ∾ Believes 1 Thessalonians 5:24: "The one who calls you is faithful and he will do it."

Looking for Leaders

Bill Hybels, pastor of Willow Creek Community Church in Chicago, looks for three C's in choosing a leadership team: character, competence, and chemistry...in that order. With character being the most important of the three, he looks for honesty, teachability, humility, reliability, healthy work ethic, and willingness to be entreated. The most important aspect of character is that the person must be committed to the spiritual disciplines and have a personal relationship with Jesus Christ. Why does Hybels put character above competence? "I have learned in church work that an occasional lapse in *competence* can be accepted. But lapses in *character* create problems with far-reaching implications. A breakdown in character tends to breed distrust and alienate team members."[1]

Let's take a look at the three guidelines of character, competence, and chemistry, along with three others—calling, commitment, and capacity.

Character

Character is the fiber inside a person that governs how they will act and react in certain situations. A person of strong character is patient and humble. This person is not looking for her own glory or trying to get attention. This person wants to deeply grow and improve, does not look to blame others, understands her own weaknesses and personality propensities, and is able to say, "I'm sorry. I handled that poorly."

Character can be seen by observing the following:

- ✑ *Family:* How does the person treat her spouse and children? Does she honor, value, and verbally appreciate her family? What a person does with her family is what she will do with her church. Family is a testing ground for effective leadership.

- ✑ *Priorities:* Does this woman have her priorities in proper perspective? God, husband, children, etc.?

- ✑ *Speech Patterns:* Speech is the microphone of the heart. Is the person slow to speak and quick to hear (James 1:19)? Observe how she talks about others. This is the way she will talk about you and the church when you are not around. Look for loyalty. Watch out for cynicism or a critical spirit.

- ✑ *Appearance:* Appearance is not a register of social classification, as in the world, but it may tell us what the person thinks about herself and how life is viewed. A leader should dress modestly, as she is being watched as an example.

- ✑ *Conduct with Others:* Does the person work well with a team? Is she submissive to authority?

- ✑ *Spiritual Disciplines:* Does the person study God's Word and pray on a regular basis?

The progress of any organization, whether it be the home, business, or ministry, highly depends on those who are in charge. If there are leaks in the roof, the entire structure is in jeopardy.

Competence

After character, Hybels looks for someone with the highest level of competence he can find. For example, if this were the model we were following as a women's ministry director, we would look for the best Bible teacher we could find to lead the Bible studies, the best organizer to head up the women's retreat, and the most hospitable woman to head up the welcoming committee. (Remember, character is always above giftedness.) In my work at Proverbs 31 Ministries, we have seen that the most competent person for a job may not be the best person for the job. There is much to be said for a willing, teachable spirit. On the flip side, if we put someone on a team or make them a leader when they do not have the gifts or talents to finish the task, we are setting someone up for failure. In that case, everyone loses. The question that needs to be asked is, Is this person capable of completing this task with excellence? If the answer is no, don't set her or your team up for failure.

Chemistry

Thirdly, Hybels looks at "chemistry." This can also be seen as compatibility. This may seem a bit difficult for some leaders to admit, but remember, this is one model among many. After working with many groups in many various situations, I believe that chemistry is a viable consideration. Hybels says, "I don't know how to say this diplomatically, but it helps if I really like being with those people! So if two job candidates have equal character and competence, I'll give the nod to the person whose personality and temperament blends with the other team members and with me."[2]

We have all been in work situations and seen how the wheels of progress slow down or come to a complete stop when there is tension on a leadership team. A healthy amount of tension is good. God has not created us all with the same temperaments, personalities, and gifts. But it is helpful if the team has the type of chemistry that honors each other's differences and utilizes each other's strengths.

Now, let's take a look at three other Cs: calling, commitment, and capacity.

Calling

There are some days when I question why I am working in women's ministry. On days nothing seems to be going right, I cry out, "Okay, God, will You remind me why am I doing all this in the first place?" Then I hear that still small voice, "Because I called you."

At times, knowing that you are called by God is the only thing you have to cling to. A calling can be described as a burning desire in your heart that is ignited by God Himself. It has nothing to do with your own goals or whether or not Aunt Betty thinks you would be really good at it.

I suspect that if you have picked up this book, God has already called you to women's ministry. I suspect He has already ignited the flame in your heart and is now fanning the embers into a full blaze!

If you begin to question your calling, pray and ask God to reaffirm. Consider the following:

1. Have you prayed and fasted about your calling?

2. Have you done everything God has called you to do?

3. Is He not telling you the next step because He is still waiting for you to do what He has already asked you to do?

4. Have you been quiet before the Lord?

5. Have you completely yielded yourself to God?

When looking for leaders, look for women who know that God has called them to ministry rather than those who simply think it would be a good idea.

Commitment

I remember when I first decided to work with Proverbs 31 Ministries as a volunteer. At the time I had no idea what God had in store for me or for the ministry. However, I committed to one year of service in the radio arm. When the tapes would break, the recording machinery would not work right, or interviews with various guests would mysteriously disappear, I questioned whether I was to continue. However, I clung to the fact that I had committed for a year, and I knew that God would not have me break my "covenant agreement."

Now I see all the mishaps as Satan's way to try to make me want to quit. I think of all the blessings I would have missed had I caved in to the trials. When gathering the leadership team, look for women who have a strong sense of commitment. Once you have asked someone to join you on a ministry team, I suggest asking them to commit to serving a certain amount of time. It may be a one-year commitment or a two-year commitment. Many suggest a two-year commitment so that the first year they are learning under someone's tutelage and the second year someone is learning under their tutelage. If she is not willing to commit, then she might not be the right person for the job.

Capacity

For women, this is a big question. Does this person have the time to invest in women's ministry? If she is a stay-at-home mom who homeschools five children, she most likely does not have the time or emotional stamina to head up a large arm of the program. If a woman is struggling with a health issue that zaps her energy, she probably does not have the capacity to be in leadership.

When choosing leaders, make sure the "want to" and the "can do" match up. Encourage those who are not at a life stage that lends itself to giving large chunks of time to volunteer for bite-sized tasks.

Spotting Leaders

Sometimes it is not always easy to know who will be a great leader and who will not. One way to find out is by simply observing the women in your church. Who tends to take the lead when a need arises? Who mobilizes women into action? Who is willing to jump in and help when there is a gap? Who seems to participate as an overflow of love and hope for the future?

On the flip side, who tends to cause dissention? Who tends to have their own agenda? Who tends to hamper unity because she always wants to get her way instead of working as a team player? Who seems to participate in an overflow of past hurt or criticism of the way things have been done in the past?

If you are unsure about someone's leadership abilities, give her a small job and see how she handles it. If she thinks she is "above" a certain job, that is cause for concern. If someone does a small job well, then she may be ready to take on a larger job. We see this principle in Jesus' parable of the landowner:

> Again, it will be like a man going on a journey, who called his servants and entrusted his property to them. To one he gave five talents of money, to another two talents, and to another one talent, each according to his ability. Then he went on his journey. The man who had received the five talents went at once and put his money to work and gained five more. So also, the one with the two talents gained two more. But the man who had received the one talent went off, dug a hole in the ground and hid his master's money.
>
> After a long time the master of those servants returned and settled accounts with them. The man who had received the five talents brought the other five. "Master," he said, "you entrusted me with five talents. See, I have gained five more."
>
> His master replied, *"Well done, good and faithful servant! You have been faithful with a few things; I will put you in charge of many things.* Come and share your master's happiness!"
>
> The man with the two talents also came. "Master," he said, "you entrusted me with two talents; see, I have gained two more."
>
> His master replied, *"Well done, good and faithful servant! You have been faithful with a few things; I will put you in charge of many things.* Come and share your master's happiness!" (Matthew 25:14-23, emphasis added).

Give a potential leader responsibility and see how she handles it. If she does well, then entrust her with more.

Dismissing a Leader

Sometimes you think you've got all the right ingredients for a fantastic team, and then you realize there is one ingredient causing trouble in the mix. Dismissing someone from the leadership team can be a difficult task. If at all possible, try to work with a woman who is causing tension to make sure you have set her up for success. Lovingly bring to her attention the behavior that is causing dissention or tension among the group, and if she is willing, discuss ways to overcome the negative tendencies.

If dismissal is the only option, consider the following phrases:

- "It seems that you're not happy here. Do you think perhaps God could be calling you to a different task?"

- "What do you love about this ministry? What do you dislike? What do you feel you are best at? How is that fitting with what you are doing now?"

We will delve into conflict resolution a bit later in chapter 46.

Job Descriptions
Defining the Call

*T*he leadership team is the organizational backbone of any women's ministry. The individual members of it are the two-by-fours that frame the rooms. The leadership team is the steering committee, policy-making body, and development group. Each woman on the leadership team must be a committed Christian who has a personal and ongoing relationship with Jesus Christ. Because churches will vary in size, there may not be a person available for each leadership position. However, the more that the responsibilities are delegated, the lighter the load on the leadership team and the stronger the sense of ownership of individual members.

In the late 1890s, Frederick W. Taylor refined the post-Industrial Revolution by advocating the standardization of tools and equipment in the factories. His ideas greatly affected Henry Ford and his development of the assembly line. Taylor's formula? *The greatest production results when each worker is given a definite task to be performed in a definite time, in a definite manner.*

While we are not working on an assembly line, the principles for efficiency still apply. Each woman on the leadership team needs a:

- ❧ Definite task or job description
- ❧ Definite time frame in which to complete the task
- ❧ Definite manner in which to perform the task

These principles are meant to serve as a guideline for various members of the leadership team; they are not carved in stone. "People first" is the motto of any effective women's ministry. Because people's lives ebb and flow, our guidelines must be flexible enough to accommodate various situations that will arise.

Below are examples of job descriptions. They are not meant to be all-inclusive, but to serve as a guide to creating the job descriptions for your various team members.

Women's Ministry Director: The women's ministry director is the general contractor for building the women's ministry. That does not mean she hammers the nails or shingles the roof. However, a good leader will always be willing to pitch in where she is needed and be willing to pick up a hammer. She...

- Organizes the informational meeting
- Stays in contact with church leadership
- Oversees planning of the overall women's ministry and individual programs
- Prepares, oversees, and presents the annual budget
- Mentors and encourages the ministry team
- Has a servant leadership style, which is influential in nature, rather than authoritative
- Feels called by God to encourage women in their many roles
- Is able to detect potential leaders and recognizes special gifts in the members of her group
- Sets up training and team-building sessions
- Sets the tone of servant leadership for the rest of the team

Assistant Women's Ministry Director: She assists the women's ministry director and assumes her responsibilities in case of her absence. She also...

∞ Is familiar with the job descriptions of each team leader

∞ Attends all leadership meetings

The assistant ministry director may be a person who is in training to be a women's ministry director in the future, either in the formation of a new group or when the current director steps down.

Bible Study Coordinator: She selects and approves Bible studies for the women's ministry. She...

∞ Meets with a team of women to discuss and review various Bible study material

∞ Assists in scheduling the various Bible study times and creates the yearly calendar

∞ Works closely with the Bible study teachers and facilitators

Bible Study Leaders or Small-Group Leaders: They facilitate group discussion during the Bible studies or small-group meetings. They...

∞ Provide a warm and sensitive environment in which the members feel welcomed and loved. In each small group, there will be women who have a deep understanding of the Bible mixed in with women who have little to no understanding of Scripture. It is the hope of every group that women who have yet to accept Jesus Christ as their personal Savior will feel comfortable.

∞ Set the tone for each woman in order for her to feel comfortable sharing her needs, thoughts, and beliefs. While they do not let false teaching pass as truth, they are sensitive to those who have not come to a complete understanding of the gospel.

∞ Follow up during the week with phone calls to check on group members or assign someone to do so

- ॐ Study the material ahead of time and are prepared to lead the group

- ॐ Are able to detect potential leaders and recognize special gifts in the members

- ॐ Are focused and able to tactfully keep others on track

- ॐ Have a servant leadership style, which is influential in nature, rather than authoritative

Finance Coordinator: She collects all monies for child care, special events, Bible study materials, etc. At all times, we must keep in mind that women's ministry exists to encourage women. Sometimes money is a delicate subject. The finance coordinator may detect someone who is having difficulty paying for her registration fee or resource material. At no time should a woman be made to feel embarrassed because of financial restraints. If at all possible, the leadership should request scholarship funds for those women who are not able to pay for certain events or for child care. There may be women who desire to encourage other women by paying for their registration or resource materials. It is sometimes a good idea to establish a "scholarship fund" into which members of the group can contribute. She...

- ॐ Handles the exchange of all money between women and the church office

- ॐ Collects money and pays the child care providers

- ॐ Collects and turns in necessary receipts for reimbursement

- ॐ Advises women's ministry teams on budget issues

- ॐ Demonstrates reliability and responsibility in handling money

- ॐ Is organized

There may be finance coordinators for each area of ministry rather than one finance coordinator for the entire umbrella.

Hospitality Coordinator: The hospitality team leader is responsible for setting a welcoming atmosphere through such things as icebreakers, refreshments, and name tags. She is a woman with a winning smile and a warm heart.

Helga Henry, wife of the late theologian Carl Henry, expresses this point: "Christian hospitality is not a choice; it is not a matter of money, age, social standing, sex, or personality. However, it is a matter of obedience to God." It is a loving response to the Lord as He exhorts us in Romans 12:13 to "practice hospitality." We have somehow confused biblical hospitality with social entertaining. In contrast, our focus should be outward, not inward. Not on ourselves or how well we do things or the status of our worldly belongings. Rather, hospitality is simply loving other people with the gifts and provisions God has given us, anytime, anyplace, and to anyone He calls us to serve.

She...

- ❧ Arrives early at each meeting to set up refreshments and name tags
- ❧ Organizes the refreshments
- ❧ Keeps the refreshments and decorations simple
- ❧ Has a sign-up sheet for others in the group to participate in bringing refreshments
- ❧ Greets each woman cheerfully upon arrival or assigns others on her team to do so
- ❧ Delegates responsibilities to others in the group
- ❧ Stays after each meeting to clean up or delegates this responsibility to someone in the group

Jesus is a wonderful example of someone who practiced hospitality. In the feeding of the 5000, He provided for their physical needs before He addressed their spiritual needs.

Many times, women rush into meetings with hearts and minds focused on all they must accomplish in their busy day. By offering refreshments at the beginning of a meeting, the members have a chance to relax and refocus.

Dr. James Dobson says that the number one problem he sees among women today is poor self-esteem. By welcoming a woman and making her feel that she is special and that you are glad she is there, you will be building her confidence and estimation of her worth.

The first part of the word "hospitality" is hospital. Think of the hospitality team as nurses in a hospital. Check the pulse and temperature of the women in the room. Not literally, of course, but get a feel for those who need extra TLC.

Special Events Coordinator: She coordinates special events such as women's dinners and conferences and selects a speaker for the events. A special events coordinator will have several people under her to take care of such things as registration, ticket sales, child care, decorations, food service, etc.

Retreat Coordinator: She leads a team of women who are responsible for planning and implementing the women's retreat. She will have several women with various duties on her team.

Volunteer Coordinator: She gathers volunteers for special jobs, such as registration for events, manning the women's information table on Sunday mornings, or setup and breakdown at special events.

Publicity Chair: She publicizes meetings in the church bulletin, makes flyers, and publicizes special events.

Child Care Coordinator: She coordinates child care workers for each event or program. She works closely with the director of children's ministry and the church administrator.

Prayer Coordinator: She leads the group in prayer and keeps a record of prayer requests and answers to prayer. This is a position that would be held in a small-group setting.

Decorations Chairman: She plans decorations for dinners or other special events and is responsible for setup before and breakdown after events.

Missions Liaison: She researches missions opportunities such as short-term missions, weekend mission projects, and support for foreign missions.

When Jesus chose His ministry team, He gave them "assignments" or "job descriptions." Over the course of three years, He trained them, invested in them, and released them. Jesus praised them when they did well and corrected them when they failed. Then He always sent them back out to minister again. Even Peter, who denied he even knew Jesus, was corrected and then released to try again. May this be our leadership model as well.

Also, when Jesus sent out His disciples, He sent them out two by two. If you have the people available, it is a wonderful plan to have two people serving in each capacity. One serves as a mentor and one as an apprentice. Each person serves for a minimum of two years, so that each time a mentor rotates off, the apprentice takes the baton and becomes the mentor for a new apprentice.

It is very important to note that just because a person is the chairperson or the coordinator, it does not mean she is responsible for doing all the work. She is the leader, and a good leader always delegates. The more people she can gather for her team, the more efficient and happier the team will be.

Gentle Reminder for the Women's Ministry Director

On many occasions I have worked with the women's ministry director for an event and I've stopped to ask her the question, "You do have a team of women working on this project with you, right? You're not trying to do all this on your own, right?" On too many occasions I have heard the words, "No, I have help," but I have seen the stress in her face or heard the tension in her voice that said otherwise.

Let me remind you of my dear friend Moses, who also tried to do it all. The account is recorded in Exodus chapter 18.

After God called Moses to lead the Israelites out of the bondage of the Egyptian Pharaoh and his taskmasters, Moses' "ministry" of over a million or so followers gathered in the desert just on the other side of the Red Sea. The folks were amazed at Moses' leadership abilities and his unique partnership with the great "I AM." But life was busy in the desert. People didn't get along very well, and there was so much to do! One day Moses' father-in-law, Jethro, stopped by for a visit. Moses recounted all that God had done, and Jethro was delighted.

On the second day of Jethro's visit, he observed as Moses took his seat to serve as judge for the people, and they stood around him from morning till evening. When his father-in-law saw all that Moses was doing, he said, "What is this you are doing for the people? Why do you alone sit as judge, while all these people stand around you from morning till evening?" (verse 14).

Moses answered him, "Because the people come to me to seek God's will. Whenever they have a dispute, it is brought to me, and I decide between the parties and inform them of God's decrees and laws" (verse 15).

Jethro saw, right away, that Moses was heading for burnout. "What you are doing is not good...the work is too heavy for you; you cannot handle it alone" (verses 17-18). Then Jethro helped Moses devise a plan to distribute the work. He suggested that Moses select capable men from all the people—men who fear God, trustworthy men who hate dishonest gain—and appoint them as officials over groups of thousands, hundreds, fifties, and tens. He suggested a rigorous leadership training program in which Moses taught the leaders God's decrees and laws and showed them the way to live. Moses distributed the workload in an orderly fashion and only handled the cases that were too difficult for his leadership team to tackle.

What a plan! We cannot do it all. God never intended the body of Christ to operate with one body part. I leave Moses and Jethro with you as a gentle reminder...disseminate, delegate, designate.

Team Building
Unifying the Members

*P*art of the ministry budget should allow for leadership training and team building. Team building is vitally important. Leaders are often pouring themselves out for others and may end up running on empty themselves. This is true for pastors, elders, and women on the leadership team. Pouring back into the team will ensure that the members will not end up spiritually and emotionally depleted. Uniting the team will ensure that they will have the greatest impact by working synergistically.

County fairs are known for their various contests. At one particular fair, a pulling contest was used to determine who had the strongest horse. The first-place horse moved a sled that weighed 4500 pounds and the second-place horse moved a sled that weighed 4000 pounds. The owners were curious as to how much the two could pull if they worked together, so they hitched them up and added more weight to the sled. To everyone's surprise, the horses pulled 12,000 pounds.[1]

The word for combined strength, which was demonstrated in the two horses working together, is "synergism." It means doing more together than one can do alone. Ten women working together as one force can accomplish exponentially more than ten women working with their own plans and agendas in mind. The purpose of team building is to help a group of people meld together as one force.

Jesus knew the importance of team building and a synergistic approach to ministry. Just before He faced the cross, Jesus prayed for His disciples, and He prayed for us as well:

> My prayer is not for them alone. I pray also for those who will believe in me through their message, that all of them may be one, Father, just as you are in me and I am in you. May they also be in us so that the world may believe that you have sent me. I have given them the glory that you gave me, that they may be one as we are one: I in them and you in me. May they be brought to complete unity to let the world know that you sent me and have loved them even as you have loved me (John 17:20-23).

Paul echoed Jesus' prayer in his letter to the Romans.

> May the God who gives endurance and encouragement give you a spirit of unity among yourselves as you follow Christ Jesus, so that with one heart and mouth you may glorify the God and Father of our Lord Jesus Christ (Romans 15:5-6).

Team building can be as simple as lunch out together or a weekend getaway. Leaders can only give out of their overflow, so do what you can to help fill them up! Here are a few ideas for team-building activities:

- Spend time praying for each other.
- Laugh and take time to get to know each other.
- Model vulnerability by sharing personal struggles.
- Ask, "What is God doing in your life right now?"
- Read a book together on leadership.
- Have dinner together.
- Take turns leading devotions.

    ∾ Get away on an overnight retreat.

    ∾ Go bowling.

    ∾ Have a manicure-and-massage mini retreat.

    ∾ Do a craft together, such as scrapbooking or pottery painting.

People long to feel significant, valued, and appreciated. The more each person on the team can learn to see their team members as children of God, created in the image of God, the more they will accept and cherish each other. Every woman on a team comes with her own personal hopes, dreams, fears, and tears. The team becomes more effective as they begin to see each other as more than a person, but as a life. Let's take a closer look at a few team-building activities.

Web of Love

One weekend the staff and several volunteers gathered at my home for a slumber party. Women were in all the beds, on all the couches, and carpeting the floor in sleeping bags. On Friday night we went out to dinner together and spent time just being friends. Saturday was a goal-setting day, so much of the morning was spent looking ahead to the future and what God might be calling us to do as a ministry and as a team. This time also included revisiting our purpose statement to make sure we were staying on target.

In the afternoon I led the group in a devotion time of Bible study and prayer. It happened to be based on the need for giving the gift of encouragement to one another. At the close of that time, I held a ball of string in my hand and explained the exercise we were about to do. It was called a "Web of Love."

"Here we have a ball of string. While holding on to the end of the string, I am going to toss the ball to someone in the circle who has been an encouragement to me in some way. When she catches it, we will have a line between us, and I will tell her what she means to me or thank her for her encouragement. Then she will hold on to the string, and toss the ball to someone who has been an encouragement to her, telling her what she appreciates about her, why she loves her, what she has meant to her, why she admires her, or simply thank her for some way she has made an impact on her life. When you catch the ball of string, hold on to the string, and then toss it to someone else, following the same pattern. Please be aware if there is someone who has not received the toss. I will start."

I began the toss while holding on the end of the string. Then for the next 30 minutes I watched and cried as women poured out their love and encouragement on each other. It was truly a web of love sprinkled with the dewdrops of tears.

The Blessing

Another team-building activity is called "The Blessing." Jacob said to the angel, "I will not let you go until you bless me" (Genesis 32:26). While Jacob asked for a blessing, most will not. However, I believe each of us longs to be blessed.

When Paul wrote to the churches, many times he prayed a blessing over them. Borrowing from Paul, pray Scripture over each team member. "Glynnis, this is what I see in you and this is the blessing I pray over you today. You are a woman after God's own heart, and He has great and mighty plans for your life. I pray that the eyes of your heart may be enlightened in order that you may know the hope to which He has called you, the riches of His glorious inheritance in the saints, and His incomparably great power for us who believe" (Ephesians 1:18-19). In preparation for this activity, earnestly ask God to show you what that person needs to hear to be encouraged.

The blessing can be a team activity where each member prays a blessing over the other or an activity in which the leader prays a blessing over each team member.

The Blessing Box

We have a blessing box in our office. When God answers a prayer or we see Him work in an incredible way, we write the blessing on a slip of paper and place it in the blessing box. Then on various days we go back and read what people deposited in the blessing box. This serves as a reminder of all that God is doing through the team on those days when we need to be reminded that ministry is much more than a to-do list to check off.

The Hot Seat

During a retreat of extended time together, place a chair in the middle of a circle. Then, one by one, put each team member in the hot seat to answer various questions. Questions should be for the purpose of getting to know the person in the hot seat on a more intimate level. They could include:

- Who has been the most influential person in your life?
- What has been the most embarrassing moment in your life?
- What is your greatest fear?
- What is one of your happiest memories?
- Which grade was your favorite in school and why?
- If you were to give your life a grade (A, B, C, D, or F) what would it be and why?
- If you could go anywhere for three weeks with anyone you choose, where would you go and who would you take along?
- Do you have a dream for your life that you are afraid to verbalize?
- What does a "safe place" look like to you?

Tombstone Testimony

There was a popular pizza commercial a few years back that asked the question, "What do you want on your tombstone?" Of course the commercial was for Tombstone pizza—and my answer was pepperoni.

This question can be the theme of a team-building activity that will give insight into what your team members see as their purpose in life.

Give each team member a gray piece of paper in the shape of a tombstone, or a piece of paper with the outline of a tombstone drawn on it, and have them write their own epitaph. Afterward, celebrate with pizza.

There are many other quick team-building exercises in chapter 23 on icebreakers. The purpose is to get to know each other and to grow to love each other. Your team does not want to know how much you know until they know how much you care.

Leadership Training
Equipping the Team

*J*esus instigated one of the first and most effective leadership training programs in history. He chose twelve men with whom to have a close, personal relationship and trained them in how to spread the gospel throughout the entire world. He did not condemn them when they made mistakes nor did He exclude them from participating in His many miracles. Jesus had a goal that His disciples would do even greater works than He did (John 14:12). That is the sign of a great leader. Let's look at some ways in which we can model Jesus' leadership training program:

- ∾ Invite
- ∾ Inspire
- ∾ Instruct
- ∾ Invest
- ∾ Intercede
- ∾ Impart responsibility

Invite

Generally, women like to be invited to join rather than volunteer for a leadership position. Jesus invited each one of His disciples to join Him in His work. "Come," He said to Peter and James, "and I will make you fishers of men" (Matthew 4:19).

Jesus did not simply ask, "Okay, who would like to sign up to be My disciples for the next three years?" No, He prayed earnestly and asked God whom He would have Him choose to be on the team. Then He invited each one to join Him.

After you have prayerfully considered whom God would have you choose to be a part of the leadership team, invite the individuals to join you in impacting your church and community for Christ. Invite each one to do a specific task and have a job description ready if at all possible. This will help a woman understand exactly what she is being asked to do and lessen the chances of disappointment. Begin by giving small tasks to see if the person is able to follow through and always be on the lookout for rising leaders.

Inspire

In his book *Leadership,* Chuck Swindoll notes, "It's much easier to describe what leaders do than to describe what they are...At the risk of oversimplifying, I'm going to resist a long, drawn-out definition and settle on one word. It's the word *influence.* If you will allow me two words—*inspiring influence.*"[1]

A great leader continually casts the vision of the ministry before the women. It is the fuel that inspires them to press on. Proverbs 29:18 says, "Where there is no vision, the people perish" (KJV). The leadership team depends on the women's ministry leadership to place before them a picture of the future. "Imagine bringing 50 women to Christ through the various arms of the women's ministry this year," she cheers.

Jesus continually reminded His disciples that He was God's Son, the Messiah. He reminded them of His purpose: "I have come that they may have life, and have it to the full" (John 10:10). They didn't always understand the vision, but it became very clear once Jesus returned to the Father.

Help the team members to see their part in making the vision of women's ministry come to fruition. Jesus said to His disciples, "I tell you, open your eyes and look at the fields! They are ripe for harvest" (John 4:35).

Many leaders wonder why their team, which was so enthusiastic in the beginning, tends to wane as the months go by. We leak. That's it! Paul wrote, "Be filled with the Spirit" (Ephesians 5:18). It is a continuous present tense verb and really should be translated, "Be filled and continue to be filled with the Spirit." Likewise, hearing the vision once and being inspired once is not enough. A leader needs to inspire and continue to inspire. Cast the vision and continue to cast the vision.

One of the best ways I know to inspire a group of women is to show them glimpses of the vision becoming a reality. Share stories of women who have been impacted by your women's ministry. At retreats, allow time for women to stand up and testify about what God has done in their lives. During leadership meetings, make time for women to share what they are learning or how they have seen God work in their congregation.

Instruct

After Jesus had spent time teaching the multitudes, He took His disciples over to the side and said, "Listen then to what the parable of the sower means" (Matthew 13:18). One day after He had finished praying, His disciples said, "Lord, teach us to pray" (Luke 11:1). Walking to the Garden of Gethsemane to pray, Jesus said, "I am the true vine, and my Father is the gardener...No branch can bear fruit by itself; it must remain in the vine" (John 15:1,4).

All through the Gospels we see that Jesus took time to instruct the disciples. Likewise, an effective women's ministry leader takes time to instruct her team, both spiritually and personally. Just as we saw with Jesus, this type of instruction involves more than how to work, it involves how to live. Your leaders may benefit from theological education, leadership skill development, and speaking and/or writing seminars. They will also benefit from encouragement, mutual sharing, and just plain being friends.

The women's ministry director may want to hold a Bible study just for leaders or spend time praying with and for the leaders. Holding a leadership Bible study or prayer time will serve two purposes. You will be helping the women grow spiritually and modeling leadership skills for them practically, showing the leaders how to lead.

Consider reading a book together as a team. (See the appendix for recommended reading.) This manual is a great resource to use in training your women's ministry leaders. Using the section on group dynamics (Part Four), you can schedule several seminars to help them be better leaders, facilitators, and mentors.

For those women who will be leading Bible studies, it is helpful to meet with other Bible study leaders and actually teach a mock lesson. The group can critique the teacher for the day, offer helpful tips, and give her lots of encouragement! For those who are new at leading a Bible study, it offers a safe place to practice.

Invest

Invest in the members of the leadership team by helping them reach their own personal and spiritual goals. One of the by-products of instructing or educating your leaders is that they understand you value them as people. By investing in your women, you are saying, "I value you as a team member. You are important to me, and I see great potential in you as a leader and as a person. I want to help you grow as a person and as a child of God, and I want to help make your dreams a reality."

Jesus invested greatly in His leadership team. He taught them how to pray, showed them how to have faith, and allowed them to participate in ministry. For example, He did not need the disciples' help when feeding the 5000, but He allowed them to participate and enjoy the mystery of the miraculous with Him.

Bill Hybels notes,

> For emerging leaders to become seasoned, wise, and effective leaders, they need proximity to and interaction with veteran leaders. This can happen in a dozen different ways, but it must happen. In Jesus' day it was common for a leader-in-training to simply follow the veteran leader around. They would talk together, walk together, eat their meals together, and sleep in neighboring tents. They would spend months, sometimes years, apprenticing. This allowed them to internalize the vision and values of the veteran leaders in ways that served them the rest of their lives.[2]

What impressed me most about women's ministry director Mary Ann Ruff was her philosophy of women's ministry leadership development. She invested in her team. By sending her leaders to training seminars, hosting appreciation dinners or coffees, sending them small gifts and cards, and giving them appropriate recognition, the women on Mary Ann's team knew they were valued, not only because of the job they could do as a member of the team, but because of who they were as a gifted child of God. Once she had invested in a person, that person felt passionate about giving back to the church.

Paul invested in his son in the Lord, Timothy, telling Timothy that he believed in him. Not only that, Paul gave Timothy great responsibility and reassured Timothy of his confidence that he could do the job. Timothy was a young man when Paul sent him to resolve several serious problems in the church at Ephesus. No doubt Paul's words of encouragement built confidence in the lad. "Let no one despise your youth, but be an example to the believers in word, in conduct, in love, in spirit, in faith, in purity" (1 Timothy 4:12 NKJV). Sure, Paul could have gone to Ephesus himself or sent someone older and more mature. Instead, he sent Timothy and assured him that he trusted him to handle the job. All the while, Paul was on the sidelines cheering, "GO, TIMOTHY!"

Another way to invest in your leaders or team members is by remembering them at tender times, such as anniversaries, birthdays, or the loss of a loved one. Weep with those who weep and rejoice with those who rejoice. Bear one another's burdens but also have fun together. The best investment you can make is with one of your most precious commodities—your time. (We'll look at more ways to invest in your leaders in chapter 15.)

Here are some investment ideas that reap big dividends:

- Attend a seminar together as a group.
- Send leaders to a leadership seminar (the church pays their expenses).
- Read a leadership or study book together as a group.
- Attend a large women's conference together as a team.
- Bring in a speaker just for the leadership team.

Intercede

An intercessor is one who prays for another. Jesus' longest recorded prayer in the Bible is found in John chapter 17, where He prayed for His disciples:

Holy Father, protect them by the power of your name—the name you gave me—so that they may be one as we are one...My prayer is not that you take them out of the world but that you protect them from the evil one...Sanctify them by the truth; your word is truth (John 17:11,15,17).

Paul opened his letters to the churches by telling them how he interceded for them on a regular basis:

For this reason, ever since I heard about your faith in the Lord Jesus and your love for all the saints, I have not stopped giving thanks for you, remembering you in my prayers. I keep asking that the God of our Lord Jesus Christ, the glorious Father, may give you the Spirit of wisdom and revelation, so that you may know him better. I pray also that the eyes of your heart may be enlightened in order that you may know the hope to which he has called you, the riches of this glorious inheritance in the saints, and his incomparable great power for us who believe (Ephesians 1:15-19).

Not only did Paul pray for others, he asked them to pray for him as well:

Pray also for me, that whenever I open my mouth, words may be given me so that I will fearlessly make known the mystery of the gospel, for which I am an ambassador in chains. Pray that I may declare it fearlessly, as I should (Ephesians 6:19-20).

When we, as leaders, ask those whom we are mentoring to pray for us, we open the door that will allow them to have the courage and freedom to share their own personal struggles and passions.

Impart Responsibility

Finally, after Jesus invited the disciples to join Him, inspired them with the vision, instructed them in how to live a life of faith, invested in their spiritual and physical well-being, and interceded for them in prayer, He imparted responsibility to them and watched them change the world. Jesus passed the baton and entrusted His leadership team with the work.

I will never forget when a group of adults in my hometown asked me to lead a Bible study for their teenage kids. I was only 20 years old, just a kid myself, but these parents invited me, inspired me, invested in me, interceded for me, and imparted the responsibility of leading their children into a closer walk with God. In my heart of hearts, I did not want to let them down. As a young adult, I grew immensely in my spiritual life because there was a group of parents who believed in me and trusted me to impact their kids for Christ. I knew that I was not capable...I just wondered if they knew it. But their trust in me gave me the boost I needed to obey God's call at such an early age.

When we pass the baton and give others on the women's ministry team the opportunity to take ownership of a project or a program, they will blossom as never before.

Right there in your own church is a woman who longs to be used by God. She is thinking...*I wish someone would believe in me, teach me, mentor me, and feel that I am worth the effort. I so want to serve the Lord, if only I knew where to start.*

Tell—Show—Do

Another model for leadership training is what I call tell, show, do. When I was in dental hygiene school many, many years ago, we learned a valuable tool for teaching patients oral hygiene instruction. First, we would tell the patient how to floss, then we would let them hold a mirror and watch us actually floss in their mouths, and finally we would hold the mirror and allow them to give it a try.

That same principle is applicable in every area of leadership training. A great leader will *tell* a team member what is expected, *show* them how to accomplish the task, and then allow them to *do* it on their own. If we stop at "telling," there may be very little effective "doing."

Tell

Telling is basically instructing the team member. "This is how you facilitate a group." "This is how you handle difficult women in a group." "This is how you reach out to those in the community." Much of this manual is for the very purpose of not only building an effective women's ministry, but also as a tool for instruction to those on the leadership team.

Show

Showing the team members how to lead happens with every move we make. Whether we realize it or not, team members are watching how leaders lead. Just as our children model their lives after what they see us do rather than what they hear us say, the members of the leadership team will emulate the leadership models they see played out from those over them.

Do

Finally, a great leader will hand over the reins of a project or a task to the team member and empower her to take responsibility for the task. She will empower her to make decisions, love her when she makes mistakes, celebrate with her when she succeeds, and encourage her to continue on in light of both.

Leadership Support

Encouraging the Team

*A*s you begin to build your women's ministry, the women on the leadership team who feel encouraged will be the ones to have the greatest impact on those around them. If their emotional buckets are empty, they will have a difficult time filling others.

I love the story in 1 Kings 17 where God sent the prophet Elijah to be ministered to by a widow. Elijah had been living by a river that dried up, so God led him to a widow to feed and house him. When Elijah approached her and asked for food, she explained that she was just now picking up sticks to start a fire. She had only enough flour in her bowl and enough oil in her jar for one more cake of bread. She was about to prepare this last supper for herself and her son, and then they were going to lie down and die. Elijah assured her if she would fix him a little cake first, then one for herself and her son, her bowl would not go empty and her jar would not run dry until the drought was over.

The widow followed Elijah's requests and her bowl and jar did not run dry; God miraculously supplied her needs. What a beautiful picture of Jesus' words in Luke 6:38: "Give, and it will be given to you. A good measure, pressed down, shaken together and running over, will be poured into your lap. For with the measure you use, it will be measured to you."

Giving the gift of encouragement is like dipping out of a bucket. If you can, visualize that we each have a bucket of encouragement. Some people have just a little in their bucket, and some have abundance. The trick is, when you dip out of your bucket to encourage someone, the Lord pours more into your bucket. However, there are many who are running low, and they try to fill their buckets by dipping out of someone else's bucket—hurting others to elevate themselves. Unfortunately, that person will always have an empty bucket as it leaks out or evaporates immediately. The only way to fill our encouragement bucket is to share with others and watch the Lord fill us to overflowing.

Perhaps one of the greatest encouragers in the Bible was Paul, writer of more than half the New Testament. In each of his letters to the various churches, Paul began with encouraging words. "I...do not cease giving thanks for you" (Ephesians 1:15-16 NASB). "I thank my God in all my remembrance of you, always offering prayer with joy...for you all" (Philippians 1:3-4 NASB). "I have you in my heart" (Philippians 1:7 NASB). "We always thank God, the Father of our Lord Jesus Christ, when we pray for you" (Colossians 1:3).

Even though Paul's letters began with encouraging words, their primary purpose was to exhort, instruct, and yes, correct. He was never known as a pushover, but his reproofs were always wrapped in love.

Businessman Charles Schwab said, "I have yet to find the man—however exalted his station—who did not do better work and put forth greater effort under a spirit of approval than under a spirit of criticism."[1] This concept is not only true in the business world, but in our homes, in our communities, and in our ministries.

Here are a few ways to encourage the women on your leadership teams:

- Ask good questions.

- Avoid the empty, "How are you?" and replace it with "How can I pray for you today?"

- Pray with them, not just for them.

∾ Listen without giving advice.

∾ Let them repeat details if they are going through a crisis.

∾ Write encouraging notes often.

∾ Invest in them by sending them to leadership conferences.

∾ Praise them or thank them in front of other people.

∾ Recognize them for a job well done.

∾ Send them a weekly e-mail of appreciation.

∾ Send them small gifts:

> • Picture frame…"Thank you for being part of our framework."
> • Mirror…"You are a reflection of Jesus Christ."
> • Candle…"You are a light to the world."
> • Hershey's hugs…"Consider yourself hugged!"
> • Hand cream…"You are God's hands to the world."
> • Flavored tea bags…"You are just my cup of tea."

Affirmation Essentials

Mary had worked tirelessly for months on the costumes and the backdrop for the Christmas musical. The stage, a heavenly array of white, reminded me of what heaven must be like. Several months after the event, Mary reluctantly told me that she received only one note of thanks from the 2000-plus congregation. She said, "I read and reread that note of thanks…I don't know how many times."

You know what broke my heart? Not that she only received only one note, as sad as that was. What broke my heart was that the note was not from me.

We do such a disservice to God's people when we do not affirm and appreciate them. In *Spiritual Leadership*, Henry Blackaby says the following:

Good leaders delegate. They resist interfering. Then, when the job is done, they give credit where it is deserved. One of the greatest rewards a leader can give people, even more than remuneration, is their recognition. Leaders ought to be constantly praising their people for their accomplishments and acknowledging their contributions to the organization. At staff gatherings and special occasions, leaders ought to be known for praising their people for their work rather than for blowing their own horns...

This need for affirmation and show of gratitude is especially acute in voluntary organizations. Volunteers don't receive year-end bonuses or increases in pay as rewards for their efforts. That's why leaders should be especially diligent to find ways of showing appreciation. At times, leaders can "spiritualize" the work done by volunteers in their organization with absurd statements such as, "They were doing it for the Lord. They don't need my recognition." Certainly some people's only motivation for serving is recognition they hope to receive, but wise leaders leave people's motivations for God to judge. True spiritual leaders assume the best of their volunteers. They understand that people want their sacrifice of time and energy to be worth the effort. Volunteers need to know they are making a positive difference.[2]

Most women working in women's ministry are volunteers. Think of ways you can encourage your team, affirm their efforts, and praise them publicly.

16

Leadership Retreats
Deepening Relationships

*A*s I was sitting in an airplane getting ready for takeoff, the flight attendant began her preflight instructions about how to use the seat belt and what to do in case of an emergency. She held up the oxygen mask and said, "If needed, oxygen masks will be released from overhead. To start the flow of oxygen, reach up and pull the mask toward you, fully extending the plastic tubing. Place the mask over your nose and mouth and slip the elastic band over your head. To tighten the fit, pull the tab on each side of the mask. The plastic bag does not need to inflate when oxygen is flowing. *Be sure to secure your own mask before assisting others.*" At this point, a video showed a mother putting on her face mask before helping her young child.

The first time I heard the message, I thought, *That seems mighty selfish...to put the oxygen mask on myself before I put it on my son.* But then I realized that if I passed out, I wouldn't do either one of us any good! The same is true as we work in women's ministry. We can only give to the degree that we are filled ourselves. We give out of our overflow, and if the cup is dry, our ministry to others will be dry as well.

A leadership retreat is designed to fill up the women's ministry team. Think about all a woman does on any given day. She is a wife, mother, friend, housekeeper, interior decorator, laundress, gourmet chef, short-order cook, chauffeur, painter, wallpaperer, seamstress, nurse, guidance counselor, financial planner, travel agent, administrative assistant, disciplinarian, preacher, teacher, tutor, spiritual advisor, dietician, lecturer, librarian, fashion coordinator, private investigator, cheerleader, manicurist, pedicurist, landscaper, hair stylist, psychologist, plumber, computer programmer, automobile maintenance expert, referee, and gift purchasing agent for both sides of the family.

And now she's added women's ministry on top of her everyday responsibilities. Calgon had the right idea with their campaign ad for bath beads several years ago: "Calgon, take me away!"

Jesus knew the importance of taking His leadership team away on mini retreats. After several days of intense ministry, Jesus gathered His disciples and said, "Come with me by yourselves to a quiet place and get some rest" (Mark 6:31).

Planning a leadership retreat is much like planning a churchwide retreat, except on a much smaller scale. The key difference is that a leadership retreat focuses on team building and seeking God for the future of the women's ministry. Let's take a look at the basic blueprint for a leadership retreat.

Dear God **Begin with Prayer:** Ask God to reveal His purpose for the retreat. Ask for wisdom and guidance in each and every detail.

Purpose: Define your purpose for the retreat. What do you see as the purpose of the leadership retreat? Is it for team building, strengthening friendships, training, evaluating, goal setting, nurturing, fun, or relaxation? Most likely, a leadership retreat will have several ingredients in the mix. When planning, make sure to have enough "white space" in the schedule for rest, relaxation, laughter, and fun!

Location: After deciding on your purpose, begin exploring location possibilities. Perhaps a hotel, a Christian camp, a Christian retreat center, a bed-and-breakfast, or a vacation home that someone is willing to let you use. If finances prohibit getting away for the weekend, why not consider having a slumber party at someone's home?

Time: There will be no perfect weekend when everyone will be available. Poll the women you want to invite and give them several choices. Then choose a time when the most women will be available. Of course, the weekends to choose from may be dictated by the location's availability.

Budget: Count the costs and come up with a budget (see chapter 6).

Theme: Choose a Bible verse and theme for the retreat that reinforces the purpose. Once the theme is decided, everything else will revolve around it. The speakers, the devotions, the songs, and the small-group activities will focus on the theme and the goals.

Icebreakers and Games: Have some fun. Icebreakers and games are a must for a leadership retreat. Two elements must be present for a great retreat: bonding and laughter! Perhaps you might want to have a Sanguine personality coming up with the icebreakers and games. It might be a stretch for a Melancholy to see the point in it all. She'll have fun doing it, but don't expect her to come up with the silly ideas.

Games such as Pictionary, Balderdash, Cranium, and Taboo will ensure lots of laughter and teamwork. Amazingly, when ladies begin competing, personality traits come to the surface that have been hiding. Games can be a very eye-opening experience. All of a sudden, sweet quiet little Barb is breaking out in a sweat...determined to WIN. Watch out. You never know who will emerge.

Gifts: As a way to encourage your team, consider giving some type of gift during the leadership retreat. It could be a journal, a T-shirt, a tote bag, or any number of items to let them know you value them.

Speaker/Speakers: Let the leaders lead. Most likely a leadership retreat will not have one keynote speaker, but rather several women participating in leading in prayer, devotion, games, and facilitation of discussion groups. The retreat can serve as an opportunity for team members to actually lead. If there are women on the team who have shown an interest in teaching or speaking but have not had the opportunity, the leadership retreat might be a wonderful place to let them spread their wings.

Cast the Vision: At a leadership retreat, the team needs to hear from the leader. This is a time for the women's ministry director to once again cast the vision, restate the mission statement, review the purpose, and then inspire the team to continue in the call God has on each of the ladies' lives. Three key words for the director—inspire, inspire, inspire!

Prayer: A retreat is a time to seek the Lord together for direction in your personal lives as well as the life of the women's ministry. In *Experiencing God Day-by-Day,* Henry Blackaby said, "Prayer is not a substitute for hard work. It is the work!"[1] We can easily get caught up in the details of running an effective women's ministry and forget why we have women's ministry in the first place. Spending time in corporate prayer helps to bring the focus back to where it needs to be…on God.

Retreat Corporate Prayer Schedule

Here is a suggested schedule for times of prayer.

- *Friday Night:* Ask the women to share various spiritual markers or milestones in their lives. Ask what one event led them to where they are today, spiritually. Ask, "Why do you want to be a part of leading women to the next step in their relationship with God?"

- Before the time of prayer begins, the women's ministry leader needs to recast the vision.

- Remind the group of the church's mission statement.

- Remind the group of the women's ministry mission statement: Example—"Moving women to the heart of God."

When the leader reminds the group of the mission statement, it helps to curtail tangents and keeps the women focused.

- ❧ Remind women of your purpose statement (how you will accomplish your mission): Example—"Through the Word of God, people, and prayer."

- ❧ Remind the women why you have women's ministry: Example— "To glorify God."

- ❧ Lead them into a time of praising God for who He is. Remind them that Jesus taught the disciples to begin prayer with praising and thanking God when He said, "Our Father, which art in heaven, hallowed be thy name" (Matthew 6:9 KJV). Also remind them that God's wrath was turned on men because, "Although they knew God, they neither glorified him as God nor gave thanks to him" (Romans 1:21).

  You may want to make a handout of the names of God found in chapter 17 to use as a guide for the praise time. Then move them to a time of thanksgiving for all that He has done.

- ❧ *Saturday Morning:* Once again, begin by having a brief time of praise and thanksgiving, and then move the women into a time of confession.

- ❧ *Saturday Evening:* Now it is time to ask what He would like to see accomplished in the women's ministry. Ask God what He would have you pay attention to this year. What are the needs that you are missing? During this time of prayer, have someone make notes on a whiteboard of any ideas that God seems to bring to mind. This time of prayer will include periods of silence as the group is now focusing on listening to God rather than talking to God.

  After the time of prayer is complete, look at what has been noted on the whiteboard. Are there recurring ideas? Does one idea seem to jump out at the group? This is not a time to make decisions, but simply gather information. Entries might include ideas such as transforming women's lives, reaching out to the world, communication, widows, discipleship, and relationships. Just like in a brainstorming session, there are no right or wrong answers. Remember, we are practicing being women who listen to God.

After looking at the ideas and seeing which ones are recurring themes, pray that God would show you how to accomplish the goal and that He would bring the people forward to accomplish the task.

Let me give you an example of how God moved through this process at a women's leadership retreat.

Mary Ann Ruff was leading a group of women in a time of prayer as mentioned above. During the prayer time, one woman said that God had led her to Acts 1:8: "But you will receive power when the Holy Spirit comes on you; and you will be my witnesses in Jerusalem, and in all Judea and Samaria, and to the ends of the earth." Someone said, "I sense that God is calling us to reach out to those beyond our borders."

The group resonated with that leading and began to ask God if this was indeed His will for their women's ministry, and if so, that He would show them the "how" to accomplish it and the "who" to head it up. They did not try to force it or make it happen on their own; they simply prayed and waited on God.

Several weeks later, Mary Ann received a call from Glenda Overstreet. "Mary Ann," Glenda said, "God has put a burning desire in my heart to reach out to women beyond our borders." She shared that God had impressed Isaiah 54:2-3 on her heart: "Enlarge the place of your tent, stretch your tent curtains wide, do not hold back; lengthen your cords, strengthen your stakes. For you will spread out to the right and to the left." God had answered their first prayer—they had the "who."

Glenda began to inquire about various global needs. The missions pastor of her church referred her to the global missions director of the denomination. Glenda discovered that there were seven churches in their denomination in Argentina, and none of them had any type of women's ministry. After taking a trip to "spy out the land" and meeting with several of the women in the Argentine churches, Glenda proposed that the women of her church hold a women's conference in Argentina. Imagine how thrilled she was to discover that they had been specifically praying for a women's conference in their country. Now they had the "how."

There are many steps that went into the preparation for such a feat, but God faithfully provided for the team at each turn. The women of Glenda's church hosted their first women's retreat for the ladies of Argentina with 21 members of the leadership attending and 100 spiritually hungry and extremely grateful Argentine women. The following year, the American women partnered with the women of Argentina to host a retreat, and the third year, the Argentine women ran the retreat on their own with the women of Glenda's church coming as supportive participants. Each year, the attendance doubled. By the fourth year, Mary Ann's team felt they had done what God had called them to do...expand their borders and lengthen their cords by encouraging and equipping women to move women to the heart of God.

They passed the baton and now their denomination's seven churches in Argentina have thriving women's ministries! And it all began as a gentle whisper from God during a leadership retreat.

17

A Leader's
*P*ersonal *F*aith *W*alk

Growing in Intimacy with God

*E*verything we do in ministry is an overflow of our personal relationship to Christ. St. Francis of Assisi said, "I am able to lead only to the extent that I follow." If we, as leaders, are not following Jesus Christ and walking in tandem with Him, we cannot effectively lead others.

As much as we long to serve Him, we may find it all too easy to become caught up in spending our time doing work *for* the Lord and neglecting our relationship *with* the Lord. We are called human *beings*, not human *doings*. God prefers that we *be* with Him before we *do* for Him. But what exactly does that look like? Jesus draws us a perfect picture.

If you knew you were going to die and wanted to leave some last words of instruction to those you loved most in the world, what would you say? What would you want them to remember long after you were gone?

Jesus faced that very situation. Just hours before His arrest, this mighty leader took His 11 disciples on a stroll down the stairs of the upper room, through the winding streets of Jerusalem, and toward the dusty road leading to the Kidron Valley. They made their way in the dark of night with lanterns and torches lighting the way. As the men walked through a vineyard that grew along the terraces of the valley, Jesus began His parting words,

> I am the true vine, and my Father is the gardener. He cuts off every branch in me that bears no fruit, while every branch that does bear fruit he prunes so that it will be even more fruitful. You are already clean because of the word I have spoken to you. *Remain* in me, and I will *remain* in you. No branch can bear fruit by itself; it must *remain* in the vine. Neither can you bear fruit unless you *remain* in me.
>
> I am the vine; you are the branches. If a man *remains* in me and I in him, he will bear much fruit; apart from me you can do nothing. If anyone does not *remain* in me, he is like a branch that is thrown away and withers; such branches are picked up, thrown into the fire and burned. If you *remain* in me and my words *remain* in you, ask whatever you wish, and it will be given you. This is to my Father's glory, that you bear much fruit, showing yourselves to be my disciples.
>
> As the Father has loved me, so have I loved you. Now *remain* in my love. If you obey my commands, you will *remain* in my love, just as I have obeyed my Father's commands and *remain* in his love. I have told you this so that my joy may be in you and that your joy may be complete. My command is this: Love each other as I have loved you. Greater love has no one than this, that he lay down his life for his friends. You are my friends if you do what I command. I no longer call you servants, because a servant does not know his master's business. Instead, I have called you friends, for everything that I learned from my Father I have made known to you. You did not choose me, but I chose you and appointed you to go and bear fruit—fruit that will last. Then the Father will give you whatever you ask in my name. This is my command: Love each other (John 15:1-17, emphasis added).

Did you notice the word, "remain"? Eleven times in 17 verses, Jesus emphasizes the importance of staying connected to Him—like a branch to a vine. "Apart from me," He said, "you can do nothing." Oh, we can be busy, but not necessarily productive. For the past three years, the disciples had been very busy men. But on the last night before Jesus faced the cross, He shared the secret to their future success. "Abide in Me, and I in you" (John 15:4 NASB).

To "abide" means to stay closely connected to, to continue in, to tarry, to dwell, to remain. If you notice Jesus' words, "remain in Me" are in the imperative tense—a command. You don't have to command a child to eat candy. You command someone to do something because it does not come naturally. Likewise, Jesus knows that our natural inclination is not to abide, so He reminds us that that is where our power lies.

All during Jesus' ministry, He moved from caring for the masses to meditation with the Master. Both are important in the life of any leader. Dietrich Bonhoeffer, a German theologian who lived during the early 1900s, wrote, "One who wants fellowship without solitude plunges into a void of words and feelings, and one who seeks solitude without fellowship perishes in the abyss of vanity, self-infatuation, and despair. Let him who cannot be alone beware of community. Let him who is not in community beware of being alone."[1]

Two of the most important spiritual disciplines for any Christian are meditation on the Scriptures and prayer.

Personal Bible Study

You run out to your mailbox and discover four envelopes: a bill from the power company, a flyer from a department store, a note from Aunt Betty, and a letter from God. Now, which one would you open first? I don't know about you, but I'd open the letter from God. And the truth is that this is a choice we face every day. God has written us a wonderful love letter full of incredible treasures, words of endearment, and instructions for equipping us for life. All we have to do is open the pages of our Bible.

Second Timothy 3:16 says, "All scripture is inspired by God and profitable for teaching, for reproof, for correction, for training in righteousness; so that the man of God may be adequate, *equipped* for every good work" (NASB, emphasis added). First Peter 1:13 says, "Therefore, prepare your minds for action" (NASB). Another version says, "Therefore, gird up the loins of your mind" (NKJV).

In my book *Becoming a Woman Who Listens to God,* I discuss encounters with God in the Word and in prayer. God promised, "You will seek me and find me when you seek me with all your heart" (Jeremiah 29:13). This is more than a casual glance before heading off to work or to the carpool in the morning. It's more than a hit-and-run encounter with God. He desires to speak to us through the pages of our Bibles, and hearing Him requires meditating and seeking Him with our whole hearts. Jesus told His followers, "If you abide in My word, you are My disciples indeed. And you shall know the truth and the truth shall make you free" (John 8:31-32 NKJV). There's that word "abide" again. It is not reading Scripture for information, but for transformation. There are many scholars who have read the Bible for information but have never entered into a relationship with Jesus Christ. This reminds me of the difference between the woman who memorizes a menu at a restaurant and a woman who enjoys the food. Only one gets fed!

Let me ask you, who can describe a sunset more accurately—a blind person who has read all about sunsets (what causes the colors, the time of day they occur, the effect of clouds on the hues) or the person who has seen and experienced the vibrant oranges, blues, pinks, and purples painted across the sky as the sun creeps below the horizon and the rays play peekaboo behind scattered clouds? I daresay the one who has experienced the sunset for herself. When we study God's Word and couple that with listening to His voice, we will come to know Him on a much more intimate level than a biblical scholar who has studied the words on the page but never taken the time to converse with the Author Himself.

When we read the Bible and savor each passage like a newly discovered treasure or a love letter from God, it becomes our very sustenance. Paul wrote, "Let the word of Christ dwell in you richly" (Colossians 3:16). Ponder what you have read. Meditate on the words. Don't be in a hurry or have a preconceived idea of how much you are going to read that day. Apply the Scriptures to what is going on in your life at that very moment in time.

Jesus told us that when we abide in God's Word, we will become a disciple, a learner, and an imitator of the Teacher Himself (John 8:31). One thing I've noticed through the years is that a Bible that is falling apart usually belongs to a person who isn't!

Prayer

Prayer is communion and communication with God. For us, as God's children, prayer includes praising God for who He is, thanking God for what He does, confessing our sin, asking for forgiveness, and petitioning God for our requests. There is also another key element to prayer—*listening for God's response*. Sometimes we tend to treat God like a celestial Santa Claus and sit down to pray with a wish list. But communion with God is much more than airing a wish list. Prayer is sitting at the feet of God with the attitude of the seraphim, who cried, "Holy, holy, holy is the LORD Almighty" (Isaiah 6:3). Prayer is coming as a child communing with her heavenly Father. Prayer is pressing our ear to the heart of God and listening to His desires.

One thing that makes the New Testament distinctively different from the Old Testament is that Jehovah God, the creator of the universe and all it contains, invites us to call Him "Daddy." It is the name of God that Jesus referred to more than any other. When the disciples asked Jesus to teach them how to pray, He said,

> When you pray, go into your room, close the door and pray to your *Father*, who is unseen. Then your *Father*, who sees what is done in secret, will reward you. And when you pray, do not keep on babbling like pagans, for they think

they will be heard because of their many words. Do not be like them, for your *Father* knows what you need before you ask him. This then is how you should pray: "Our *Father* in heaven, hallowed be your name" (Matthew 6:6-9, emphasis added).

If you are a parent, you can imagine how discouraging it would be if your children only talked to you when they wanted something. Quite the contrary, we talk to our children to discipline, instruct, nurture, train, comfort, encourage, guide, and teach. Our relationship with our heavenly Father is much the same. We are called children of God, and He longs to gather us under His wing like a mother hen and speak to us in the quietness of prayer. Our heavenly Father is always available and attentive, compassionate and caring, interested and involved.

Sometimes God simply wants to tell us how deeply He loves us. I will never forget a time of prayer I spent with a group of women just before I was to speak at an event. I had flown to Tennessee, and moments before I went out to minister to the women who had gathered at the church, the leadership team held hands and prayed together. As one woman prayed, she said that God had shown her that very day that I was very precious to Him. God's love washed over me and tears began to spill down my face. God loved me! He loved me! See, that's the message that I was going to share with those women at the conference, but in the hustle and bustle of preparation, God wanted to remind me that He loved me too.

Prayer is not meant to change God's mind, but to change us and align our thinking with His. When we begin our prayer with praise, we take the focus off of ourselves and on to God. When we pray for God's will to be done, we take the focus off our desires and on to God's desires for our lives.

Prayer turns our focus toward God and allows Him to rearrange our priorities. It is more than unloading our burdens and enumerating our desires. Prayer sets our agenda. Did you ever notice that Jesus didn't set His agenda and then ask God to bless it? No, He did only what the Father told Him to do. He "had to go" to Samaria, the next town, and to Zacchaeus' home for dinner. He also had to delay His journey to see His ailing friend Lazarus until he had been dead for four days. Why? Because that's what His Daddy told Him to do.

How did Jesus know what He was to do on any given day? I believe He was in direct communication with His Father at all times—both talking to and listening to Him. We see how God directed Him in prayer in Mark 1:35. After Jesus had performed many miracles, "in the early morning, while it was still dark, Jesus got up, left the house, and went away to a secluded place, and was praying there" (NASB). Here we see several facets of Jesus' time with His Father. What did He do? He prayed. When did He do it? In the early morning. Where did He go? Off by Himself. Why did He have a quiet time with God? He spent time talking to His Father and setting His priorities for the day.

Notice that when the disciples looked for Jesus, they always knew where to find Him—praying. It's interesting that Mark 1:36 says that while Jesus was praying, Simon and his companions searched for Him, found Him, and said to Him, "Everyone is looking for You" (verse 37 NASB). And He replied, "Let us go somewhere else to the towns nearby, so that I may preach there also; for that is what I came for" (verse 38 NASB). That was His focus for the day. He had received His "marching orders" from God, and He was going to stick to them. Would it have been a noble cause to go back to Capernaum and heal a few more people the way He had the day before? Yes. But it wasn't what God had planned for the day.

I don't know about you, but by 8:30 in the morning my phone is ringing with all kinds of requests and demands that threaten to pull me in several directions. By spending time with God first thing in the morning, I am able to set my priorities and say yes or no with confidence. When we start our day with God, it helps us keep our focus on what He has called us to do and not what everyone else wants us to do. As women's ministry leaders, this is the only way to keep our focus on what God would have us do.

Jesus' Pattern for Prayer

Some of the greatest moments in a Christian's life are a result of time spent in prayer. Jesus spent all night in prayer before He chose His disciples (Luke 6:12). He defeated Satan's temptations after praying and fasting for 40 days (Matthew 4:3-10). Prayer preceded His miracles (John 11:41-43) and gave Him the strength to go to the cross (Luke 22:39-43). The disciples observed Jesus' prayer life and asked Him to teach them to pray the way He did (Luke 11:1). He gave them seven simple steps:

1. *Our Father which art in heaven.* Acknowledge that you are a child of God and He is your almighty Father with whom you have a relationship.

2. *Hallowed be thy name.* Praise God for who He is and the holiness of His name and character.

3. *Thy kingdom come. Thy will be done in earth, as it is in heaven.* Pray for His will to be done in your life and the lives of those for whom you intercede. Praying the Word of God is praying the will of God. Pray for God's will to be done in your family, church, nation, and the world.

4. *Give us this day our daily bread.* Pray daily for your needs and the needs of those for whom you intercede.

5. *And forgive us our debts, as we forgive our debtors.* Pray for God to forgive you for your sins, as being in His presence will bring conviction of sin. Also, give your grudges over to Him and forgive those who have offended you.

6. *And lead us not into temptation, but deliver us from evil.* Pray for protection from the world, the flesh, and the devil.

7. *For thine is the kingdom, and the power, and the glory, for ever.* God is the eternal King of Kings whose rule knows no end. He is omnipotent, omniscient, and omnipresent. End by praising God once again. Amen (Matthew 6:9-13 KJV).

Did the disciples learn how to pray? Yes, they did! In Acts 1, during their time in prayer at Pentecost, the Holy Spirit descended on the disciples and gave them power to spread the gospel throughout the entire world.

Prayer is not designed to change God's mind. It is designed to change us and align our thinking with God's. Just as God worked through Jesus' life by prayer and through His disciples' prayer lives, so He works through ours.

Praising God for Who He Is

Some people are unfamiliar with spending time praising God for who He is. However, it is as simple as saying, "Lord, I praise You that You are the Creator, that You are the Provider, that You are the Healer." If this is an unfamiliar aspect of prayer, consider using the names of God listed below. This list is also a wonderful tool to copy and handout to the leadership team for extensive times of prayer and praise.

Old Testament Names of God

Throughout the Old Testament, we see various names of God that reveal His character and His ways. Many times, when God worked mightily in a person's life, he or she called God by a new name. For example, when God took care of Hagar after being cast away in the desert, she came to know him as El Roi—the God who sees. When God provided the ram in the thicket for Abraham, he came to know God as Jehovah-jireh—the LORD will provide. And when God revealed Himself to David as the Shepherd, David came to know Him as Jehovah-rohi—the LORD our shepherd.

Many are comfortable thanking God for what He has done but are not accustomed to praising God for who He is. One way to spend time praising God simply for who He is, is by praying His various names found in the Old Testament. Below is a partial list:

- ❧ Jehovah—The Self-Existent One (Exodus 3:13-15)

- ❧ Jehovah-jireh—The LORD will provide (Genesis 22:14)

- ∾ Jehovah-rapha—The LORD who heals (Exodus 15:26)

- ∾ Jehovah-nissi—The LORD is my banner (Exodus 17:15)

- ∾ Jehovah-mekoddishkem—The LORD who sanctifies you (Leviticus 20:8 NKJV)

- ∾ Jehovah-sabaoth—The LORD of hosts (Joshua 5:13-15 NASB)

- ∾ Jehovah-shalom—The LORD our peace (Judges 6:22 NASB)

- ∾ Jehovah-elyon—The LORD most high (Genesis 14:17-20)

- ∾ Jehovah-rohi—The LORD our shepherd (Psalm 23:1)

- ∾ Jehovah-tsidkenu—The LORD our righteousness (Jeremiah 23:6)

- ∾ Jehovah-shammah—The LORD is there (Ezekiel 48:35 NASB)

- ∾ Elohim—The Creator (Genesis 1:1)

- ∾ El Roi—The God who sees (Genesis 16:7-8)

- ∾ El Shaddai—The All-Sufficient One (Genesis 17:1-8)

- ∾ Adonai—The LORD (Genesis 15:1-2)

- ∾ El Olam—Everlasting God (Genesis 21:33 NASB)

- ∾ The Rock of My Salvation (2 Samuel 22:47 NASB)

- ∾ The Glory and the Lifter of My Head (Psalm 3:3 NASB)

- ∾ The King of Glory (Psalm 24:7)

- ∾ My Strong Rock (Psalm 31:2 NASB)

- ∾ My Fortress (Psalm 31:3 NASB)

- ∾ The Chief Among Ten Thousand (Song of Solomon 5:10 NKJV)

- ∾ Wonderful (Isaiah 9:6)

- ∾ Everlasting Father (Isaiah 9:6)

- ∾ A Nail in a Sure Place (Isaiah 22:23)

- ∾ The Righteous Branch (Jeremiah 23:5)

👁 The Ancient of Days (Daniel 7:13)

👁 King over All the Earth (Zechariah 14:9)

Be Encouraged in the Lord

Next to Jesus Christ, King David was one of the greatest leaders in the Bible, and yet he faced great struggles throughout his reign. In 1 Samuel 30, we read of a time when the enemies came into David's camp and took his and his soldiers' wives and children captive. His men were devastated and many could not go on. David faced a crisis of leadership, and he knew that in order to lead his men, he had to be encouraged himself. But with everyone around him falling apart, where could he go? There was only one place…to God.

"But David strengthened himself in the LORD his God. Then…" (1 Samuel 30:6-7 NASB). Notice that first he spent time with God, and *then* he took action. Be encouraged, dear friend, by the One who longs to encourage you most!

—PART FOUR—
Group Dynamics

*M*y dictionary defines the word "dynamic" as "active, energetic, and capable of giving a sense of power and transmitting energy." It also means "endowing with divine power." Group dynamics describe how people in a group relate to one another, and so much of that is dependent on the group leader. She sets the tone, guides the discussion, and provides a safe environment for women to take that next step closer to God. Our purpose, as Paul wrote to the Colossians, "is that they may be encouraged in heart and united in love, so that they may have the full riches of complete understanding, in order that they may know the mystery of God, namely, Christ, in whom are hidden all the treasures of wisdom and knowledge" (Colossians 2:2-3).

Our prayer is that God will fill us with the power of the Holy Spirit in order to see each woman as a dearly loved child of God, love each woman as sister in Christ, and guide each woman to the knowledge of the truth of Christ Jesus.

In the last section we looked at how the leadership team relates to one another. Now let's take a look at how the leadership team relates to others in order to have a dynamite group experience.

∽ ∽ ∽

Fabulous Facilitators

*A*uthor William Barclay notes, "It is only when truth is discovered that it is appropriated. When a man is simply told the truth, it remains external to him and he can quite easily forget it. When he is led to discover the truth himself it becomes an integral part of him and he never forgets."[1] The purpose of a group facilitator is to serve as the guide, leading women on a journey to unearthing treasures of truth in the Scripture. A teacher is one who instructs; a facilitator is one who leads. One of the greatest joys of a facilitator is when a group member "hits a vein" of gold or silver and discovers a truth for the very first time.

A facilitator encourages an environment of trust, respect, love, and support. She encourages spiritual growth without trying to control it, understanding that it is the Holy Spirit, not the leader, who brings about life change. She moves the group discussion along, helping members become more reliant on their own abilities to study the Bible and less reliant on a particular teacher to spoon-feed them.

As with all relationships, a facilitator must create an atmosphere of trust among the group members. Factors that affect trust are nonverbal and verbal messages presented by the leader. Attitudes are communicated through verbalization, tone of voice, body language, facial expressions, and posture. A simple hug or pat on the back communicates volumes to a woman who is starved for acceptance.

Discussion Destroyers

Whether it is in a small-group discussion, an event-planning session, or a leadership team meeting, our goal should always be to keep the channels of communication open rather than damming up the flow. There are many communication styles that stop discussion cold. Below are just a few.

Advising: "What you need to do is put your child in a time-out every time he misbehaves and that will solve your problem." An advisor tells the person what he or she should do and appears to have all the answers. This makes the group member feel as though her problems are easily solved and foolish for asking the question.

Preaching: "Jesus said to love your neighbor, so you should ignore the fact that she is cutting down your bushes and parking her car in your yard. After all, what would Jesus do?" Preaching at someone makes them feel spiritually inept. Preachy words to avoid are: *should, ought, all Christians…, no Christian would…, you need to…*

Blaming: "If you just loved your husband better, he wouldn't want to stay out late at night with the boys. You must be doing something wrong as a wife or he would love you better." The blamer gives an explanation to show the group member that her past actions have caused the present situation. Thus, she is the guilty party.

Judging: "If you were a Christian, you wouldn't feel that way about your mother-in-law. Christians don't talk that way or act that way." The one who judges puts that group member on the defensive and implies that a Christian does not struggle with sin. The judger puts herself in the place of God, and the group member feels condemned rather than loved. When someone is openly judging, the group is no longer a safe place to grow.

Probing: "What happened in your childhood to make you feel this way? Have you ever had an abortion or been sexually abused?" The leader (or detective) is eager to track down all the facts in the case. She grills the group member about the details of what happened instead of listening for how the member was feeling. Facts over feelings will forfeit group discussion and trust. This type of questioning is inappropriate in a small group setting and will terrify the group members...if they even dare to come back again.

Arguing: "Evolution is a lie. God created the earth in seven days, and I don't care what you say—evolution is a tool of the devil." (Now, evolution is a lie, but that's probably not the best way to handle the situation when someone in a group believes it.)

Analyzing: "Why do you feel that way?" In a small group, it is best to leave psychoanalysis for psychotherapists.

Shaming: "The Bible tells us to be anxious about nothing but pray about everything. I do not sense that you are praying at all, but are simply worrying. Don't you trust God to handle your problems?" Shaming makes the person feel guilty by ridiculing her for her actions, thoughts, or emotions.

Having a Yes Face

I love the story of Thomas Jefferson's crossing of a flooded river.

> During his days as president, Jefferson and a group of companions were traveling across the country on horseback. They came to a river which had left its banks because of a recent downpour. The swollen river had washed the bridge away. Each rider was forced to ford the river on horseback, fighting for his life against the rapid currents. The very real possibility of death threatened each rider, which caused a traveler who was not part of their group to step aside and watch. After several had plunged in and made it to the other side, the stranger asked President Jefferson if he would ferry him across the river. The president agreed without hesitation. The man climbed on, and shortly thereafter the two of them made it safely to the other side. As the stranger slid off the back of the saddle onto dry ground, one in the group asked him, "Tell me, why did you select the president to ask this favor of?" The man was shocked, admitting he had no idea it was the president who had helped him. "All I know," he said, "is that on some of your faces was written the answer 'No,' and on some of them was the answer 'Yes.' His was a 'Yes' face."[2]

A facilitator has a "yes" face that welcomes the joy of discovery among the group members. She asks good, open-ended questions, listens well, and shares as a fellow traveler and not as an expert. Now, let's delve into a few of the qualities of a fabulous facilitator.

The Power of a Question

One of our most powerful tools as a group leader is the question. Jesus was a master at asking questions, and He began at an early age. When He was 12 years old, He traveled with His parents to celebrate Passover in Jerusalem. Three days into His parents' journey home, they noticed that Jesus was missing from the caravan. Panic-stricken as any parents would be, they rushed back to the city to look for their son. Where did they find Him? "After three days, they found him in the temple courts, sitting among the teachers, listening to them and asking them questions. Everyone who heard him was amazed at his understanding and his answers" (Luke 2:46-47).

Jesus is referred to as a healer and teacher, but He was also a master at asking questions and attentively listening. He asked questions of lawyers, invalids, mothers, politicians, fishermen, rabbis, demons, a blind man, Roman officers, a leper, and the disciples. In the Sermon on the Mount alone, He asked 14 questions. He asked the woman caught in adultery, "Where are your accusers?" He asked the scribes, "Why are you thinking evil in your hearts? For which is easier, to say, 'Your sins are forgiven,' or to say, 'Rise and walk'?" Obviously, since Jesus is omniscient, He knows everything. He did not ask questions to gather information. He used questions to get people to think, and many times to help them come to their own logical conclusions.[1]

By asking questions, the leader encourages the students to think, make new discoveries, and explore possibilities. "This teacher guides the group through the lesson in a way that lets them see the scenery for themselves and enjoy the trip personally."[2] This type of leader often discovers that she learns as much from the group members as they learn from her.

Robert Crosby, author of *Now We're Talking!* said, "Ambassadors use questions to build bridges between countries that are oceans apart. Teachers use questions to build bridges to their students. Spouses use questions to build intimacy with one another. Managers use questions to cultivate teamwork and productivity among employees. Wise parents use questions to bridge the generation divide with their children, whether en route to nursery school or on the way home from a soccer game."[3] We, as women's ministry leaders, need to ask good questions to draw women out and draw women in. But what makes a good question good?

Open and Closed Questions

There are many types of questions. One is a closed question that can be answered in one word, such as yes, no, or okay. Then there are open questions. For example:

Closed question: "Did you like the sermon on Sunday?"

Open question: "What did you like about the sermon on Sunday?"

A good discussion group leader will ask questions that draw the members out. She will ask open questions that guide the members into deeper discussion and discovery. She also uses questions to clarify a response, such as, "Are you saying that you believe Jesus died for all people?"

Jesus asked many questions, not because He didn't know the answers, but because He wanted the person to come to the realization on his or her own. He used what are called "guiding questions."

Some Dos and Don'ts of Asking Questions

Dos

- ❧ Encourage group members to ask each other questions.

- ❧ Ask questions that deal with both facts and feelings.

- ❧ Ask open-ended questions.

- ❧ Follow up an incorrect answer with other questions that lead to the right answers without embarrassing the one who gave the incorrect answer.

- ❧ Ask questions to clarify a response.

- ❧ Ask questions that cover only one idea at a time.

- ❧ Ask questions that are appropriate for your "students" spiritual maturity level.

- ❧ Direct questions to the entire group.

- ❧ Give positive verbal responses such as: "wonderful insight," "great answer," "wow," "Jan, that's great."

Don'ts

- ❧ Don't ask obvious questions.

- ❧ Don't fear silence or jump in with an answer if there is a period of silence.

- ❧ Don't dominate the discussion.

- ❧ Don't combine two questions, but do restate.

- ❧ Don't ask closed questions.

- ❧ Don't ask questions that are too personal unless that relationship has been cultivated (usually with time).

- ❧ Don't single out one person and ask them a personal question unless you have let them know you'd like to do that ahead of time.

- ∾ Don't look at your watch when the person is answering a question.

- ∾ Don't fish for an answer.

How to Respond to a Wrong Answer

In every group situation there is the possibility of someone giving an answer that is simply wrong. What do you do in order to steer the group in the right direction, while at the same time not embarrassing the member who gave the incorrect response? Here are a few suggestions:

- ∾ Affirm the person without affirming the answer.

- ∾ "Thank you, Melissa, for sharing that answer. Does anyone have another thought or a different answer?"

- ∾ "Does someone else have another idea?"

- ∾ "That is an interesting way to look at it."

- ∾ "Why do you think that?"

- ∾ "What other information are we given?"

- ∾ "Does anyone else have a different interpretation?"

St. Augustine once said:

In essentials *unity*.
In the non-essentials *liberty*.
In all things *charity*.

20

The Art of Listening

While it is important to know how to ask good questions, it is equally important to respond by listening. Some years ago I was struck by an article in my local newspaper. Joanne Ivancich was described as a friend for hire, earning as much as $500 a month to sit and listen to whatever a person wanted to talk about. She is called a "personal development coach" who helps people focus and make decisions. Basically, she receives payment for two things: asking good questions and telling the truth. She is described as "part consultant, part motivational speaker, part therapist and part rent-a-friend."[1]

An ad in a Kansas newspaper read: "I will listen to you, without comment, for 30 minutes for $5." The person who placed the ad received 10 to 20 calls per day.[2] Everyone wants to feel valued and significant. Perhaps nothing speaks louder than a listening ear. As philosopher Voltaire once said, "The road to the heart is the ear."

Characteristics of a Poor Listener

- ∾ Regularly interrupts the speaker
- ∾ Jumps to conclusions quickly
- ∾ Finishes sentences for the speaker
- ∾ Has poor posture

- Does not make eye contact
- Changes the subject prematurely
- Doesn't give verbal response
- Looks away or at her watch while someone is talking
- Is impatient
- Loses emotional control
- Fidgets with pen or papers and/or shakes hands or feet nervously
- Doesn't listen, but only waits for the other person to stop talking so that she can have her turn

Characteristics of a Good Listener

- Looks at the person who is speaking
- Asks questions to complete the loop or clarify
- Repeats to clarify ("What I hear you saying is…")
- Doesn't interrupt
- Stays on the subject until the person is finished
- Shows concern by asking questions about the speaker's feelings
- Ensures confidentiality
- Doesn't give advice without being invited
- Is emotionally controlled
- Asks questions to encourage the person to tell more instead of less

Body Language of a Good Listener (Offer R.E.S.P.E.C.T.)

- Relax while being attentive
- Eye contact is important

∾ Sit in an open body posture without crossing your arms

∾ Position yourself so you can face the one speaking

∾ Engage by leaning forward

∾ Connect by nodding your head at appropriate moments

∾ Touch the speaker's shoulder or arm

Respect is important. Many women are reluctant to share in group settings. Perhaps they are insecure or have been embarrassed in the past. In order to be an effective group leader, one must show respect to each individual group member.

Listening Exercise

Listening does not come easily for most of us. The following is a fun and effective exercise to use in leadership training to sharpen listening skills.

Break the group up into pairs.

∾ Decide which person in the pair will speak first.

∾ The first speaker completes the following thought in two or three sentences: "When I think about my purpose in life, I think about…"

∾ Then the second speaker repeats in her own words what the first speaker has just said. The first speaker must be satisfied that she had been heard accurately. Continue with the exercise, rotating speaker and listener.

Below are other statements to use for this exercise:

∾ When I enter a room full of people, I usually feel…

∾ When I am feeling anxious in a new situation, I often…

∾ What I look for in a friend is…

∾ When I encounter a truth in God's Word, I…

∽ Group settings that make me feel uncomfortable are those where…

∽ When I am alone, I usually…

∽ I feel closest to God when…

∽ The emotion I find most difficult to control is…

∽ One day I would like to…

∽ I am afraid of…

∽ Right now, this exercise is making me feel…

Listen

When I ask you to listen to me
And you start giving advice,
You have not done what I asked.

When I ask you to listen to me
And you begin to tell me why I shouldn't feel that way,
You are trampling on my feelings.

When I ask you to listen to me
And you feel you have to do something
To solve my problem,
You have failed me,
Strange as that may seem.

So please listen and just hear me.
And if you want to talk,
Wait a minute for your turn;
And I'll listen to you.

—AUTHOR UNKNOWN

Personality Puzzle

*W*hile working in various women's ministries, I have witnessed the beauty of God's unique design among women who work well together. Like an intricate jigsaw puzzle, each woman adds to the completion of a beautiful picture. Some women form the borders, some the corners, and some fill in the middle. When I put a puzzle together, I usually look at the box top to get the completed picture in mind, and then I gather all the pieces together that have similar hues and colors—all the pieces that look like water go in one pile, all the pieces that look like the pink blooms of the cherry tree in one pile, and all the pieces that look like the stone house in the background in another pile. Then I look for the corners and the borders. From there, I begin to fill in the puzzle to form a beautiful picture.

Working with women and their many personalities is a lot like that. By now you have an idea of what you want your women's ministry to look like. You've gathered your corners and borders, and it's time to fill in the rest of the puzzle with the women who will form a beautiful work of art. But who goes where and which women should be grouped together? This is the personality puzzle.

Van Walton is a master of working with various personalities, and I asked her to explain this piece of the puzzle for *Building an Effective Women's Ministry*. Van is a certified personality trainer through

CLASS (Christian Leaders, Authors and Speakers Services), and a member of the Proverbs 31 Ministries speaker team.

Ministering with Personality

Van Walton

As you search for and select your team, chances are you will be looking for women who have great personalities. Typically, people known for their great personalities are positive performers, productive participants, and people pleasers. They are energetic, enthusiastic, and encouraging. They are known for their bright eyes, bubbly actions, and smiling faces. Yes, you do want women with great personalities serving on your team. But not all great personalities are bubbly, smiley, and bright-eyed.

Everyone has a personality. Personalities were first studied and categorized 400 years before Christ. Hippocrates, the father of medicine, theorized that personality styles play a major role in an individual's reactions to certain circumstances. People operate out of their own unique personalities. After researching this fascinating subject, Hippocrates determined that there were four basic personality styles or temperaments, and being a Greek philosopher, he gave each one a Greek name: sanguine, choleric, melancholy, and phlegmatic. Each personality style functions in a unique way; however, most people have a dominant personality with a sprinkling of another. A well-balanced team has a combination of several personality types, making the most of each particular strength.

Let's take a look at various aspects of each personality. The following chart is a personality diagram that gives lots of information at a glance. Take time to study and think of people you know who fit into the different categories. See if you can identify yourself. If you can't readily decipher your personality, don't worry. Remember, we will be directing you to an evaluation of sorts that will further aid in finding your personality.[1]

POPULAR SANGUINE

Extrovert • Talker • Optimist

happy and fun-loving
adventurous
inventive
pleaser
cheerful
charming
show off
gets along with others
joiner
works best with a group

- Is not interested in routine, details, minute tasks

- Best suited for ministry that is visible, active, people inclusive, and creative

- Works well with decoration, hospitality, drama, vision casting, crafting

POWERFUL CHOLERIC

Extrovert • Leader • Optimist

controlling and directing
eager to work hard
productive
goal-oriented
quick
independent
aggressive
responsible
problem solver
works best in charge

- Is not interested in taking breaks, mindless chatter, listening to complaints

- Best suited for ministry that is labor intensive, in need of organizing and leadership

- Works well with delegation, planning, teaching, decision making

PEACEFUL PHLEGMATIC

Introvert • Follower • Pessimist

easy-going
flexible
content
witty
good listener
mediator
relaxed
leads when encouraged
observer
works best quietly

- Is not interested in conflicting situations or high energy activities

- Best suited for ministry that is behind the scenes and slow paced

- Works well with service to others, support

PERFECT MELANCHOLY

Introvert • Thinker • Pessimist

serious
scheduled
talented
loyal
intense
responsible
smart
researcher
neat
works best alone

- Is not interested in "frivolous" events or "mindless" activities

- Best suited for ministry that is intellectually stimulating, requires numbers, orders, and detail

- Works well with budgeting, music, worship, teaching

As you build the women's ministry in your church, remember, a house isn't all doors, walls, or shingles. Many supplies are needed to create a structure. Because Hippocrates' terms are literally Greek to us, we are going to borrow Sharon's use of the house model to understand the personalities.

The most important portion of a home is its *foundation*. It is a solid surface with deep footings that are mathematically laid out so the entire house will fit together as it is built. Every ministry needs a good foundation, which is often displayed in the melancholy personality. Like the foundation, the melancholy is rarely noticed, but the ministry rests upon her. It is important that the foundation be near perfect in all its calculations.

A house cannot be put together without *nails*. Nails are constructed of iron and steel. Although most nails are never seen, they serve a very important purpose; they keep the house together. Like the nails, the phlegmatic person gets the job done, and yet many times goes unnoticed. Every ministry needs people who keep the vision and people together. They are known as peacemakers. They also work behind the scenes in many capacities and do not like drawing attention to themselves.

Of course the *roof* is very important. Like the roof, the choleric personality controls the environment within the house, keeping heat and cool in or out. Under the roof the house is organized into various rooms for different functions. Every ministry needs someone powerful and decisive who will not be afraid to put the pieces together and keep it functioning. A house must have a roof, or it would be vulnerable to outside destructive elements. It is the same with a women's ministry. Boundaries must be defined so unforeseen issues can be addressed and quick decisions made when the ministry finds itself in stormy weather.

Finally a house needs a *door*—the sanguine personality. An open door sends a message of hospitality. A door decorated with a wreath tells people they are welcome. Doors come in all styles and colors, yet they have one thing in common. People enter and leave through them. The door can set the emotional tone for a home. People who enter will at once feel a cheerful high or a mournful low depending on the attitude the door displays. A home, or ministry, that is warm and friendly is a safe place for women to gather, grow, and give.

With every strength comes a potential weakness. For each personality we'll see the following: three positive personality traits, three ideal jobs, and three potential weaknesses. When we understand each other's weaknesses, we are better able to extend grace without being surprised or disappointed.

Interestingly, each of the four personality types thrives in different situations.

The Popular Sanguine

Thrives on: attention, approval, affection, acceptance, presence of people, and activity

Positive personality traits: friendliness, creativity, and enthusiasm

Ideal jobs: decorating, hospitality, or special events

Possible weaknesses: lack of follow-through, overcommitment, and a talkative nature

The Powerful Choleric

Thrives on: appreciation for achievements, opportunity for leadership, participation in ministry decisions, and something to control

Positive personality traits: delegating abilities, working hard, and decisiveness

Ideal jobs: director, leader, or chair

Possible weaknesses: bossiness, impatience, and knowing it all

The Peaceful Phlegmatic

Thrives on: peace and relaxation, attention, praise, self-worth, and loving motivations

Positive personality traits: forgiveness, servanthood, and kindness

Ideal jobs: prayer coordinator, team member, or behind-the-scenes worker

Possible weaknesses: procrastination, undercommitment, and passivity

The Perfect Melancholy

Thrives on: sensitivity to deep desires, satisfaction for quality achievement, own space, security, stability, separation from noisy and messy situations, and support

Positive personality traits: evaluation, stabilization, and being thorough

Ideal jobs: tasks in finance, an advisory capacity, or in coordination of people and projects

Possible weaknesses: overly high expectations, lack of compassion, and negativity

In Dr. Gary Chapman's book *The Five Love Languages,* he notes five different ways that people feel loved: acts of service, words of affirmation, quality time, physical touch, and gifts. What says "I love you" to one person may be totally different from what says "I love you" to another. Likewise, various personalities have similar reactions to discouragement and similar ways that they are encouraged. How can we tell that someone is discouraged? And what brand of encouragement suits the various personalities? Below are a few examples:

     ~ The *sanguine* team member will turn to the other women on the team to fill her inner vacuum. She will want them to affirm her by joining her in the frenzied decorations for the next event. She may go overboard, spending too much and making a big deal of the "just right" theme, so much so that she will turn others off. She will in effect be screaming for attention and at the same time causing her teammates to run away. She wants to feel good about herself. What she needs from you is some affection and attention.

∾ The *melancholy* member will move deeply into her inner self, attempting to perfect her life with lists and charts so she can check off what she has accomplished. She might remove herself and her much-desired talents from your team if she doesn't feel others' satisfaction in her contributions. What she needs from you is some sensitive words telling her how important her contribution is to the ministry.

∾ The *choleric* team member will try to take more and more control, but will soon find herself losing control. She will become more manipulative, assertive, disagreeable, and even insulting when she doesn't feel appreciated for all her hard work. What she needs from you is your listening ear after you have asked her to explain the plusses and minuses of the organizational structure. This will allow her an opportunity to lead.

∾ As your ministry's programs gear up becoming busier and more active, you might find the *phlegmatic* female completely avoiding all women's activities. She needs peace. She is looking for self-worth. If she can't find it, she would rather be at home in her quiet, non-challenging environment. What she needs from you is some quiet time alone, just the two of you working on a simple yet important task: stuffing envelopes, running errands, visiting a new mother in the hospital. The time you spend with her will make her feel valued and loved.

There are many resources available to help women in ministry to understand the various personality types and bring out the best in people. Personality assessments are a fun team-building activity and provide many "aha" moments as women begin to recognize various personality types on their team. When each team member understands her personality profile and the personality profile of those on her team, she will be able to "pursue the things which make for peace and the building up of one another" (Romans 14:19 NASB) and the ministry of your church.*

---

* See the appendix for personality assessment information and additional personality resources.

*T*roubleshooting
*D*ifficult *P*ersonalities

A little leaven leavens the whole lump of dough" (1 Corinthians 5:6 NASB). Likewise, one self-centered and disruptive group member hinders the growth and openness of the entire group. Below are some ideas for coping with common problems and difficult personalities. These suggestions hold true whether in a leadership team meeting, committee meeting, or small-group Bible study.

Disruptive Behavior

Disturbed Darlene

Uses the group as a counseling session. Shares at length at each meeting, the latest developments in her ongoing saga.

Solution

Tactfully interrupt the explanation of the problem and say, "We'd better get back to the lesson, or we may not finish today." Afterward, offer to meet with the person to discuss her problems. Don't feel that you can solve all her problems. You may need to refer her to a professional counselor.

Blocker Bertha

Blocks the flow of discussion with argumentative statements and tangents.

Refocus on the passage or question at hand. Ask someone to restate the question at hand.

Talker Tammy

Shares long illustrations and answers. Interrupts others and monopolizes the conversation.

Have Tammy sit beside you instead of across the table or circle. Speak with her afterward and say something like, "Tammy, your answers are wonderful, but I think we need to give others in the group an equal opportunity to share."

Silent Sue

Does not speak up in the group. Sits passively on the edge of the group.

Direct a question to Sue that you know she can answer. Just being able to answer correctly may give her the confidence to speak up again.

Arguer Angela

Challenges the discussion leader. "But" is her favorite word. Becomes combative and defensive if others in the group do not agree with her.

Remind her that the Bible is the final authority. Do not enter into an argument.

The Holy Spirit is capable of defending Himself. While the leader must not allow anyone to teach anything other than the truth, do not become angry. This will alienate the group.

Expert Edna

Thinks she is a Bible authority. Lectures the group using theological jargon that may be intimidating to those who have limited Bible knowledge. Robs members of the joy of discovery.

Privately applaud Edna's Bible knowledge, but remind her that people learn best by discovering truths themselves. Explain that the ultimate goal of the group is for members to feel encouraged and experience spiritual growth. Ask her to join you in prayer for the individual members.

Pleasing Paula

Always gives the "right" answer, even though it may not be how she truly feels.

Always share honestly with the group, revealing your own weakness and struggles. Express appreciation when she shares an opposing view.

Complaining Cathy

Constantly complains about the people in the group and the way the group is run.

Assign her a job to do. Remind her that everyone is doing the best they can.

Superficial Sara

Shares on a very superficial level. Not willing to go deep or reveal too much about her true feelings.

Perhaps the leader is not sharing on a personal level. Be open and specific in your own sharing, and ask for specifics when the members share.

Late Lucy

This is leaven that will quickly affect the entire group. If it is not dealt with quickly, the whole group will begin to consistently arrive 15 minutes late.

Set a time and begin promptly, even if there is only one other person present. If tardiness continues to be a problem, ask the group if the meeting time is too early and needs to be changed.

Confronting a group member can be very difficult. Remember, everyone has the desire to be loved and encouraged. Before confronting a group member, the leader should pray and ask God to give her an attitude of love. End the conversation with praise for what the member is doing well in order to leave her on a positive note.

Too Much Information

Another situation that comes up often in small-group sharing time is TMI...too much information. What do you do when a woman in the group begins sharing very intimate details of her life and you notice other group members beginning to squirm in their seats?

- ∽ Don't feel as though you have to give advice. The person sharing usually wants to simply be heard, not necessarily fixed.

- ∽ Avoid cutting her off by saying, "Jane, we'll pray about that," and then moving quickly to another subject.

- ∽ Avoid saying, "I understand" if you really don't.

- ∽ Avoid trying to cheer her up. The Bible says to mourn with those who mourn and rejoice with those who rejoice (Romans 12:15).

- ∽ Try not to express shock. (I learned this skill when I was a counselor at a Crisis Pregnancy Center. Your whole being may be thinking, *I'm not believing this!* But do your best to remain calm...as though you've heard the scenario a thousand times.)

- ∽ If the woman keeps going on and on, manipulating the group time, ask her if it would be okay for the two of you to get together afterward.

- ∽ Have the group stop and pray for her right then and there.

∾ Refer her to a trained professional if her problems are beyond your training.

When to Refer to a Professional

∾ If the person asks for professional help, always refer her to someone.

∾ If the person is in a dangerous or life-threatening situation.

∾ If the person is involved in self-destructive behavior, such as sex, drugs, alcohol abuse, self-induced vomiting, cutting oneself.

∾ If the person mentions thoughts of suicide.

∾ If the person exhibits a physical change in appearance, such as rapid weight loss.

Icebreakers

Getting to Know One Another

*A*n icebreaker is simply a means of getting to know one another that encourages an atmosphere of warmth, acceptance, and sharing among team members. Your group may want to spend a few minutes each session asking a "get to know you" type question. To make it interesting, you may want to change the order of answering the questions. Following are some suggestions. There are several possibilities for choosing the order in which ladies will share. It is important before you choose any of these suggestions to be sensitive about your group.

Order Variations

- Simply go around the circle. Each one shares.

- Place numbers on name tags. Call out a number to designate who is the next to share.

- Designate the first to share. She in turn chooses someone who is wearing one of the same colors she is wearing. Continue until all have shared.

- Give everyone a piece of paper. Each lady writes her name on it. The names are placed in a basket. Designate the first to share. She then reaches into the basket, choosing a piece of paper, and reads the name of the next lady to share.

∾ Share in the order of closest birthdays already celebrated and go backward until everyone has shared.

∾ Share in the order of number of siblings.

∾ For a change, which will allow ladies to spend more time talking and growing deeper, divide the group into smaller groups using one of the following:

  • long-haired blondes, short-haired blondes, long-haired brunettes, short-haired brunettes, redheads, and those with gray hair
  • divide according to children's stages: infants, toddlers, preschoolers, grade school, middle school, high school, college, adults
  • painted fingernails by different shades, including those unpainted
  • one ring, two rings, three rings, or more
  • eye color: brown, blue, green, hazel, gray

Seasonal Icebreakers

∾ Collect cards that relate to the season: Christmas, Valentine's Day, and Easter. You will need cards that are different. Cut the card into four or five pieces using curved lines, creating a puzzle. Mix the pieces up. As each woman arrives, give her a piece and tell her she is to find the other three to four pieces she needs to put her card back together. Once each lady has found the other pieces to her card, she has reached the desired goal.

∾ Share a favorite memory or tradition related to the season.

∾ Ask a trivia question. The one who answers asks the next trivia question.

∾ Create an acrostic using a seasonal word and items that can be found in the room where ladies are gathered. For example, using the word FEAST: Fireplace, Entry table, Apple, Stool, Teacup.

∾ Give each lady a piece of tissue paper. Tell her to hold it behind her back. Give instructions, telling the ladies they are in a contest to see who can come the closest to tearing their tissue paper into one of the following: the shape of a heart, a Christmas tree, snowflake, angel, Easter bunny, lamb, cross, etc.

∾ Play charades using seasonal songs or sayings.

Childhood Icebreaker Questions

1. Where were you born?
2. How many brothers and sisters do you have?
3. How old were you when you learned to ride a bike?
4. What was your favorite room in the house as a child?
5. What was your mother's/father's occupation?
6. What was your favorite subject in school?
7. What is your favorite childhood memory?
8. How did your family celebrate Christmas and/or Thanksgiving?
9. What was one of your favorite holiday traditions?
10. Who was your first boyfriend?

Family Icebreakers: Fill in the Blanks

1. I was initially attracted to my husband because...
2. I chose the name _____ for my firstborn because...

3. The trait I most admire in my (mother, father, sister, brother) is…

4. Our favorite family pastime is…

5. Our favorite place in the house to hang out is…

6. My last child was born in (name of town) at (name the hospital).

7. My most obvious physical trait is my _____. I inherited it from my _____.

Spiritual Icebreakers: Complete the Sentences

- ∾ My first memory of hearing about God is…

- ∾ The person who introduced me to Jesus Christ was…

- ∾ The first church I ever attended was…

- ∾ The Bible verse that most speaks to me is…

- ∾ My favorite Bible story is…

- ∾ My first Bible was…

- ∾ When did God first become real to you?

Personal Icebreakers: Getting to Know You

- ∾ Before I arrived here today, I had to…

- ∾ My favorite toy when I was a child was a…

- ∾ Ten years ago, I spent most of my time doing…

- ∾ My name is (Van). V stands for VICTORIOUS. Each lady tells what the first letter of her name stands for.

- ∾ If I could do or be anything at all, I would…

- ∾ As a child my favorite daydream was…

- ∾ My favorite thing to do these days is…

- When did you pierce your ears? How? Why haven't you pierced your ears?

- I volunteer in the community by...

- Name everything in your purse. The lady who has the most stuff listed dumps her purse and tells all!

- What is one thing you are good at doing?

- Who was the most influential person in your life?

- If you could be a fictitious person in a book or movie, who would you be and why?

- If money were no object and you knew you could not fail, what would you try to accomplish over the next five years?

Relational Fun and Games

As ladies arrive put them together in groups of two or three. Either group them together as they come through the door or assign numbers or match name tags. Have them work together doing one of the following:

- Locate 26 items in the room, each starting with a different letter of the alphabet.

- Give them a storage bag filled with Legos and see what creation flows from the individual groups. Tell them to name their creation.

- Find out three things about one another that you each have in common.

- Make a commitment and a plan to get together sometime within the next two weeks.

- Choose a volunteer project of a couple of hours you can work on together.

More Get-to-Know-You Ideas

- ∾ *Two Truths and a Lie:* Get each person to tell two true facts and one falsehood about themselves. Then let the others guess which one is not true.

- ∾ *Today's Special Guest:* Ask each team member to pull out a picture from her wallet and tell about the person.

- ∾ *Testimony Time:* Have various team members share their testimonies. Never call on someone to do that on the spur of the moment. Ask them ahead of time or have them sign up in advance.

- ∾ *Pet Peeves:* Ask everyone to share their pet peeves. Complete the following sentence: "It really bothers me when someone…"

- ∾ *To Tell the Truth:* The leader collects one fact about each member and types up a list of facts. These are facts the person has shared freely and does not mind the others knowing. Pass the sheet out and try to guess which fact goes with which person.

- ∾ *Timeline Trail:* Have each person draw a timeline of their spiritual life and mark the high and low points. Start at age one and go to the present. (This is a wonderful exercise for those who are nervous about sharing their testimony. By explaining their timeline, they will be sharing their testimony. It will also make some realize that they have never asked Jesus to be their Savior.)

- ∾ *Self-Portrait:* Give everyone a large sheet of paper and a few crayons. Have each member draw a self-portrait without letting the others in the group see. Then have the group leader collect the pictures and hold them up one at a time. See if the group members can match the drawings with the correct person. When the person is identified, have her tell a bit about herself.

∾ *M&Ms:* Place a bowl of M&Ms on a table and ask each person to take four to five. Then have them share the following for each color selected:

Brown—Share about the house you grew up in.

Yellow—Share about your favorite summer vacation.

Blue—Share about your first airplane ride.

Green—Share about your first date.

Red—Share about your first ticket for breaking the law.

Orange—Wild card. Share any of the above.*

* See the appendix for more resources of icebreaker ideas.

24

Creative
Ways to Lead Prayer

*P*rayer is one of the most important parts of any women's ministry meeting. Whether in a small group or evening event, prayer should be the bookends of the gathering.

In a small group setting there may be many women who are not accustomed to praying with other people, so the leader must be sensitive and not put someone on the spot or make them feel uncomfortable. A leader leads by example. It is exciting to watch a timid woman approach the throne of grace with confidence because she has watched others lead her there.

A women's ministry leader or a small-group leader has a wonderful opportunity to model prayer. Jesus often prayed aloud, not that He needed to for the Father to hear Him, but so that those around Him could eavesdrop on the conversation and learn how to pray themselves. He prayed aloud when He raised Lazarus from the dead (John 11:41-42), when He served the Last Supper (Luke 22:19), and when He gave thanks before feeding the 5000 (Matthew 14:19).

As you participate in corporate prayer, you will see God answer and lives changed. Keep a list of requests and praises and encourage the women to pray for each other throughout the week.

Let's take a look at several creative ways to lead prayer.

Six S's of Prayer

In her book *What Happens When Women Pray,* Evelyn Christenson gives six simple reminders for corporate prayer. These are particularly helpful when leading a group that is not accustomed to praying aloud.

Short Prayers: Long prayers may be intimidating. Offer short prayers, perhaps two or three sentences for each subject.

Simple Prayers: Pray just as if you are talking to a friend. Use simple words, omitting King James vocabulary and elaborate words. Use a normal conversational tone right from the heart.

Small Groups: Pray in small groups rather than in the larger group. A woman may feel more comfortable praying with two or three other women. "Where two or three come together in my name, there am I with them" (Matthew 18:20).

Silent Periods: Prayer is a two-way conversation. What God has to say is more important than what we have to say. Don't worry if there is a period of silence. God may be speaking to someone's heart. Explain this to the group to help those unfamiliar with times of silence feel more comfortable.

Specific Requests: Be specific with your requests. Avoid prayers such as "We pray for world peace" or "We pray for all the sick children in the world." Instead, pray for personal issues, such as Aunt Betty, who has pneumonia, a daughter who is straying from the Lord, a marriage that is struggling, or for more patience.

In order for a woman to share specific personal requests, she must feel a sense of trust and openness. Establish a confidentiality policy right from the beginning. "We covenant together that nothing said in this prayer time will be repeated outside of this group." The way for the group to be honest in their sharing is for the leader to model by being honest and personal with her requests.

Subject by Subject: Pray for one subject at a time. Some people call this "praying through." As one person prays aloud, others pray silently on the same subject, adding their own prayers in turn. Make sure to include praises in your prayers.[1]

ACTS

Another simple and effective way to lead prayer is using the ACTS pattern. Assign a prayer leader to lead the group through the four aspects of prayer: Adoration, Confession, Thanksgiving, and Supplication. During the adoration time, the group members spend time praising God for who He is (you may want to refer to the names of God in chapter 17). During the confession time, group members confess any sin that might be standing in the way of their relationship with God or other people. This can be done silently or verbally. The third aspect of the ACTS pattern is thanking God for what He has done. And finally, the fourth aspect is supplication: petitioning God for various needs. The purpose of the prayer leader is to sense when it is time to move from one phase of prayer to the next. For example, she simply says, "Lord, now we come to You with prayers of thanksgiving."

Other Creative Ideas for Group Prayer

1. Pick a portion of Scripture to pray for one another during the week (Colossians 1:9; Ephesians 3:14-19).

2. Pray a psalm.

3. Begin the prayer time by praying the Lord's Prayer.

4. Spend some prayer time just thanking and praising God.

5. Break your group into prayer couplets and pray for each other's requests during the week.

6. Hold hands when you pray.

7. Take the group outside for prayer.

8. Spend time in silent prayer.

9. If someone is having a particularly difficult time, stop and pray for them right then and there.

10. Pray about the principles you studied during the discussion time.

11. Use 3 x 5 cards to record requests. Give each woman a card to take home and pray for during the week.

12. To overcome fear, have each person complete a sentence with one word. For example: "Lord, forgive me for_____." "Lord, help me be more_____." "Lord, help me let go of_____." The leader states the first part of the sentence and the members simply say the one word or words to complete the sentence.

13. Have the members write out their prayer requests before they come. This cuts down on the time it takes for them to make their requests and helps the members state the requests in a concise manner.

14. Have the members write their prayer requests on 3 x 5 index cards. Write the date at the top of the card. Have a facilitator collect and read the cards one at a time. As a card is read, stop and have someone pray for that request.

Prayer and the Leader

As a leader, there are some proven ways to facilitate a meaningful prayer time in your group:

∾ Model prayer for the group.

∾ Respect the intimacy level.

∾ Guide the prayer time by taking them from praise to confession to thanksgiving to requests and back to praise.

∾ Avoid lengthy discussion of prayer needs.

∾ Avoid giving or allowing others to give advice during prayer time. It belittles the prayer need by saying, "Oh, we can fix this for you. That's easy."

∾ Include prayer time at each meeting.

∾ Pray the Scriptures. When you pray the Word of God, you pray the will of God.

∾ Suggest that members write down the prayer requests and pray for the members during the week.

∾ Avoid going around the circle for open prayer so as to not embarrass someone who is not comfortable praying aloud.

∾ Don't try to sound superspiritual or pray in King James language. Just speak to God as you would speak to a friend.

PART FIVE

Programs
and Special Events

*I*n chapter 5 we walked down the aisle of the programs and saw a variety of options and ideas. Now let's pull a few off the shelf and take a closer look.

Like the rooms in a house, each program will serve a different purpose with specific goals and expectations. Through surveys, brainstorming, and astute observation, various needs will surface. Programs are devised to meet the women where they are spiritually as well as mentally, physically, and emotionally. This section will deal with programs that are geared to encourage and equip women of the church. The following section will deal with programs that target those outside the church body.

Remember, the goal is effectiveness for life change. As women in ministry, we are striving to lead women to the next step in their relationship with God. No matter where she is on the continuum from new believer to seasoned saint, these programs are for the specific purpose of taking her hand and walking side by side to the next step in her journey.

I encourage you to look at these ideas as springboards for your own innovative programs rather than as exact blueprints to follow. Pick and choose. Adapt and adopt. Consider what will work best for your women's ministry—and don't be afraid to try something new!

❧ ❧ ❧

Bible Studies

"In the beginning was the Word, and the Word was with God, and the Word was God" (John 1:1). As we begin to look at various programs for women's ministry, we will start where God started...with the Word.

Choosing Bible study material is a decision a group will need to make many times during their life together. So let's begin by looking at an orderly method of evaluating and choosing material.

Group Considerations When Selecting Study Material

When a small group first forms, the material used should be highly relational, assisting the group in getting acquainted and building a significant level of understanding, care, respect, and trust. With hundreds of resources on the market, choosing study material can be confusing. Here are some questions to consider:

1. What is our group's makeup?

2. What is our group's purpose?

3. What are the spiritual needs of the women in the group?

4. What material would give balance and variety to what we have previously studied?

5. Has the Holy Spirit been pointing the group to a deeper understanding of a new area?

6. Did questions come up in a previous study that warrant further study in a certain area?

7. Is the material biblically based?

8. Would the study lead us to a better understanding of the Bible?

9. Is the study in line with our church's doctrine?

10. Is the depth of the material appropriate for the group?

11. Does the amount of homework coincide with what our group has agreed to tackle?

12. Can the study be completed in the time frame allotted for the group to meet?

13. Is the material a study of the Bible rather than the study of an author's opinions?

14. Do we want to do an inductive Bible study or a topical Bible study?

Study Guide Criteria Selection

Below are guidelines to consider when making a final selection of the study material.

The Publisher

Is the publisher a reliable source for solid biblical doctrine? While not all-inclusive, reliable publishers would include:

- NavPress
- Victor Books
- InterVarsity Press
- Word Publishing
- Tyndale House Publishers
- Gospel Light
- Zondervan Publishing House
- Moody Publishers

- ∿ Multnomah Books   ∿ Harvest House Publishers
- ∿ Harold Shaw   ∿ Life Way
- ∿ Precept Ministries   ∿ David C. Cook

The Study Guide Format

Areas to look at in any potential study guide are the format, initial questions, content questions, application, and additional leader helps. Are the questions clear and concise? Are the questions challenging to one's thinking rather than asking for simple responses? Do the questions assist in studying the Bible inductively, including observation (what does it say), interpretation (what does it mean), and application (what does it mean to me and how can I apply it to my life)?

Purchasing the Material

Once the group or committee has selected a study guide, it is important to allow enough time to obtain copies. The books can be ordered from a Christian bookstore, online bookstore, or directly from the publisher or ministry. For example, Proverbs 31 Ministries and Precept Ministries study guides may be ordered directly from the ministry home office. Often Christian bookstores will allow bulk books to go out on consignment or will give credit when the unwanted books are returned.

Order the books about three weeks in advance. It is better to overestimate the number rather than place a special order for one or two books at the last minute. Again, most bookstores will give credit for extra books returned in a reasonable amount of time. It is best to discuss the return policy with the store ahead of time so there will be no misunderstanding.

Group Evaluation for Ongoing Studies

The major focus of a small-group Bible study is the study of Scripture. However, the health of the group is also an important factor to consider as the group continues. Building relationships, honest sharing, meaningful prayer, application of truths to life, and significant service projects all play a role in what the group chooses to do for their time of Bible study.

Thus, it is important to evaluate how the group is doing as a whole in order to select the proper curriculum. The process of selection should begin four to six weeks in advance of concluding a current study so that materials can be obtained in time for the group to continue on schedule the following year or "semester."

Bible Study Material Review

One way to evaluate Bible study material is to distribute various study guides to members of a Bible study committee for review. Have the women review the material and report their findings.

Another way to evaluate Bible study material is to have each group leader complete a review after the study is complete and keep the reviews on file for future consideration. On page 179 is a helpful guide for review.

When reviewing material, keep your purpose and target group member in mind. For example, if you are selecting material for beginners, make sure the material is not too in-depth, the time it takes to complete the material is not too lengthy, and the questions are not too complicated. On the other hand, if you are selecting material for a group of women with advanced biblical knowledge, make sure that the material is challenging and the questions penetrating. Studies that are too complex for the beginner will lead to discouragement, and studies that are too simple for the more advanced will lead to boredom.

Is the purpose of the group fellowship and encouragement, with Bible study as the springboard for discussion? Then the study may require only an hour a week. Is the purpose of the group in-depth Bible study? Then the participants may expect and enjoy lessons that take an hour a day. Oscar Feucht once said, "The difference between reading [the Bible] and study is like the difference between drifting in a boat and rowing toward a destination." The key is to know your hoped-for destination for each group and select material accordingly.

Bible Study Material Review

Book/Study Guide:_____ Reviewed by: _____

Author: _____Date: _____

Series: _____Publisher: _____

Bible study group spiritual level:

_____Beginner _____Intermediate _____Mature

The material was oriented most for:

_____Beginner (new Christians)

_____Intermediate (those with some Bible
knowledge)

_____Mature (mature Christians with more
advanced Bible knowledge and experience)

Overall evaluation of the material:	lowest			highest	
1. Positive response from the group	1	2	3	4	5
2. Good introduction	1	2	3	4	5
3. Content spiritually challenging	1	2	3	4	5
4. Practical application of the material	1	2	3	4	5
5. Quality of questions for personal study	1	2	3	4	5

List the strengths of the material:_____

_____

_____

List the difficulties of the material: (too complex, too simple, too theological, etc.) _____

_____

Would you recommend this study to another group?

_____ yes _____ no

Inductive Bible Study

Not every Bible study leader will choose to use a study guide. One of the most effective ways to study the Bible without a guide is called inductive Bible study. (It is important to note that many study guides do follow the inductive pattern.) The beauty of inductive Bible study is that the members are guided on a journey of discovering God's truth for themselves, rather than being told what the teacher has learned.

The word "inductive" means the process of drawing a conclusion. Some may feel that the inductive approach feels very mechanical at first. However, just as a pianist learns the keys and the scales of the instrument so that music can flow from her fingertips with little effort, the tools and methods of the inductive approach will help the reader to understand the deeper truths of the Scripture and allow the Holy Spirit to work freely to bring fresh insight. The three elements of inductive Bible study include:

Observation: What does the passage say?

Interpretation: What does the passage mean?

Application: What does the passage mean to me?

Observation—What Does the Passage Say?

Just as a scientist makes no interpretation until he has collected all his data, a Bible scholar makes no interpretation until she has gathered all her facts. Observation is the process of seeing and writing down what the passage says. Observation has been defined in several ways: the act, power, or habit of seeing and noting; thorough and careful notice; to watch closely; to look intently; to give full attention to what one sees; to be mentally aware of what one sees. When observing Scripture, begin by reading the passage and noting what the author has to say. No interpreting. No applying. Simply observing. This could be several verses or a whole chapter. If the focus is just a few verses, read the surrounding text to make sure that the passage is kept in context.

Read straight through the passage. If questions of interpretation come to mind, jot them down and come back to them later.

While reading the passage, look for the following:

- ∾ Key words—important or repeated words

- ∾ A theme or themes—such as salvation, holy living, use of the tongue, etc.

- ∾ Contrasts and/or comparisons—used to compare a new idea to something familiar

- ∾ Illustrations—parables and stories

- ∾ Advice, warnings, promises, admonitions—things the author tells you to do

- ∾ Lists—such as fruit of the Spirit listed in Galatians 5 or the armor of God in Ephesians 6.

- ∾ Reasons or results—look for "if" and "then"

- ∾ Questions—questions introduce an idea or challenge the reader

- ∾ Important connectives—"therefore," "but," "if," "in order that"

- ∾ Audience—to whom was the passage written?

- ∾ Time—what was going on at that point in history?

- ∾ Who—who wrote it?

- ∾ What—what are the main themes?

- ∾ When—when was it written?

- ∾ Where—where did it happen? Will it happen?

- ∾ Why—why was it written?

- ∾ How—how is the truth illustrated?

Interpretation—What Does the Passage Mean?

After you have dissected the passage to understand what it says, then move to interpretation to discover what the passage means and the purpose behind the author's words. Notice, not what the passage means to us (that comes later with application), but what the author means to say. Interpretation will vary from person to person, commentary to commentary. The idea is to discover, with the guidance of the Holy Spirit, what God is saying through the author who held the pen.

Below are some helps for interpreting Scripture:

- ∼ Pray. The Bible is clear that it is the Holy Spirit who opens our eyes to see the truth. We should never try to interpret Scripture on our own, but rely on the Holy Spirit to lead us into all truth (1 Corinthians 2:9-16; Ephesians 1:15-17; Psalm 119:18).

- ∼ Define key words. Use a dictionary or a Hebrew/Greek dictionary to gain insight into the meaning of key words.

- ∼ Cross-reference. The best interpreter of the Bible is the Bible. Use a concordance or cross-references listed in the margin to look up verses that relate to the same subject matter. There are many wonderful concordances available, including inexpensive CDs for the computer.

- ∼ Read the passage in various Bible translations to gain greater insight.

- ∼ Read the surrounding verses to keep the passage in proper context.

- ∼ Finally, read commentaries to expand on what you have already learned. I strongly encourage students of the Bible to resort to commentaries after they have studied the passage on their own. It is very exciting to experience the Holy Spirit revealing truth to us directly!

Application—What Does the Passage Mean to Me?

Finally, after you discovered what the passage says and what the passage means, apply what you have learned. The ultimate purpose of Bible study is to know God and His design for your life. James warns us not to be merely hearers of the Word, but doers of it (James 1:22-25). God desires life change—for us to be transformed into the image of Christ by the renewing of our minds. That happens when we study the truths of Scripture and apply them to our lives. The basis of application is found in 2 Timothy 3:16-17: "All Scripture is inspired by God and profitable for teaching, for reproof, for correction, for training in righteousness; so that the man of God may be adequate, equipped for every good work" (NASB).

When leading a Bible study, don't be surprised if the applications are very different for the different group members. God's Word is living and active (Hebrews 4:12). How exciting that He uses His Word to minister to people right at their point of need.

Below are questions we can ask ourselves when applying Scripture to our lives:

- What am I to do?

- What am I to believe?

- How am I to act?

- What am I going to change about my life to make this Scripture a reality in my life?

Bible Study Team Leaders

A Bible study team will vary depending on the people available to serve. Below are suggestions for positions to consider:

- *Bible Study Coordinator:* She chooses the Bible study material and coordinates the calendar for the various studies throughout the year.

- ❧ *Bible Study Review Coordinator:* She gathers a group of women to evaluate various Bible studies and presents recommendations to the Bible study coordinator.

- ❧ *Administration Team Leader:* She organizes and plans registration, creates rosters, places members into small groups, and handles money for materials.

- ❧ *Hospitality Coordinator:* She coordinates refreshments, name tags, hugs, and makes sure each attendee feels comfortable. She arrives early to make sure the refreshment area is set up when the ladies arrive.

- ❧ *Worship Leader:* She leads the group in singing and creates an atmosphere that prepares the women to experience God's presence.

- ❧ *Prayer Leader:* She leads the group in corporate prayer and teaches prayer by modeling.

- ❧ *Child Care Coordinator:* She coordinates the babysitting, hires sitters, collects money, or plans the schedule for group member rotation. She works with the church in arranging child care and the facilities.

Sample Bible Study Schedules

Sample Morning Bible Study Schedule

8:45–9:15	Fellowship and refreshments
9:15–9:20	Welcome and announcements
9:20–9:30	Singing
9:30–10:00	Prayer
10:00–11:00	Teaching and small-group discussion
11:00	Close in prayer
11:30	All children are picked up by this time

Sample Evening Bible Study Schedule

6:45–7:00	Fellowship and refreshments
7:00–7:10	Welcome and announcements
7:10–7:20	Singing
7:20–7:50	Prayer
7:50–8:50	Teaching and small-group discussion
8:50	Close in prayer
9:10	All children are picked up by this time

26

Programs for *Moms*

Mary Ann Ruff was a newly married woman attending a large church in Kansas City, Kansas. While her husband worked as an associate pastor, Mary Ann worked with women who were college- and career-aged. Being very tuned in to the women at her church, Mary Ann began to observe young moms in their congregation and noticed a few common threads. They appeared exhausted, lonely, and frazzled. Her heart went out to these women, even though she had no children of her own.

Mary Ann went to the leadership of the church and asked, "What is the church doing for young mothers? Are there any programs specifically targeted for their unique needs?"

Mary Ann discovered that there were circles and a few Bible studies sprinkled throughout the week, but nothing specifically targeted for young mothers. The staff agreed to allow Mary Ann to begin exploring the possibilities for such a program. God, in His providence, gave Mary Ann the training and insight she would need to accomplish such a task—she discovered she was pregnant with her first child.

During the beginning stages of exploring possibilities, Mary Ann did exactly what is outlined in this manual. She began with prayer. Two other women joined her and agreed to spend time seeking God as to what He would have them do to help young mothers grow in their relationship with Him, as well as what they could do to reach out to young mothers who did not have a relationship with Him at all. After a few months, the trio decided to offer a summer Bible study.

The first Bible study was held in a woman's home. The group commissioned college students to babysit the children in the basement while the mothers gathered upstairs for their Bible study time. Ten women, eager for adult interaction and hungry for God's Word, gathered that day. The group met for ten weeks during the summer and came to a close in late August.

The following fall, Mary Ann and her team set out to duplicate their summer effort. However, there were no college students to help with child care. They met with the children's director at the church, and she agreed to provide the needed facilities and workers. That fall, the same ten women attended. But God had a much grander idea in mind.

Before the winter/spring semester, the "tireless ten" wanted other young mothers to experience the love and care they were privy to in such a group, so they decided to host an event. They invited a speaker, passed out flyers, and invited their friends to attend a luncheon. Much to their surprise (and the surprise of the child care workers), 50 women showed up. From that event, three other Mornings for Mothers groups were begun. The leaders of the groups were Mary Ann and her two original prayer partners.

Because child care became a major issue, Mary Ann approached the church leadership and presented Mornings for Mothers as an outreach opportunity. They all agreed that this was a unique opportunity to reach out to the women in their community and offered child care out of the church budget. This also allowed the Mornings for Mothers committee to work closely with the children's director.

Over the next several years, Mornings for Mothers continued a pattern of hosting an outreach event with a speaker, followed by sign-ups for the following semester. The speaker events were changed to evenings due to the increased child care needs. Having the event at night allowed for attendees to find their own child care. After ten years the Mornings for Mothers ministry had grown to include five groups, five days a week. There were 25 groups meeting every week!

Mary Ann and her family moved to Charlotte, North Carolina, and the process began again.

The Mornings for Mothers Bible studies are designed to provide much-needed support for mothers of young children. The leadership team believes that motherhood is a high calling and that today's society does not place the importance on motherhood that it so duly deserves. Because many stay-at-home moms feel isolated during this phase of their lives, Mornings for Mothers provides an outlet for both spiritual growth and social interaction—both of which bring refreshment and rejuvenation into the hearts and souls of moms.

Building Your Own Program

Now let's take a look at some of the specifics. More than a "how to" for beginning a ministry for young mothers, I want you to see that this pattern can be followed to begin any ministry.

Begin with Prayer

Dear God

Remember, Mary Ann began with prayer. God put a passion in her heart, and then she gathered several other women to pray with her as she asked for direction and wisdom.

Develop a Mission Statement

Mornings for Mothers Mission Statement: To firmly root women in the fundamentals of the Christian faith and deepen their relationship with the Lord Jesus Christ while building relationships with other women.

Define Your Purpose

Purpose: To connect mothers within small groups in order to form friendships while growing in the knowledge of God's Word as it applies to their lives.

State Your Principles

Principles: In order to accomplish the mission statement, Mornings for Mothers incorporated four principles into each small group: prayer, Bible study, fellowship, and service. These are the same elements found in the relationship between Jesus and His disciples.

1. *Prayer:* "Be anxious for nothing, but in everything by prayer and supplication with thanksgiving let your requests be made known to God" (Philippians 4:6 NASB).

   ~ *Corporately:* Pray together as a group each week. The amount of time allocated for prayer should be under the direction of the Holy Spirit, never rushed. Teach group members that prayer is a form of communication with the Lord, and as such, it requires listening as well as petitioning Him with requests. Encourage group members to pray aloud and to listen to the Lord's voice during prayer. Give Him time to respond and do not be afraid of silence (Psalm 27:14; 46:10 NLT). Keep prayers simple and to the specific requests guided by the Holy Spirit (2 Kings 19:15-16,19).

   ~ *Individually:* Each group member should pray individually throughout the week for the prayer requests presented within the group.

   ~ *Leaders and Coleaders:* Leaders and coleaders oversee the small group and have a certain amount of authority over the group. They are responsible for what is taught and discussed within the group. Therefore, they are encouraged to pray together for and over the group each week. Praying together for the group can be done in person or over the telephone. Their continually seeking the Lord's guidance for the Bible study and for His truth to prevail are critical to thwart Satan's attacks that aim to kill, steal, and destroy what the Lord desires to do within the hearts of each member (Luke 10:1; Ecclesiastes 4:9-12).

2. *Bible Study:* Studying God's Word is necessary because Scripture is our final authority and reveals God's truth. Encourage group members to study God's Word for themselves and participate in open, free flowing discussion (Proverbs 27:17; 1 Thessalonians 5:21; 1 John 4:1).

3. *Fellowship:* God is a God of relationship. He purposefully designed us to desire fellowship with Him and with each other. Encourage relationships within the group by being vulnerable and asking others to share ideas, thoughts, feelings, and experiences regarding the material we are studying. Also, schedule two times during the year where group members can gather for the sole purpose of fellowship and getting to know one another.

4. *Service:* Serving provides the opportunity to put faith into action, allowing Christ to express Himself through us. Mornings for Mothers has a designated service coordinator who will communicate ideas for service to the small groups throughout the year.

Design Job Descriptions

The following are guidelines for various job descriptions in a Mornings for Mothers program. Again, depending on the size of the church and the availability of leaders, job descriptions will vary.

Mornings for Mothers Group Leader: The leader must be a member of the church and share in the mission of Mornings for Mothers. She must complete the small-group training and attend the annual leadership retreat. The leader models the four principles of prayer, Bible study, fellowship, and service within the group and establishes goals, format, and ground rules for the group (confidentiality, punctuality, accountability).

Coleader: The coleader is a member of the church and shares in the mission of Mornings for Mothers. The coleader is a leader in training, prayer partner with the leader, and assistant to the leader.

Administrator: The administrator is responsible for maintaining reports for the appropriate staff member. She coordinates all room assignments and compiles the directory or registrants. She is responsible for ongoing communication with the group leaders and coleaders, maintenance of the leadership directory, and compilation of the curriculum list.

Special Events Coordinator: The special events coordinator plans speaker events for the calendar year (fall, winter, spring). She coordinates the room setup, coffee, food, advertising, and speaker selection.

Promotions Coordinator: The promotions coordinator is responsible for the promotion of the Mornings for Mothers groups through the church weekly newsletter. She is also responsible for coordinating volunteers for the information table on Sunday mornings to hand out flyers or answer questions about Mornings for Mothers.

Communications Coordinator: The communications coordinator compiles and creates the monthly newsletter and calendar.

Child Care Coordinator: The child care coordinator serves as a liaison to the mothers who have children in child care in order to communicate their needs to the children's director.

Service Coordinator: The service coordinator is responsible for organizing service projects. She finds out how many people would be needed for each service project that arises and calls the leaders to fill the needs. She also works with the child care coordinator as needed.

Leadership Training Coordinator: The leadership training coordinator is responsible for training new leaders before the fall groups begin. She sets up times of encouragement for leaders and coleaders to get together and share needs as well as refresh leadership skills. Leadership huddles should occur at least two to three times a year.

Curriculum Coordinator: Researches new book and study guides for future study.

Mornings for Mothers Group Covenant

It is a good idea to prepare a group covenant at the beginning of each year. Some groups may want to review the covenant again in January to reestablish the ground rules and refresh everyone's mind about why they're in a small group.

Mornings for Mothers is a sample of a ministry that ministers to moms. If your church is considering a similar ministry, keep the following points in mind:

- ⁓ Choose a name that has a broad appeal. For example, Mornings for Young Moms rules out the mom who may feel she is too old to come.

- ⁓ Allow ample time for fellowship.

- ⁓ Be flexible. Mom never knows what a new day will bring. Give her grace as she struggles through the throes of increasing demands.

- ⁓ Provide service projects so that she can feel she is a part of something bigger than her small world.

- ⁓ Keep small groups at 10 to 12 members.

- ⁓ Consider having a leader and coleader (or shepherd) for each small group.

Mornings for Mothers is a type of need-driven ministry. Just as Mary Ann saw that young mothers in her church were struggling with their new roles and responsibilities, there are probably moms in your church who are struggling as well. One thing is truly universal; mothers of young children need a break!

Women in
the Workplace

Over the past several generations, a new segment of the church family has emerged—women in the workplace. An effective women's ministry considers the special needs of women who work outside the home.

Women in the Workplace offers two opportunities for ministry: providing meaningful programs and events specifically geared toward Christian women in the workplace and providing meaningful outreach opportunities for women in the workplace.

Amanda Bailey worked with small groups in her church. While taking phone calls in regard to small-group opportunities, Amanda noticed an abundance of calls requesting Bible studies for women who worked outside the home. At the time, her church did not have such a Bible study available. Amanda began to keep a list of inquiries. When the list grew to 50 names, she felt God calling her to provide a nighttime Bible study to meet the growing need.

Amanda began with prayer, enlisting several others to pray with her about the who and the where and the how of forming a ministry specifically geared toward women in the workplace. After a time, she put an announcement in the church bulletin about the new opportunity and contacted the women on her inquiry list. Twenty-five women showed up for the first Women in the Workplace Bible study.

After the first year, Amanda felt that God was calling her to pass the ministry baton to someone else. Her role had been to explore the need, begin the process, and now she felt that God was calling someone else to expand the Bible study into a comprehensive ministry. Following the patterns set out in chapter 11, Amanda looked for someone with character, competence, chemistry, calling, commitment, and capacity.

Mary Reitano exhibited each of the six C's, so Amanda took the next step—she invited. Amanda approached Mary and asked if she would be willing to develop the ministry for women in the workplace. Mary was a career woman who already had a passion for these women with unique needs, God had already begun fanning the flames of desire, and all she needed was the invitation. Over the next four years, Amanda followed the steps lined out in chapter 14. She invited, inspired, instructed, invested, interceded, and imparted responsibility.

"I had a concern for the woman in the workplace," Mary explained, "because she often seemed outside the inner circle of church life. Yet she is on the front lines of one of the richest mission fields today. Looking around me, I noticed that she frequently looked stressed, exhausted, and lonely. Also, I noticed women in the workplace who were raising children alone and women working out of necessity and not by choice. The woman in the workplace is just like other women, with a wonderful mixture of emotions, talents, hurts, sins, and hunger for God, but her schedule and current role in life create unique challenges and opportunities.

"I wanted to reach out to the working woman and affirm her as a person and a child of God. She needs specific validation in her role. Understanding our calling energizes us. Being understood connects us. First John 4:19 states, 'We love because he first loved us.' God ministered to us first by giving, not by asking. A working woman doesn't need another to-do list from the church. She often already feels guilty about not doing more. She needs encouragement that her work and her family (if she has one) are also her ministries."

The following suggestions outline how Mary began reaching out to women in the workplace through a program she called On-the-Job Training.

Dear God **Begin with Prayer:** Begin by gathering women who have a passion to reach out to the women in the workplace to pray. Ask God to send the right leaders who care about and connect with the unique needs of this special group of ladies. In Mary's leadership team, they pray for 15 to 20 minutes of the one-hour planning session. All aspects of the ministry are prayed for—leaders' purpose, women attending events, topics, service projects, training, outreach, and timing.

Develop a Mission Statement: On-the-Job Training's (OJT's) mission statement dovetailed with the church's mission statement: To help women become fully devoted followers of Christ.

Decide on Guiding Principles: Because of the complexity of a woman in the workplace's schedule, consider the following guiding principles:

- ❧ KISS (Keep it Simple, Sister)—the women's lives are already complex.

- ❧ Grow slow—the women's lives are fast paced.

- ❧ Be flexible—the women are constantly dealing with deadlines and need flexibility. (Mary's group met every other week rather than every week.)

- ❧ Have fun—the women need to release stress by laughter and enjoyable activities.

Choose a Ministry Theme Verse: "Whatever you do, work at it with all your heart, as working for the Lord, not for men" (Colossians 3:23).

Develop the Leadership Team: Form a leadership team of women who understand the unique needs of women in the workplace and the opportunities they have been given. Each team member has a significant voice on major decisions. The leaders meet once a month (on alternating weeks when the group does not meet) to pray, plan, and prepare. Because we have described the various job descriptions in previous chapters, we will simply list them here. The team might include the following:

- ❧ Director or coordinator
- ❧ Co-director or co-coordinator
- ❧ Prayer coordinator
- ❧ Social events coordinator
- ❧ Outreach trainer
- ❧ Newsletter editor
- ❧ Small-group leaders coordinator
- ❧ Publicity leader
- ❧ Service coordinator
- ❧ Administrator

Make a Schedule: Because of the packed schedules of women in the workplace, consider meeting every other week rather than every week. Meeting bimonthly will take longer for women to connect, but that will give them the flexibility they need.

Choose the Topics: Ask the women what topics they would like to see addressed. Most likely you will see balance, guilt, children, diet, stress, schedules, business, and spiritual growth.

Develop the Programs: Below are some program ideas to consider implementing with your women in the workplace:

- ❧ Quarterly Saturday breakfast with a speaker
- ❧ Bimonthly small-group Bible study
- ❧ Lunchtime weekly Bible study

ᐯ Simple newsletter for women in the workplace with articles applicable to their specific challenges. (Mary Rietano's newsletter was called *Renewed on the Run.*)

ᐯ Sunday school for women in the workplace

ᐯ Group service projects

Here's what a few women had to say about the impact of a ministry for women in the workplace:

ᐯ I chose Women in the Workplace because as a single woman I wanted to be in a place that didn't define who I am only by my being single (i.e., singles groups), especially since I define my role in life primarily as a working woman whose ministry is at my job. I love getting to know woman of all ages and backgrounds in the small groups, yet we all share many of the same struggles balancing careers with life.

Marion—Occupational Therapist

ᐯ I got involved in a Women in the Workplace Bible study because it fit my time frame and I wanted to be with other working women. As a mother who works outside the home, sometimes you can feel condemned—but there was no condemnation here, only acceptance.

Allyson—Trainer

ᐯ If truth be told, I probably came to my first event because of the friendliness of the person behind the women's ministry table when I saw the brochure and approached her about it. Had she been stuck-up or cold, I may not have pursued it. Many times leaders seem too busy for the new person and more eager to talk to their existing friends. She seemed genuinely interested in me and her welcome was sincere. Beyond that, I longed to connect with other Christian women in the workplace. Having been in the workplace for over 30 years at that point, and having been a Christian just a few years longer than that, my experience in churches was often that the women I met were stay-at-home moms with children, and it was often tough to relate. That role also seemed to be honored by the church more than that of a working woman. The personal experiences we could exchange in this ministry, and the feedback and support from others in similar daily environments, proved invaluable.

Lauri—Compliance Specialist/Employment and Benefits

We have a unique opportunity to impact the culture for Christ right in our own backyards. When Paul traveled to Athens, he ministered in the synagogue (in the church) "as well as in the marketplace day by day with those who happened to be there" (Acts 17:17). What a wonderful challenge for us today—to minister in the church and in the marketplace with those who happen to be there.

28

ℛetreats and 𝒢etaways

𝒫lanning your first women's retreat is much like planning a wedding. You spend months making all the arrangements, sending out the invitations, and then praying that all those you hold dear will attend. A women's retreat is a wonderful opportunity to escape from the hustle and bustle of everyday life and retreat for spiritual and physical renewal. To "retreat" means to draw back to a place of refuge, privacy, or safety, sometimes to escape danger or difficulty.[1] Paul wrote to the Thessalonians, "We are determined to share with you not only the gospel of God but also our own selves" (1 Thessalonians 2:8 NRSV). Likewise, a retreat provides a relaxed atmosphere to share the hope of Jesus Christ and our very lives.

Most retreats are one-night/two-day events or two-night/three-day events. The purpose is to gather together for a time of spiritual growth coupled with food, fellowship, and fun. Retreats serve as a time of uninterrupted fellowship among believers as well as a time for unbelievers to be exposed to and loved by Jesus through their believing friends. Common elements include a speaker, breakout speakers, an activity, music, prayer, and lots of fun. Let's take a look at the basic elements of planning a women's retreat.

Before you begin planning a retreat, or any event, keep the following in mind:

- ❧ Today's woman longs to be a balanced woman.

- ❧ Today's woman longs to know her purpose in life.

- ❧ Today's woman is under stress and needs a break from the hectic pace of our culture.

- ❧ Today's woman longs for meaningful relationships but often does not know how to find or cultivate them.

- ❧ Today's woman wants to participate in activities that are worth the investment of her time and avoids those that are not (or that she perceives are not).

- ❧ Today's woman wants to know "What's in it for me?"

With the above cultural trends in mind, begin the planning by starting with...you guessed it...prayer.

Dear God Begin with Prayer

Once again, we always begin with prayer. "Unless the LORD builds the house, its builders labor in vain" (Psalm 127:1). A successful women's retreat is one in which God orchestrates the details. From the smallest details to the largest, we want to be women who listen to God. Ask Him to reveal the retreat location, the speaker, the theme, the publicity ideas, the best activities that foster openness and sharing, and who should serve on the retreat committee.

Form the Retreat Committee

Many hands make light work. Break down the various tasks into bite-sized pieces. The following are some various retreat team suggestions. But keep in mind, they are simply *suggestions*. Most churches do not have the volunteer base to fill each of these positions. Please don't let this list paralyze you by thinking that you can't get started unless each position is filled. Remember, God chose to change the entire world with a ragtag bunch of 12 uneducated men! With that said, here are some *suggested* job descriptions.

- ∽ *Chair and Cochair:* These ladies oversee the big picture and coordinate the various team members. They help the team determine the schedule, the speaker, and the breakout sessions. They look for any gaps and see that they are filled.

- ∽ *Prayer Leader:* She organizes prayer time for the retreat and during the retreat. If there is a "prayer room" for the retreat, she plans the schedule for those who are serving as prayer warriors and sets up the room.

- ∽ *Promotions Coordinator:* She assembles brochures, advertises in the church bulletin, and posts flyers in strategic places around the church, such as inside bathroom stall doors, etc.

- ∽ *Keynote Speaker Coordinator:* She gathers speaker information and serves as a liaison with the speaker once she is selected.

- ∽ *Speaker Shepherd:* The speaker shepherd takes care of the speaker at the retreat. She takes the speaker to and from the airport (or arranges the transportation), makes sure her room is prepared adequately, escorts her to the meeting rooms before each session, assists in the setup of the book table, provides water up front, and assists with any minor emergencies (runs in panty hose, need for Tylenol, forgotten toothbrush).

- ∽ *Book Sales Coordinator:* She oversees the book table, arranges volunteers to work the book table, and stays in contact with the speaker if she brings books to sell.

- ∽ *Worship Leader:* She plans the worship time, including arranging for the musicians and singers. She determines special music, prints handouts of worship songs, and provides music for transition times (tapes or CDs).

ᴥ *Audiovisual Coordinator:* She coordinates audiovisual needs such as the overhead, PowerPoint, microphones, lapel mic, video equipment.

ᴥ *Drama Team:* They plan and perform skits to reinforce the retreat theme.

ᴥ *Breakout Session Coordinator:* She coordinates the various breakout sessions, gathers their handouts, and coordinates the meeting space with the chair. She clears the breakout leaders with the women's ministry director before these leaders are invited. She sees that each approved breakout session leader signs the church's statement of faith to avoid any conflicts in theology during her presentation.

ᴥ *Small-Group Coordinator:* She plans activities and questions for small groups and invites approved women to be small-group leaders. She plans a training session/or sessions for small-group leaders.

ᴥ *Decorations Coordinator:* She plans the decorations for the meeting rooms, dining room, and even the bathroom. She is responsible for taking down the decorations as well.

ᴥ *Greeters:* They welcome the ladies when they arrive at the retreat center. With the many responsibilities that women are leaving behind, they will trickle in for several hours. Attending a retreat is risky for some women, and how they are received at the beginning can set the tone for their entire retreat experience. This is a very important job!

ᴥ *Games and Icebreakers Coordinator:* She plans icebreakers and games for free time and before keynote sessions.

ᴥ *Snacks Coordinator:* She coordinates snacks for breaks and late night nibbles.

ᴥ *Accommodations Coordinator:* She deals with the retreat center and hotel to arrange and confirm all room reservations, meals, and meeting rooms. She lets the facility liaison know of any special needs. She sets up a special room for any VIPs, such as the speaker. She arranges check-in and check-out times.

∾ *Registration Coordinator:* She keeps a record of registration and places women in rooms together. She processes registrations and turns in money to the treasurer for deposit.

∾ *Treasurer:* She collects monies paid for the retreat and turns it in to the proper person in the church. (This might be the same person who does the registration. If not, the two work closely together.) She keeps track of all the receipts turned in for expenses and reimbursements.

∾ *Gifts and Door Prizes Coordinator:* She gathers door prizes for giving away during the retreat and also items for goody bags.

∾ *Packet Coordinator:* She gathers the materials for and stuffs the attendees' packets.

∾ *Name Tag Coordinator:* She collects the names from the registration coordinator and makes name tags to be given out when the women arrive. She could make a really cute name tag that reinforces the theme of the retreat.

∾ *Follow-up Team:* The follow-up team contacts women who attended the retreat who are not members of the church or who made a first-time commitment to Christ. They help the newcomers get plugged in to the church.

Secure a Location

Select a location that suits the needs of the women in your group. I have been at retreats in luxury hotels, retreat centers, and youth camps. Each retreat has taken on a different flavor depending on the location. If you choose a rustic location, make sure the accommodations are suitable for older women.

Retreat centers book out far in advance, so begin checking out various locations at least one year before the event. You will want to consider the sleeping arrangements (how many to a room), the food (do they prepare all the meals, what is the quality of the food), the capacity (can it hold the number you will be expecting, is there a limit), the meeting room (can it hold a large group, do they have the audiovisual capabilities you require), breakout rooms (do they have breakout rooms for small-group meetings), recreation options (do they have tennis courts, hiking trails, swimming pools, shopping, etc.), cost (is the cost within your budget), and dates (do they have the dates available you are interested in).

Once a decision has been made, secure the date with a deposit.

Select a Time

When planning a retreat, check with school and church calendars. We always need to keep in mind that the women's ministry is one spoke in the wheel, not a wheel of its own. Check the church calendar to be sure that no other major church event is happening during the proposed retreat date. Once a date has been decided, put it on the master church calendar right away so that the rest of the "spokes" know not to schedule a conflicting event.

Also, make sure to check school calendars. Stay away from teacher workdays (many families take long weekends during those times), holidays, and spring or fall breaks.

Prepare a Budget

The budget is a major consideration in planning any event. The best-case scenario would be to have a retreat budget designated in the women's ministry budget that is established at the beginning of the calendar year. However, if there is not a retreat budget, bring a committee together to count the costs. The registration fee for the attendees should defray most of the cost, and a budget is the best way to determine what the fee should be. Below are three scenarios.

Retreat Budget (200 women—two nights/three days)

Scenario #1

Publicity (including postage)	$ 350
Retreat materials (handouts, speaker packets)	$ 500
Coffeehouse and free time activities	$ 250
Registration expenses (name tags, phone calls)	$ 250
Deposit for next year's retreat	$ 500
Speaker fee	$ 2000
Creative (music dramas, sound, photos, videos)	$ 150
Speaker's room, food, travel	$ 500
Planning retreat and team meeting costs	$ 100
Facility ($65 x 2 nights x 200 ladies)	$ 26,000
Total	**$ 30,600***

* To break even, the registration fee should be $153. If the committee wanted to keep the cost at $99 each, the women's ministry budget would need to pay $10,800, or $54 per person, and the attendees would each pay $99. Note that this budget does not include any scholarship money or any free rooms for the women on the committee.

Retreat Budget (70 women—one night/two days)

Scenario #2

Publicity (including postage)	$ 250
Retreat materials (handouts, speaker packets)	$ 200
Craft supplies	$ 35
Registration expenses (name tags, phone calls)	$ 50
Deposit for next year's retreat	$ 500
Speaker fee	$ 3000
Creative (music dramas, sound, photos, videos)	$ 150
Speaker's room, food, travel	$ 500
Planning retreat and team meeting costs	$ 100
Decorations	$ 100
T-shirts (6x70)	$ 420
Facility ($60 x 70)	$ 4200
Total	**$ 9505***

* Registration must be $136 to break even. Again, let's say you did not want to charge the women $136. If you dropped the price to $95, then the women's ministry would need to pay $2870 or $41 per attendee.

Scenario #3: Let's say you do not have any money budgeted for a retreat. That's when you get creative. Make a list of everything you will need for the women's retreat, and then begin to pray for men and women to come forward to donate their time or tangible resources. It is amazing what people will give if they are made aware of the needs and are given the opportunity.

Select a Theme

Every retreat needs to have a theme. Most speakers have favorite topics and can help the committee come up with a theme. However, some committees already have a theme in mind...usually as a springboard for what they will be studying in the future or as reinforcement to what they have been studying in the past. To go along with the theme, select a theme Bible verse for the weekend. Decorations, music selection, breakout sessions, and keynote sessions all revolve around the theme.

For example, a theme might be Ultimate Makeover, and the theme verse might be from 2 Corinthians 5:17, "I am a new creation in Christ, the old is gone and the new has come."

Invite a Speaker

After you have determined the budget, the date, and the location, you are now ready to secure a speaker. The speaker selection is one of the most important elements of a retreat. If the speaker is wonderful, the attendees will not remember that the room was too cold, the chicken was too done, or the beds were too hard. They will simply revel in how God impacted their lives. However, if the speaker is poor, even the best food and greatest facility will be overlooked and the attendees will leave disappointed.

One option is to have someone in your church or community serve as the speaker for the weekend. Ask the speaker if she requires an honorarium or if she has a set fee. Even if she does not have a set fee, be as generous as your budget will allow. All of the cost for the speaker, such as food and lodging, should be covered by the hosting church.

If you are choosing an outside speaker, there are many options. Speakers' bureaus and ministries have highly trained, godly speakers available. Proverbs 31 Ministries, CLASS, Speak Up Inc., and Milk and Honey are just a few (see the appendix for contact information). Most speakers' bureaus offer a range of speakers to fit any budget. When choosing a speaker, it is important to keep in mind that speakers vary in experience, expertise, availability, and biblical knowledge. You are not simply paying her for the weekend. You are paying for messages she has taken years to develop. The more experienced speakers will most likely have a higher fee. If the speaker is a published author, you can expect her fee to be higher than one who is not.

Typically, a well-known speaker will draw a larger crowd. She will also be booked further ahead, so make sure you contact her well in advance.

Another way to look for a speaker is to take a trip to your local Christian bookstore. Many authors are also speakers. Take a look at some of the books and topics to see if something piques your interest. The author's contact information is usually included in the back of the book. If it is not, her contact information can be obtained from the publisher. When contacting a speaker, whether through a speakers' bureau or on your own, it is always a good idea to request an audiotape or CD to hear a sample presentation. Also, make sure that the speaker's message is in line with your church's doctrinal beliefs. After the speaker's second session is not the time to discover that her beliefs do not line up with the church's.

Set the Goals

I've always heard, "If you don't know where you're going, how will you know when you get there?" As with any event, it is good to have certain goals and expectations. Write down the goals for the retreat and then use those goals in the reevaluation time afterward. Example goals could be to provide:

∽ An overall enjoyable retreat for those in attendance

∽ A relevant topic that is applicable to the attendees

∽ An excellent speaker who is knowledgeable, transparent, challenging, and Spirit-led

∽ A safe place where attendees feel welcomed and loved

∽ A safe place for seekers to learn more about Christ

∽ Effective small groups with fabulous facilitators

∽ A variety of interesting, relevant breakout sessions

∽ An appealing choice of activities during free time

∽ Enough downtime or unscheduled time for relaxation

∽ Intentional activities for fun and laughter

∽ Intentional prayer activities for group and individual prayer

∽ A time for women to make a commitment to follow Christ

As a speaker, I always ask the retreat coordinator what she would like to see happen during the retreat. Share your goals with the speaker so she can know how to pray for God's leading.

Breakout Sessions
Choosing Breakout Leaders

Not all retreats have breakout sessions, but these smaller gatherings add variety and interest to the event. If your committee has decided to offer breakout sessions, begin by making a list of potential breakout speakers. Once the list is compiled, have the names approved by the women's ministry leader. Invite the various women to lead a breakout session about five to six months prior to the event. Let each leader/speaker know she will need to turn in a title and brief description of her session a few months prior to the retreat. This will give the publicity committee time to complete the brochure with breakout information or perhaps post it on the church website.

Scheduling Breakouts

One or two breakouts seem to work well for most retreats. This allows for some variety and movement among the ladies. One breakout could be before lunch (after the morning keynote session) and one after lunch (before the afternoon keynote session).

The rooms and times should be decided before everyone arrives at the retreat. Most retreat centers or hotels have room maps and layouts available for selection ahead of time.

Directing Traffic to Breakouts

The room assignments for the breakouts should be listed on the schedule. At the retreat, clearly mark the breakout rooms with brightly colored signs. Post the title of the breakout and the leader's name in large print. You may need additional signs to place in the hallway to direct women to breakout sessions that are in out-of-the-way places.

Assisting the Breakout Leaders

It is very helpful to have a "shepherd" or assistant for each breakout leader. This could be someone on the retreat committee who does not have a job at that particular time. The assistant would go by the breakout room just before the session begins to make sure the breakout leader has everything she needs (handouts, enough chairs, a podium, tape recorder, a hug, etc.).

Taping Breakout Sessions

Because the women can only attend one or two breakout sessions, you might want to consider taping the sessions and having them available for purchase.

Small Groups

Another option for a women's retreat is to have one or two small-group times. The groups could come together to answer questions pertaining to the speaker's topics (speakers can provide discussion questions), "get to know you" type questions, or time for group prayer. The leaders should be members of the hosting church and preferably graduates of some type of small-group facilitator training. The training could be part of the retreat planning. The best size for a small group is around eight women.

At some time before the retreat, gather the small-group facilitators together. Give them the questions or icebreakers and make sure everyone knows what to do. Remind them how to be a "fabulous facilitator" (see chapter 18).

The groups are assigned ahead of time by someone on the registration committee or someone assigned specifically for small groups. It is helpful to keep roommates together to ensure the woman will know at least one other person in her group. It is also a wise idea to mix mature Christians with new believers or seekers. There will always be changes in the registration at the last minute, so print out the small-group assignments the day before the retreat.

If someone shows up at the last minute and is not preregistered, cheerfully allow her to be in a group with her friend. In no way imply that she is an inconvenience.

Note the attendee's small-group assignment on her name tag. It can be anything from a number to a cute sticker.

Planning Schedule Timeline

We've all said it dozens of times: Time flies! Since the retreat planning can be spread out over several months, it is a good idea to set up a timeline to make sure everyone stays on target. This will eliminate some of the last-minute hassles...but not all of them. No matter how well you plan, there will always be some last-minute glitches. Below is a sample timeline for a spring retreat. It begins the previous spring.

May 2	Team leaders, date, and location finalized
July 2	Speaker confirmed
August 1	Theme confirmed
August 4	Brunch for team leaders for a planning session
September 6	Retreat organizational meeting
September 25	Women's ministry kickoff dinner—retreat to be announced
October 14	Team leaders' meeting
October 31	Breakout leaders' topic finalized
November 18	Team leaders' meeting—finalize the schedule
November 19	Contact the speaker and let her know how the retreat is progressing. Send her a copy of the finalized schedule.
December 1	Brochure content finalized and given to designer, mailing list generated
December 8	Team leaders' meeting
January 13	Full committee meeting
January 20	Brochures available on the women's ministry table and mailed to women on the mailing list
January 27	Registration begins
February 2	Outlines for breakout sessions finalized and sent to chair
February 10	Team leaders' meeting
February 24	Announcement from the podium on Sunday morning (show video of last year)

March 1	Small-group facilitator training
March 17	Deadline for registration
March 17	Send an e-mail to all committee members, breakout leaders, and small-group leaders to encourage them, generate excitement, and help everyone feel a part of what's going on.
March 20	Team leaders meet to stuff packets and pray
March 20	Request checks for speaker fees or honorarium from the church secretary
March 22-24	RETREAT!
April 1	Complete thank-you notes to all volunteers
April 13	Follow-up brunch

Publicity Timeline (for a Spring Retreat)

September: (two Sundays in the bulletin) "Ladies, mark your calendars for the spring women's retreat on March 22-24. A meeting will be held in Room 309 on Thursday, September 20, from 7:00 to 8:00 P.M. for anyone interested in helping to plan this event. For more information call..."

December: (two Sundays in the bulletin) "Only a few more months until the spring women's retreat. 'Life in the Faith Lane' is the topic for this year with Susan Smith as the speaker. You don't want to miss this one! Forget the 'fast lane' and let's get in the 'faith lane.' The retreat will be at Blue Ridge Assembly in picturesque Black Mountain, March 22-24. Continue watching for further details."

January: (one Sunday in the bulletin) Run a full-page insert that reflects the same theme and graphics as the retreat brochure.

February: (through the Sunday before the retreat in the bulletin) "Women's Retreat registration has begun! Brochures are available at the women's ministry table. Come join us for relaxation and rejuvenation on March 22-24 at Blue Ridge Assembly in Black Mountain. Cost is $110. For more information contact_____ at_____."

February: Place a full-page retreat insert in the bulletin.

March: (two Sundays prior to the event in the bulletin) "The women's retreat is just around the corner! Never been on a women's retreat? You're not alone. Last year we had 90 first-timers! Don't let being new stop you from getting connected to other women while growing closer to God. Register at the women's ministry booth today! Cost is $110, double occupancy, meals included. For more information call_____ at_____."

Other Publicity Ideas

In addition to the above timeline, you might want to consider the following:

- ∾ Advertise on your local Christian radio stations.
- ∾ Place an announcement in the local newspaper.
- ∾ Send an invitation to other churches in the area.
- ∾ Place an announcement in your denomination newsletter.
- ∾ Place brochures or posters in local bookstores.
- ∾ Place posters or announcements on the inside door of ladies' bathroom stalls.

Personal Invitations

While publicity is very important for a successful retreat, nothing means more than a personal invitation. Women love to be invited and are more likely to sign up if they know they have one "buddy" with whom they can attend. Church statistics show that 95 percent of first-time attendees came because someone invited them to come.

Sample Retreat Schedule

Friday

4:30	Arrivals and check-in
6:00–7:00	Dinner
7:00–7:30	Announcements, icebreakers, giveaways
7:30–7:50	Special music and/or worship
7:50–8:50	Session one (speaker)
9:00	Snacks, games, fun activities

Saturday

6:45–7:45	Exercise class (totally optional!)
7:45–8:45	Breakfast
9:00–9:15	Announcements, icebreakers, giveaways
9:15–9:35	Worship (music)
9:35–10:45	Session two (speaker)
11:00–11:45	Breakout sessions (or small groups)
11:55–12:45	Breakout sessions
12:45–1:45	Lunch
2:00–5:30	Free time and optional activities
5:30–6:30	Dinner
6:30–7:00	Announcements, icebreakers, giveaway
7:00–7:30	Worship (music)
7:30–8:30	Session three (speaker)
8:30–9:00	Special activity
9:00	Fun and games

Sunday

8:00–9:00	Breakfast
9:00–9:30	Worship (music and prayer)
9:30–10:00	Testimonies

10:00–11:00	Session four (speaker)
11:00–11:15	Retreat wrap-up
11:30–12:30	Lunch

Attendee Packets

When the attendee arrives at the retreat, she should receive a name tag and a packet. It is nice to include sheets of paper in a double-pocket folder, and place the folder in the packet. The packets could include:

- ∾ Welcome letter from the committee

- ∾ Map of the grounds and surrounding area

- ∾ Retreat schedule

- ∾ Small group assignments (if applicable)

- ∾ Breakout session descriptions and room number

- ∾ Prayer request form (if applicable)

- ∾ Handouts for the main sessions

- ∾ Song sheets (if an overhead or PowerPoint is not used)

- ∾ Women's ministry brochure

- ∾ Evaluation form

- ∾ Pen

- ∾ Notepad or sheets of paper for notes

- ∾ Kleenex

- ∾ Small gift

- ∾ Chocolate

Remember, these are just suggestions (but the chocolate is pretty important!).

Taking Care of the Speaker

Much of the success of a retreat depends on the speaker. So it only makes sense that she needs to feel welcomed, informed, and cared for. Here are some tips on how to take care of your speaker.

Before the Event

- Obtain a contract so the expectations are clear. Most professional speakers generate contracts and send them to the appropriate contact person at the church. The contract should outline the speaker fee or honorarium, travel and lodging arrangements, audiovisual requirements, book table needs, and any other details for the weekend.

- Most speakers require a deposit to secure the date. Return the deposit with the signed contract.

- Tell the speaker the exact times she will be speaking and the time allowed for each session.

- Ask the speaker to provide master handouts or outlines to be copied for each attendee.

- Inform the speaker of any special needs of the women. For example: dissention in the church over an issue or women who are hurting because of death of a loved one or divorce.

- Let the speaker know the goals of the retreat and what the committee hopes to see happen as a result of the retreat.

- Request biographical information on the speaker and a picture to use for publicity.

- Make sure she has the name and phone number of her contact person for the event.

- Send her a copy of all promotional material.

- Arrange her airfare or have her arrange the airfare and reimburse her upon request.

- Provide a driver to pick her up and take her back to the airport.

- If she is driving to the event, send her a map with clear directions to the church or retreat facility.

- Provide a "goodie" basket for her room with items such as bottled water, chocolate, and any other treats you think she might like.

- Pray for the speaker often and send her a note of encouragement before the event.

During the Event

- Assign a "shepherd" to take care of the speaker at the event. The shepherd will make sure she gets to each of her sessions on time and to the dining hall.

- Review how she would like to be introduced. A good introduction creates an air of excitement.

- Have her podium and microphone of preference ready.

- Allow her times of rest and reflection during the event.

- Keep an eye out if she appears to be cornered by an attendee. She may need for someone to gingerly rescue her from an awkward situation.

- Pay the speaker the remainder of her speaker fee or honorarium.

After the Event

- It can be very difficult for a speaker to go in for a weekend, fall head over heels for the group she is ministering to, and then never hear from them again. Encourage the attendees to write notes of appreciation or e-mails of thanks, letting the speaker know of her impact on their lives.

- Return photographs.

Scholarships

Unfortunately, sometimes the women who need to attend a retreat the most are the very ones who cannot afford to go. Whether they are a single mom, the wife of an unsupportive husband, or a woman struggling just to make ends meet, the registration fee may be prohibitive. Consider offering a scholarship program for such women.

Make an announcement to the church members, inviting them to participate in giving to the scholarship fund. Retreat leaders who have done so have discovered that many are delighted to give. I remember one man who gave because he saw the change in his wife from the previous year and wanted to say thanks. Some give because they know someone in particular they want to sponsor and some give to the general scholarship fund for anyone who needs a helping hand. See the sample scholarship request form on the next page.

Kaleidoscope of Women

The hope of any women's retreat is to welcome women from many walks of life and at many stages in their spiritual journey. The authors of *Women's Retreats* mention several groups of women who make up the kaleidoscope of faces attending: the nonbeliever, the stressed-out woman, the newcomer, the woman in crisis, the fence-sitter, the outcast, the wallflower, and the potential leader. Below is a brief summary of each:

> ∾ *The Nonbeliever:* Women in the church are encouraged to invite their nonbelieving friends to their retreat. They are the "Oprah generation," many seeking spiritual alternatives and buying into radical feminism. But living in the midst of authentic community for several days is a powerful tool to reveal the true Christ and cause women to reflect on God, their lives, and choices.

Confidential Scholarship Request

If you are unable to pay the registration fee, but would like to attend the women's retreat, please complete this form and turn it in with your application. Once the form has been received, it will promptly be forwarded to a member of the benevolence committee for review. After review, a retreat committee member will contact you. It is the goal of the retreat committee to allow every woman a chance to attend. Please spend time in prayer before completing this form and remember that this request will be kept confidential.

Name_____

Address_____

_____

Phone number_____

Please indicate the appropriate response:

❑   I would like to request a full scholarship.

❑   I would like to request a partial scholarship in the amount of $_____. I can pay the remainder.

❑   I would like to make payments of $_____ per month for _____ months to make attending easier on my budget.

Please use this space to provide any comments or information you may have regarding your request:

_____

_____

_____

_____

_____

_____

∾ *The Stressed-out Woman:* A women's retreat is one way to help women who need prolonged mental and spiritual rest. It provides solitude, time meditating on God and His works, unscheduled hours for naps, games, reading, and moments to share with friends.

∾ *The Newcomer:* Forty-four million Americans move every year. For Christians, that means leaving behind a history, finding a new church, and acclimating to a new community where no one knows them, their gifts, or ministry experience. A retreat can jump-start the adjustment, especially when the leaders are trained to reach out.

∾ *The Woman in Crisis:* Shattered marriages, abuse, layoffs, runaway teens, cancer, infertility—there are hundreds of circumstances that afflict women today. Where can they go for healing, direction, and energy to persevere? Several days with a group of supportive women that point to an ongoing intimate relationship with Jesus can make all the difference.

∾ *The Fence-Sitter:* A fence-sitter lives with one foot in the world and one foot in the church. She may attend church on Sunday and yet have a live-in boyfriend. The Holy Spirit can use a retreat setting to break through resistance. A block of time in the midst of committed women and hearing biblical, convicting messages from a gifted speaker can get women off the fence and change the direction of their lives.

∾ *The Outcast:* There may be women who attend a retreat who have pasts that they are ashamed of. A retreat is a place where they can find love, forgiveness, and acceptance—perhaps for the first time.

∾ *The Wallflower:* A women's retreat provides a safe place for women who have been hiding in the shadows to come out into the light and reveal their spiritual gifts and talents. Women who may not feel comfortable making a long-term commitment to serve at the church may welcome a chance to serve for a weekend event. Often a wallflower will burst into full bloom after a retreat.

෴ *The Potential Leader:* As mentioned earlier in this book, always be on the lookout for leaders. A retreat is a wonderful place to watch volunteers in action and spot potential leaders.[2]

Post-Retreat Evaluation

At the close of the retreat allow each attendee to complete a women's retreat evaluation. This will let you know what worked well, what needs to be continued for next year, eliminated for next year, and tweaked for next year. Of course, each form will be different as it reflects the events that took place during your particular retreat.

After the evaluations have been completed, have one member of the team summarize the comments for the rest of the team. (See sample evaluation form on next page.)

One-Day Retreat

A one-day retreat is a day when women come together at the church for a time of spiritual growth and renewal. The day usually begins on Saturday morning and ends by about 4:00 in the afternoon. This is a great alternative to a weekend retreat and offers those who are not able to leave town for a night or two another option to connect with women in their church and community.

Once again, begin with prayer. Pray that God will reveal who the speaker/teacher needs to be, the theme, the publicity ideas, and the best activities to foster openness and sharing, and who should serve on the committee.

The basics of planning a one-day on-site retreat is much like planning a weekend getaway. Go back to the beginning of this chapter and review the steps for planning a weekend event. Note that

Women's Retreat Evaluation

In order to help us plan for next year's retreat, we would greatly appreciate your honest feedback. Please respond to the following questions, circling the rating number which applies and/or state your answers in the available spaces. Note: "5" is the highest rating and "1" is the lowest. Thank you for taking the time to complete this evaluation. Our goal is to provide the best retreat possible and your input allows us to continue doing what we do well and change what needs improvement.

1. Overall, how would you rate your weekend?　　1　2　3　4　5

2. Did you feel welcomed and comfortable?　　1　2　3　4　5

3. Did you enjoy the topic?　　1　2　3　4　5

4. Was it relevant to your current struggles?　　1　2　3　4　5

5. Did you enjoy the speaker?　　1　2　3　4　5

6. Did you enjoy the music?　　1　2　3　4　5

7. Do you feel that you grew spiritually?　　1　2　3　4　5

8. Did you enjoy the Friday night activity?　　1　2　3　4　5

9. Did you enjoy your free time?　　1　2　3　4　5

    What did you do?_____

10. Did you enjoy the drama?　　1　2　3　4　5

11. What was your favorite part of the retreat?

    _____

    _____

12. How can we improve for next year?

    _____

    _____

many of the same elements will be present in a one-day event, but on a smaller scale.

Because one of the main reasons for planning such an event is to allow women in the church to connect as well as grow spiritually, there needs to be time in the schedule for women to relate to one another through some sort of small group activity or icebreaker.

Below is a sample schedule for a one-day, in-house retreat.

Saturday Seminar Day Schedule

8:00–8:30	Doors open
8:00–8:45	Continental breakfast
8:45–9:15	Welcome, announcements, door prizes,
9:15–9:25	Skit
9:25–9:35	Special music and worship (two songs)
9:35–10:35	Session one (speaker)
10:45–11:35	Breakout session
11:45–12:35	Breakout session
12:45–1:45	Lunch and book table shopping
1:45–2:45	Session two (speaker)
2:50–3:35	Breakout session
3:45–4:15	Close

Variations could include a concert in the afternoon rather than a breakout session, an added speaker session in the morning rather than a breakout session, or any number of combinations.

Dinner/Speaker Events

Special events, as with each program in a women's ministry, are geared toward meeting a specific need among the women in your church and community. When deciding on which special event to tackle, always begin with...you guessed it...prayer.

> *Dear Lord, we come before You today asking that You will guide us as we plan for our special event. We pray You will go before us to select and prepare the speaker, the women who will serve, and the women who will attend. We pray we will be women who listen to Your still small voice in the smallest to the largest details. Lord, we pray that Your Holy Spirit will go before us and prepare the hearts of the women who will attend this event. We pray that many will bring their unchurched friends and that many will come to know You in a personal way. In Jesus' name, amen.*

Define Your Purpose

The purpose of your event will determine your course. Is the event to draw in seekers or disciple and encourage Christians? Is the event for teaching, encouraging, or entertaining? An event that is specifically geared toward reaching out to seekers will be (should be) very different from an event that is specifically geared toward equipping those who are already believers.

Decide on a Theme

The theme of the event will determine your speaker, music, and decorations. If you have a speaker in mind, she may determine your theme for the event and be able to suggest music and decorating ideas. Decide on a theme and then proceed. Below are options for dinner-event themes:

Women Under Construction	Operation Resuscitation
Ultimate Makeover	Girlfriend Gatherings
Spring Fling	Yaweh Sisterhood
Fall Fest	Spa for the Soul
Festival of Tables	Christmas Tea
Celebrating the Season	Girls' Night Out
Dreams of a Woman	Hats Off to Moms

When giving the event a title, consider words that will encourage a non-Christian to attend. For example, "Understanding Your True Identity" might be inviting for a Christian, but "Ultimate Makeover" would be more inviting for a non-Christian. Also, "Celebrating a Christ-Centered Christmas" might be intriguing for a Christian, but "Preparing Your Heart and Home for the Holidays" might be more inviting for the non-Christian.

Delegate Duties

The job descriptions for a special event are much the same as the job descriptions for a retreat. However, the longevity and the complexity of the task will be less involved.

> ∾ *Chair:* She oversees the big picture and coordinates the various team members. She looks for any gaps and sees that they are filled. She is available the night of the event to help out

where needed. She works very closely with every member of the event team.

∽ *Prayer Leader:* She organizes prayer times before, during, and after the event. She coordinates the prayer team, who will pray with those who come forward to accept Christ or with a prayer need.

∽ *Food Coordinator:* She plans the menu for the event and works with the kitchen crew, catering company, or the volunteers who will be preparing the meals.

∽ *Promotions Coordinator:* She assembles brochures, advertises in the church bulletin, posts flyers in strategic places around the church.

∽ *Keynote Speaker Coordinator:* She gathers speaker information and serves as a liaison with the speaker once she is selected.

∽ *Worship Leader:* She plans the worship time, including arranging for the musicians and singers. She determines special music, prints handouts of worship songs, and provides music for transition times (tapes or CDs).

∽ *Audiovisual Coordinator:* She coordinates audiovisual needs such as the overhead, PowerPoint, microphones, lapel mic, and video equipment.

∽ *Drama Team:* They plan and perform skits to reinforce the event theme.

∽ *Decorations Coordinator:* She plans the decorations for the meeting room, dining room, and even the bathroom. She is responsible for gathering volunteers to set up and take down the decorations.

∽ *Greeters:* They welcome the ladies when they arrive at the event and tell them they are glad they came! These ladies help attendees feel comfortable and see that a woman who comes alone is paired up with someone who will befriend them for the evening.

∞ *Registration Coordinator:* She keeps a record of registration and places women at tables together (if tickets are required).

∞ *Treasurer:* She collects monies paid for the event and turns it in to the proper person in the church. (This might be the same person who does the registration. If not, the two work closely together.)

∞ *Gifts and Door Prizes Coordinator:* She gathers door prizes to give away during the event.

∞ *Follow-up Team:* The follow-up team contacts women who attended the event who are not members of the church or who made a first-time commitment to Christ. They help newcomers get plugged in to the church and answer any questions they might have regarding the church or developing a relationship with Christ.

Plan the Budget

Estimating the budget for a dinner/speaker event is much easier than for a retreat.

Decorations	$ 100
Door prizes	donated
Sound and audiovisual	$ 50
Speaker	$1500
Food (200 attendees x $6)	$1200
Tablecloth rental (25 tables)	$ 50
Dinner for team leaders and speaker (10 x $6)	$ 60
Publicity (flyers and brochures)	$ 200
Miscellaneous printing (cards, tickets, etc.)	$ 50
Total	**$3210**

If the tickets sell for $10 apiece, the remaining cost to the women's ministry budget would be $1210.*

---

* Money-Saving Tip: At the close of the event, offer the centerpieces for sale. Announce that anyone who would like to purchase the centerpieces and take them home to enjoy can leave $5 on the table.

Invite a Speaker

I have attended many events where the publicity committee had slick, enticing brochures, beautifully presented and deliciously prepared food, and decorations that looked as if they were straight from *House Beautiful.* However, the speaker's presentation marred the entire evening. I cannot stress this enough. Today's busy woman does not want to feel that she has wasted her time. You may have to cut corners on some dinner aspects of your event, but try your best not to cut corners on the speaker. The women who attend will quickly forget the decorations and the yummy chicken divan, but the words of the speaker will linger for a lifetime. If your speaker is a disappointment, it will affect the attendance of events in the future.

When choosing a speaker, make sure that someone has heard the speaker before or has listened to a tape. (Most speakers can provide sample tapes.) One of the best ways to find a speaker is by word of mouth. Ask other churches about great speakers they have had in the past and visit websites to gather more information. (See the appendix for ministries that have speakers available.)

Call various speakers and chat with them about what their topics are, what you are hoping to see happen at your event, and what their fee or honorarium usually is. Let them know the length of time you will need them to speak and how you would like for them to close out their time (with an altar call or a simple prayer). The speaker you choose needs to feel she is part of the event team. Invite her to join you in prayer for the event and for the women who will attend.

Once you have selected a speaker, ask her to send you a photograph and a biography for publicity and any other material that might be helpful for you to use in promoting the event. If she is a published author, your local radio station might like to do an interview or your local newspaper might consider writing an article about her book(s).

Make sure the speaker has a contact person for the event. She is there to serve you, but remember, she is also a visitor.

Promote the Event

Remember, of all the various ways to promote an event, nothing is as effective as a personal invitation. Here's how one church had a telephone campaign to invite women to their women's ministry kickoff dinner. A letter and script were sent to key members of the women's ministry team along with a list of members and phone numbers.

Letter to Ministry Team Members

Dear Friends:

As someone who is involved with women's ministry, you surely realize the need to reach out to all women of our church and extend to them opportunities to experience God's love and mercy through participation in various programs and groups offered within our church family. With that in mind, we'd like to ask for your help in extending to them a personal invitation to take part in the women's ministry kickoff dinner.

Enclosed you will find a list of approximately 20 names for you to call between September 3 and September 10, along with a page of information to give you an idea of what to tell them. Feel free to leave them a voice mail message if they are not available.

Last year we heard from several women who appreciated a personal invitation to the kickoff. If you are unable to make your calls, please let me know as soon as possible. Thank you in advance for your help and dedication to reaching all the women of Forest Hill Church for His glory.

Key information:
Date: September 27
Time: 6:30 P.M.
Speaker: Mary James
Cost: $6.00
Tickets required

Phone Invitation Script

Hi, _____. This is _____ from the women's ministry and I'm calling to invite you to our kickoff event on Tuesday, September 27. We're going to have dinner and hear about all the opportunities available in the women's ministry here at the church—everything from Bible studies to missions trips to support groups. Each group will have a booth, and you'll be able to walk around and find out about everything that's going on. Also, Mary James is going to speak on prayer. She has a way of making you feel inspired instead of feeling guilty!

Tickets will be on sale for the next two Sundays at the women's ministry booth in the lobby of the church. The cost is $6.00 and will include a prayer journal.

You can get your tickets on your own or with a group. We hope you'll come—whether you've been coming to church for one week or ten years.

Table Hostesses

One way to approach ticket sales is to ask women in the church to be table hostesses. One woman purchases eight tickets and is then responsible for inviting seven other women or selling her tickets. This works particularly well when a church member is responsible for filling the table with her unchurched friends.

Door Prizes and Giveaways

There's something about free stuff that sets a woman's radar in motion. For some reason, I'll buy makeup that I don't necessarily need to get the "gift with purchase" that I probably won't use. So what can we learn from Estée Lauder and Lancôme? *If you give something away, they will come!*

During a special event, let the ladies know there will be door prizes given. Include the mention of door prizes in the publicity material as an incentive for attendance. If the door prize is particularly enticing (such as a day at a spa) mention it on the flyers or brochures. The names for the drawing can be generated from the registration or you could use their response cards for a drawing at the end of the event.

There are many creative ways to choose the recipient of a door prize, such as putting a sticker on the bottom of someone's chair or plate—a blue sticker is door prize number 1, a red sticker is door prize number 2, etc. Of course, simply drawing names from the registration cards works just as well.

Businesses are usually very agreeable to donating door prizes for such an event. They see this as an advertising opportunity as well as being a good neighbor in the community. Also, a business can often write the gift off on their taxes as a gift to a charitable organization. You might want to mention the tax donation when soliciting for giveaways.

Sample Schedule

6:15–6:45	Doors open and women are greeted with a name tag and table assignment
6:45–6:55	Welcome and announcements
6:55–7:40	Dinner is served
7:40–7:45	Door prizes while women are finishing dessert
7:45–7:55	Special music
7:55-8:55	Speaker
8:55	Close

Schedule for Dinner Setup and Cleanup

(Consider asking the men to help with this area of the event. The women get a kick out of having the men serve.)

9:30–11:30 A.M.—Setup
- ❑ Place tablecloths on all tables
- ❑ Set up server station with pitchers and extra table supplies (flatware, napkins, etc.)
- ❑ Set up centerpieces
- ❑ Place flatware, napkins, and cups on table
- ❑ Align chairs with place settings
- ❑ Put number signs on tables
- ❑ Make sure trash cans are in the kitchen
- ❑ Have drink pitchers ready

5:00–6:30 P.M.
- ❑ Fill pitchers with tea and water
- ❑ Assist the cooks and servers if needed
- ❑ Fill ice in cups around 6:10
- ❑ Light candles around 6:15

6:30–7:30 Dinner Duties
- ❑ Man food stations
- ❑ Serve water and tea
- ❑ Fill empty pitchers with water and tea
- ❑ Provide extra ice to cups if needed

7:30–8:00
- ❑ Clean up plates, flatware, napkins
- ❑ Clean up drink station
- ❑ Man the coffee station
- ❑ Eat if possible

8:00–9:00 During the Speaker Time
- ❑ Clean up the coffee station
- ❑ Dispose of filled garbage bags

❑ Collect and dispense of extra liquid in pitchers
❑ Condense leftover desserts
❑ Clear tablecloths from coffee station and booths if possible
❑ Eat if you haven't already

9:00 Finishing Up
❑ Take out the garbage
❑ Finish cleaning up the food and drink stations
❑ Break down the stage
❑ Eat the desserts

Response Cards

Perhaps an invitation to accept Jesus Christ is extended at your dinner/speaker event. If so, you might want to have response cards on each table. A response card can have many uses, such as collecting information about visitors who attended the event, surveying who attended, discovering who would like follow-up to find out more about the church or a relationship with Jesus Christ, or allowing a place for someone to tell that she accepted Christ.

Response Card

❑   I would like to receive information about this church and the women's ministry.

❑   I would like to know more about having a personal relationship with Christ.

❑   I have several questions and would like to have someone from the women's ministry call me.

❑   Tonight, I prayed to ask Jesus Christ to be my Savior and Lord.

❑   Tonight, I prayed to rededicate my life to Christ.

Name: _____

Address: _____

City/State/Zip: _____

Phone Number: _____ E-mail: _____

Prayer Request: _____

Immediately after the event, collect the response cards and pray for the needs mentioned. Also, use the cards for planning future events and following up with the women who wanted to know more about the church or about Jesus Christ.

Festival of Tables

A Festival of Tables is a wonderful way to take care of the decorations and give women an opportunity to participate in the event in a small way. At a Festival of Tables event, various women sign up to be table hostesses. The table hostess is responsible for decorating her table according to the theme of the evening. For example, if it is a Christmas event, a table hostess would use her own Christmas china and decorate the table anyway she chooses. It could be elegant or fanciful. The variety of styles and personalities are what make the decorations fun!

The church should provide the basics: a white tablecloth, silverware, napkins, and possibly glassware.

Women love looking at a beautifully set table, so make sure to allow enough time for the attendees to peruse the room to see the various table settings.

Women's Ministry Kickoff Dinner

A women's ministry kickoff dinner is an exciting way to usher in the beginning of the "academic" year. Most programs follow the school calendar year, September to the end of May. A kickoff dinner showcases the programs and events that will take place during the year, and casts the vision for the women's ministry in general. A kickoff dinner might include a keynote speaker, but will also include a time for various team leaders to share about programs and events that will take place during the year.

The following are ideas to consider for a kickoff dinner.

- Either before or after the dinner, have booths or tables set up in an accessible area to showcase the various opportunities available throughout the year.

- Post team leaders at the booths to answer questions, help with sign-up sheets, and give out ample smiles.

- During dinner, show a video of some of the previous years' events.

- Include a skit of the hectic pace of a woman's life and the need for women to support each other.

- Consider giving each woman a small gift, such as a prayer journal or a bookmark.

- Give each woman a printed calendar of events for the year.

- Have sign-up sheets at the various ministry tables for both attendees and for those who would like to volunteer to serve.

Sample Invitation

Are you looking for a place to connect within the women's ministry?

The annual Women's Ministry Kickoff Dinner,

Celebrating Women: A Festival of Ministry

is the perfect place for you!

The fair will showcase a tour of all women's ministries.

The dinner will be held September 17, 2005, at 6:30 p.m. in the dining hall.

Tickets are $6 and can be purchased on Sundays at the women's ministry table or in the church office.

Our special guest speaker will be Mary James

Mentoring

$\mathcal{S}$ome years ago I was sitting in a cross-generational discussion group on the need for mentoring among Christian women. A young lady in her twenties expressed how desperately her peers needed older women to come alongside them and share from their experiences and wisdom as wives, mothers, and friends. I was nodding my head in agreement as if to say, "Yes, yes, we do." Then all of a sudden I came to the shocking realization that she was looking at me, not as a peer who needed mentoring, but as the older woman who needed to be doing the mentoring!

After I got over the initial shock of being considered an "older woman" and trying to figure out how this happened (I was 39 at the time), I started to think seriously about Titus 2:3. "Likewise, teach the older women to be reverent in the way they live, not to be slanderers or addicted to much wine, but to teach what is good. Then they can train the younger women to love their husbands and children, to be self-controlled and pure, to be busy at home, to be kind, and to be subject to their husbands, so that no one will malign the word of God."

I asked myself a few questions. What is a mentor? What exactly is a mentor supposed to do? What does the Bible have to say about mentors? Who can become a mentor? How "old" is older?

What Is a Mentor?

Let me share some insights on mentoring taken from *A Woman's Secret to a Balanced Life*, a book I coauthored with Lysa TerKerust. Have you ever been driving down a country road when the fog was so thick you couldn't see ten feet in front of you? It can be a terrifying experience. But if another car pulls out in front of you, and you can follow its taillights, suddenly the driving in the fog isn't so scary. I think that is a beautiful picture of a mentor. She is like a light, guiding a fellow traveler down a sometimes foggy, rocky, bumpy, or rough road of life. Win Couchman described it this way, "A mentor is someone further down the road from you, who is going where you want to go, and who is willing to help you get there."[1] Webster calls her "an experienced and trusted friend and advisor." Did you notice neither Titus 2 nor Webster said she had to be an expert or an authority? That should be a relief to us all.

Susan Hunt, author of *Spiritual Mothering*, describes mentoring this way:

> Spiritual mothering [mentoring] is to be impressed on younger women as you prepare the fellowship supper together at church, as you make blankets for the home for unwed mothers, as you sort clothes for the homeless shelter, as you talk about how to maintain a devotional life with three preschoolers competing for your attention as you walk through the factory making deliveries or into the courtroom to defend a client. Spiritual mothering has more to do with demonstrating "the shape of godliness" than with teaching lesson plans.[2]

Spiritual mothering takes place when...

> A woman possessing faith and spiritual maturity enters into a nurturing relationship with a younger woman in order to encourage and equip her to live for God's glory.[3]

As you can see, mentoring and discipleship go hand in hand. However, while discipleship teaches one how to understand God's Word and pray, mentoring demonstrates how to live life.

Mentor Model

During Cheri Jimenez's time as women's director in Raleigh, North Carolina, she and her pastor's wife, Cathy Horner, shared a passion to connect younger and older women. They gathered a leadership team and followed the pattern suggested in Janet Thompson's book, *Woman to Woman Mentoring*. The following is how Cheri and Cathy introduced the program.

Orientation Coffee

Women who were interested in becoming part of a mentoring relationship were invited to an informational meeting and asked to fill out a one-page profile form and have their picture taken. A photographer was on hand to snap Polaroid pictures of the potential mentors and mentees. The profile card included: name, address, phone number, e-mail address, birth date, age, occupation, work phone number, spouse's name, children's names and ages, church attendance history, and whether she would like to be a mentor or mentee. During the meeting each woman was invited to share why she wanted to be in a mentoring relationship. After the sharing time, if a woman felt especially drawn to someone she would like to mentor, she was asked to note that on her card. However, no guarantees were made.

Women were asked to make a six-month commitment to the relationship (except in the summer—then only a three-month commitment). They were to phone each other at least once a week and meet twice a month.

The mentoring relationship was not meant to necessarily be a Bible study (although it could be if both parties desired it). It often included life skills or mutual interests (i.e., cooking, crocheting, gardening, and parenting). It basically was designed as an "arranged friendship" for either a six-month or three-month period. The leaders gave the mentors a list of suggested Bible study materials and beneficial books that had been previously reviewed.

Administrative Team Prayer Day

The following day (Sunday), the women's mentoring administrative team gathered together to pray over the profile cards, and in a continued spirit of prayer, invited the Holy Spirit to match the women into pairs. Prayerful consideration was given to each woman's background, personal interests, and stated needs. Then each mentor was assigned a mentee.

Mentoring Kickoff Dessert

On the following Thursday night, the pairs were revealed. The mentors were asked to come the first hour, at 6:30 P.M., for a mini-training session. They were given the profile cards of their mentee and the mentor/mentee booklets. Around 7:15 or so, the mentees began arriving in another room.

At 7:30 the mentors were asked to go to their mentee (whose picture they had already seen), introduce themselves, and guide them back to the training room for dessert and coffee. After a brief 30-minute training time for the mentees (i.e., the mentor is not your mother or your best friend, she is not on call for you 24/7, etc.), the formal program ended and the women were given time to drink coffee, get to know one another, sign their commitment covenants (in their booklets), and schedule their next meeting time.

The pairs were assigned a prayer warrior who had agreed to support them in prayer for the commitment period. The prayer warrior was asked to make regular monthly calls to each pair she had been assigned so that she could ask for prayer requests and see how things were going. This was an attempt to keep a finger on the pulse of the ministry and be advised of any problems in any of the relationships.

Mentoring Covenant

As with any small group, it is advisable to have a covenant agreement. Below is the covenant suggested by Janet Thompson.

Mentoring Covenant

We will make a six-month commitment to the
mentoring relationship.

We will contact each other once a week and meet a
minimum of twice a month.

We will pray for each other and ask the Lord to deepen
our bond of friendship.

We will do things together, such as work on spiritual disciplines,
learn a new skill, attend church functions
(retreats, seminars, or women's activities).

We will take walks together, go out for a meal or coffee together,
and spend time in each other's home.

We will make an effort to keep our relationship
ongoing, consistent, and fun.

We will always ask God to be part of it and to bless it.

We will take our relationship seriously and make time
for it in our schedules.

We will keep our sharing confidential—just between the two of
us—unless we agree it is okay to share with someone else.

We will talk only about ourselves.[4]

Halftime Refresher for Mentors

As its name suggests, the Halftime Refresher is an evening scheduled halfway into the program for mentors to come together to ask
questions, share tips, and pray over problems. Confidentiality is
highly stressed. This is basically an open forum that is essentially led
by the mentors themselves for mutual encouragement.

Celebration Supper

At the end of the commitment period, everyone was invited to a
catered meal to celebrate what God had done. After the meal and
some brief announcements, pairs were invited to give testimonies.

Developing Your Own Mentoring Ministry

Each mentoring ministry will take on the personality of the home church and the leaders who are guiding it. The basic blueprint will follow the steps we have seen throughout the book.

Begin with Prayer:

> *Dear Lord, thank You for the privilege of being Your hands and feet to a hurting world. Just as You sent Jesus to earth to show us how to live, You send us out into the world to be heavenly ambassadors for You. Just as You sent Mary to Elizabeth, You continue to use women to encourage and equip other women. Your Word instructs the older women to teach the younger women. We pray that You will lead and guide us as we implement a program to facilitate spiritual mothering principles in our church. We ask that You will bring godly mentors forward who have a passion and love for the next generation. Give them the confidence they need to fulfill the call of Titus 2. We also pray that You will bring younger women who need a helping hand to guide them down the path You have chosen for them.*
>
> *We give this ministry to You. Help us to be women who listen to Your still small voice and heed Your gentle nudges. In Jesus' name, amen.*

Define Your Purpose: The scriptural foundation often used for a mentoring ministry is Titus 2:3-5. "Teach the older women to be reverent in the way they live, not to be slanderers or addicted to much wine, but to teach what is good. Then they can train the younger women to love their husbands and children, to be self-controlled and pure, to be busy at home, to be kind, and to be subject to their husbands, so that no one will malign the word of God."

Develop a Mission Statement: The mission statement for the mentoring program of Saddleback Church in California is as follows: "To give the women of Saddleback Church the opportunity to experience joy and growth in their Christian lives by participating in one-on-one supporting and encouraging mentoring friendships."[5] Saddleback went on to define mentor and mentee: "A mentor will be a woman who is a practicing Christian, regularly attends Saddleback Church, and has the desire to let her life be an example and godly role model. A mentee will be a Saddleback Church woman who is young in her walk with the Lord. Women of all ages are welcome."[6]

Select a Leadership Team: The leadership team could include a ministry director, kickoff coordinator, prayer coordinator, registration coordinator, greeter coordinator, hostess coordinator (for coffees or teas that occur in homes), publicity coordinator, etc. Cheri found that it was very helpful to have someone older on her committee who would have the ear of potential mentors in the church. In her case, it was the pastor's wife. She knew the potential mentors and they responded well to her invitation to serve.

Develop Job Descriptions: After you have decided on the leadership team positions, clearly define the various roles. Remember, this will help potential volunteers know exactly what they are signing up to do.

Decide on a Schedule: A beginning and an ending to a mentoring program will help both mentor and mentee feel more comfortable entering into such a relationship. Janet Thompson, in her book *Woman to Woman Mentoring,* suggests a six-month program. "This lets those who may be nervous about mentoring know that this is not necessarily a lifetime commitment. In case there are some relationships that never quite gel, they can learn and grow but still have the opportunity to move on in six months."[7]

Publicize the Ministry: After you have decided on a plan of action, publicize the mentoring ministry by including information in the church bulletin, by placing flyers throughout the church (don't forget the back of bathroom stall doors), by inserting a note on the church's website, by having information at the women's ministry information table, or by any other means available.

Plan a Kickoff Event: A kickoff event could be coffee or tea in someone's home or at the church. The main attraction is the meeting and pairing, so keep the refreshments simple.

Reevaluate: After one season of the mentoring program, reevaluate the process. Find out what worked and what didn't work, and then make the necessary adjustments for the following year.

Who Can Be a Mentor?

Who can be a mentor? We all can. Chances are if you are reading this book, you know women who are younger than you who could benefit from your life experiences. You probably also know women who are older than you from whom you could benefit.

Looking back at my own life, I see woman after woman who helped me on my journey. It began with the mother of a friend of mine, Mrs. Henderson, who shared Jesus Christ with me. Then it was a group of women who were the portrait of godly womanhood. As a new mother, Mary Marshall Young helped me understand my true identity in Christ. Cissy Smith taught me how to press on in the face of adversity. Newley Lindsey showed me how to be creative with a paintbrush and a pair of scissors. And, well, the list goes on and on. I am a product of the women who have impacted my life.

"Mentoring means using the wisdom that comes from life's experiences to help others who are encountering similar experiences in their lives. Christian mentors share how God guides and supports, counsels and consoles, in both the good and the bad times."[8] Your life experiences are much like the treasures or talents that are mentioned in Matthew 25. Let's not bury those treasures in the ground, but invest them in the lives of others.*

---

* In the appendix I have included several mentoring resources. Because mentoring can be a complex issue, I suggest further study before you begin.

$\mathcal{H}$annah's $\mathcal{H}$eart
Developing a Need-Driven Program

$\mathcal{J}$esus always paid attention to the needs of the people around Him. He looked up into a tree and noticed a tax collector who needed some love and encouragement. He walked into town and noticed a woman in a funeral procession for her only son and saw someone who needed a miracle. He turned His ear to men crying out for healing and gave sight to the blind. Likewise, as women in ministry, we must keep our eyes open and our ears pressed to the heart of God to hear the cries of the women in our church and community. If we see a group of individuals who are on the fringe or have unique needs that are being unmet, perhaps we need to draw them in by establishing specific ministries or need-based ministries.

Women relate best to those who understand their particular struggle. They are drawn to "been there, done that, lived to tell about it." Need-driven programs are usually begun by women who have experienced the particular life experience or struggle.

In this chapter, I would like to introduce you to Amanda Bailey. Amanda struggled for years with infertility and began to see that many other women in her church and community were struggling as well. God called Amanda to create a specific ministry to meet the needs of those who were experiencing the pain of empty arms.

As we look at how Amanda started a program for women experiencing infertility and miscarriage, we can see a pattern for beginning any need-driven ministry. Now let's let Amanda share how she began her program, Hannah's Heart.

Amanda Bailey

I was married at 39, and soon after that my husband, Bill, and I discovered I was pregnant. We were both happy and stunned. We told the good news to everyone who would listen, made sweeping plans about our future, and shared with all our friends the loving grace of a God who made this possible. Nine weeks later I started spotting and had a miscarriage. I had started a journal to save for our child, but the pages were as empty as the longing in my heart. As I dealt with my grief and puzzlement at what God was doing in my life, I began to fill this journal instead with poems and letters reflecting the many emotions that ran rampant through my mind. A few months later I once again discovered I was pregnant and once again had a miscarriage.

A year later I was pregnant a third time, but this pregnancy also ended in a miscarriage. Fetal testing showed that this baby was a boy with genetic developmental defects. This time my heart went numb, my prayer life went numb, and my life felt as though it were on hold. Still in a state of spiritual shock, I found that I was pregnant a fourth time, barely two months after the loss of my third child. This time my husband and I did not dare to rejoice, as the pattern of miscarriage echoed in our minds. There were hints of problems from the beginning, and we did not get our hopes up or allow ourselves to love this child. But the ultrasound showed a fetus that was more childlike than any that had come before, and a small glimmer of hope and a seed of love were planted in my heart. Ten weeks later we lost this child as well. I strongly felt the ache of God's heart for me and for the death of His little one. My husband and I grieved for this child, but at the same time I felt a real joy knowing this child was with God and was to be eternally comforted by the heart of God. How did I come to this point of strength in the midst of such disappointment? God gave me two other women who understood my pain.

Three Women—One Struggle

Less than a year after my first miscarriage Tracey Storie, Wendy Davis, and I got together to share our frustrations over our infertility, medical questions, and spiritual struggles. After our time of sharing and praying, we felt comforted by God and by each other. Tracey turned to 2 Corinthians 1:3-4, and we realized that God had personified that verse in our time together. "All praise to the God and Father of our Lord Jesus Christ. He is the source of every mercy and the God who comforts us. He comforts us in all our troubles so that we can comfort others. When others are troubled, we will be able to give them the same comfort God has given us" (NLT).

After reading the account of Hannah's infertility in the opening chapters of 1 Samuel, we agreed that we wanted to respond to God the way she did, as women who were passionate in our relationship with God and who were able to praise God no matter what. Hannah cried out to God, "My heart rejoices in the LORD" (1 Samuel 2:1). We wanted a heart like Hannah's, so we called our ministry Hannah's Heart.

The Birth of a Ministry

As we began to pray for ways to reach out to other women who were experiencing infertility, God began to reveal a plan. Let me walk you through the process.

Dear God ***Begin with Prayer:*** A multitude of things must work properly in a woman's body and a man's body for conception, implantation, and a healthy birth to take place. My favorite infertility doctor always reminds his patients, "Only God can make a baby!" Likewise, only God can make a healthy ministry...and prayer is essential.

Develop a Mission Statement: Our mission statement was as follows: "To reach women on the journey of infertility and to offer transforming opportunities as they connect more deeply with God and each other."

Develop a Ministry Strategy: Certain ministry values we wanted to establish at the inception of Hannah's Heart became our nonnegotiables. We started working on these ministry values by starting with the five emphasized words below. Then we wrote out sentences to accompany them. Please feel free to use the following in establishing your own group.

- Children are a *gift* from God, and God alone is the source of life. We deny that the conceiving and bearing of children are indications of greater character, spiritual maturity, or merited divine favor.

- Seeking of God's will through *prayer* is a valid and powerful means of understanding the heart of God concerning infertility, miscarriage, or adoption.

- God does not want us to struggle alone and has designed the *community* of the body of Christ to help bear our burdens and encourage us to remain steadfast in our love of God.

- God wants us to *share* the grace He offers to us with all women so that they may come to know Him in this journey and for their whole lives.

- Being first *adopted* into God's family and chosen by Him, we affirm that every member of our earthly families (whether through biology, adoption, or blending) is an integral part of God's plan in the lives of His children.

- MOTTO: We are a network of women experiencing infertility but seeking a fertile life.

We asked additional questions to determine where the ministry would fall in the church structure. If this is new territory for you, ask your pastoral staff or women's director to help map out the different options for you. Of course, as your ministry grows and changes, these may fluctuate over time. Below are questions to consider:

- ❧ Will you mostly be ministering to individuals or to groups?

- ❧ Will your meetings model teaching principles or counseling principles?

- ❧ Do you primarily see yourself as an outreach ministry (evangelism) or an "inreach" ministry (discipleship)?

- ❧ Will you be a small group ministry (6 to 12 people in a group), hold medium-sized events (average 30 people), host large events (over 100 people), or a combination of all three?

You and your ministry partners must develop your own vision for the ministry and determine the nonnegotiables. If they are not clearly stated from the beginning, those who join the ministry team later may desire something totally different, and you may find yourself leading a ministry that has very little resemblance to what God called you to form. For example, if you feel that weekly meetings should include Bible study, but the majority wants to share and pray, you will grow frustrated and ineffective. Your nonnegotiables should be developed from the following areas:

- ❧ Your vision—Stay true to the vision God has given you.

- ❧ Your gifts—Determine how He can use your ministry partners' and your gifts most powerfully.

- ❧ Your time—Carefully prioritize and set aside time that is realistic with clearly defined boundaries.

Besides offering a safe place for women who are experiencing infertility, we saw three key areas where we could impact women's lives:

∾ *Evangelism:* Because infertility is a journey that tends to draw people to God, we saw that this ministry could be a vital part of our church's evangelism strategy.

∾ *Discipleship:* Because women on the journey of infertility often feel left out of the regular community of the church, they tend to bond very quickly. They develop close friendships, and desire to be together often for Bible study and prayer, thus spiritual growth will be easily sparked! (See Hebrews 10:24.)

∾ *Leadership:* Because the needs of women experiencing infertility will be met within the group, it provides a natural environment for helping someone take a leadership role and help someone else in return.

Decide on a Target Audience: Who is your target audience? Who are you trying to reach out to in this ministry? Your answers to these questions will help you figure out where you fit within your church's structure. You may want to do a women-only group and be a part of your women's ministry. You may want to include husbands and be a part of the church's marriage ministry. Although our Hannah's Heart ministry is predominately for women, we do have events in which we invite the husbands to participate. Our public forums, conferences, and social events are for both men and women. Here are trends we've noticed along the way:

∾ Women's groups initiate bonding quickly, develop community more deeply, and function best when the number is kept to 6 to 12 women per group.

∾ Couples' groups work well when both spouses are united, when the lead couple is willing to be vulnerable and open, and when the number is kept to 3 to 4 couples per group.

∾ Men's groups need a discerning vulnerable leader and an active agenda. This type of group functions best when the number is kept to 3 to 4 men per group.

Present the Ministry Idea to the Church Leadership: Different churches have different procedures that you must go through to start a new ministry. We made sure to have the blessing and support of our church first. Ideally, your time of preparation prayer will have alerted them and they will be open and ready to help you. Be flexible with the kind of ministry that best fits your church's structure. God will be the one to grow your ministry as He sees fit. So don't worry about this stage. Respect your church's decisions and honor their spiritual and financial accountability. Your church has many resources that will add to the success of your ministry: money, meeting room, counseling, and prayer.

Set Up an Organizational Meeting: Set up several times for you and your ministry partners to share the vision of the new ministry. Extend personal invitations, but also put an open invitation in your church bulletin, on bulletin boards, at the women's ministry table, or in any informational publications.

Develop Relationships: A need-driven ministry thrives upon personal relationships that develop within the ministry and outside of the ministry. Relationships are what keep people coming back. Developing relationships and nurturing friendships outside the group will be the fertilizer to make the groups grow.

The longevity of your ministry will live or die depending on the depth of the community. An infertility ministry can be made up of a very transient group. Some women may need support for a short time, some women may need long-term support, and some women will graduate out of the group by having children or adopting. For those who do conceive and have a child, encourage the group to celebrate! You might have a woman who is experiencing secondary infertility and feeling embarrassed that she is struggling when she already has a child. Let the group know that her pain is just as real as their pain and that she is clearly welcome in the group. Some tips for building a strong sense of community include:

- ∽ Share each other's story.

- ∽ Explore the Bible.

- ∽ Pray together.

- ∽ Contact each other during the week via phone, e-mail, or phone calls.

- ∽ Meet for lunch or coffee.

- ∽ Share journal entries.

- ∽ Celebrate births.

- ∽ Celebrate holidays. (Holidays are particularly difficult for couples who long to have children. Consider hosting a Christmas party for the spouses or sending a card at Mother's Day.)

Concluding Words: The journey of infertility, as with many need-driven ministries, includes disappointment, despair, and devastation. But a ministry based on encouragement, support, and biblical teaching can make a tremendous difference. You can be a part of impacting women by meeting them at their point of need to share the hope and healing of Jesus Christ and nurturing a personal ongoing relationship with Him.

Examples of Need-Driven Ministries

Women in the workplace

International students ministry

AIDS ministry

Infertility ministry

Women who struggle with depression

Ministry to families with disabled persons

Newcomers ministry

Women struggling with cancer

Single parent ministry

Ministry to shut-ins

Ministry to widows

Weight loss ministry

Married women who worship alone

Prison ministry

Women's shelter ministry

Hispanic, Vietnamese, or other ethnic group ministry

Gathering Volunteers

or we are God's workmanship, created in Christ Jesus to do good works, which God prepared in advance for us to do" (Ephesians 2:10).

Building, growing, and maintaining an effective women's ministry is a monumental task, and one thing is for sure—one woman or even a handful of women, cannot do it alone. It takes a team of women working in unity for common goals, and it requires many helping hands. In a word: volunteers.

The prophet Nehemiah was a master at gathering volunteers. He had a great task before him, the rebuilding of the walls of Jerusalem, and he knew he could not do it alone. He needed 100 percent participation. As we mentioned earlier, Nehemiah first began with prayer, asking God to give him clear direction. Second, he assessed the situation to see what needed to be done (Nehemiah 2:11-16) and decided who needed to do what. Third, he cast the vision, "Come, let us rebuild the wall of Jerusalem, and we will no longer be in disgrace" (Nehemiah 2:17). He let the men and women know what was in it for them and how God was going to be with them each step of the way. Fourth, he called for volunteers and gave specific job descriptions (Nehemiah 3). Throughout the book of Nehemiah we read how he prayed for, encouraged, and directed the volunteers. Finally, at the close of the book, Nehemiah celebrated those who had participated in the building project. He listed their names (the heads of the families) and hosted a big party!

Let's take a look at each of these volunteer principles and see how we can apply Nehemiah's strategy of gathering volunteers and keeping them motivated to the completion of the task. First we'll begin with prayer.

> *Dear Lord, we come to You today thanking You for the privilege of serving the women in our church and community. We know that You created each of us for good works that You planned beforehand that we should do. We come to You asking that You reveal to us those whom You have chosen to join with us in this mission of reaching out to the women through various means. We pray You will show us how to help women feel fulfilled by serving You with passion and purpose. In Jesus' name, amen.*

Nehemiah's Volunteer Strategy

- ✑ Assess what needs to be done.

- ✑ Cast the vision of the project.

- ✑ Assign specific, clearly defined tasks. (Rather than "Would you like to work on the retreat committee?" ask, "Would you like to help plan the brochure for the retreat?" Women are hesitant to commit if they are unclear about what you are asking them to do.)

- ✑ Train the workers or show them what to do.

- ✑ Encourage them along the way.

- ✑ Pray for them regularly.

- ✑ Celebrate when the job is complete.

Volunteering in Teams

Women long to be in relationship with other women. That is one reason women's ministry is so vital to the life and health of the church. While women may volunteer because they want to contribute or help, many will volunteer in hopes of developing relationships along the way. A menial task, such as stuffing envelopes, can be the highlight of someone's week if they get to do it with someone they enjoy spending time with.

I remember many years ago when I gathered with a group of volunteers to fold newsletters. The room was pulsating with energy and enthusiasm as young mothers listened to instruction on collating, stamping, and bundling newsletters by zip codes. Everyone settled into their little work space, surrounded by piles of papers and boxes for mail. There was about 30 seconds of silence before the real purpose of "mailing night" began. No one said, "Let's begin." It just happened naturally.

"Meredith has started having temper tantrums!" one mother exclaimed. "I don't know what's gotten into her."

The room buzzed with, "Meredith? You've got to be kidding. She's always been such a little angel."

Then the sound of temper tantrum stories and ample advice began to fill the room. Meredith's mom was encouraged to know that her little girl was not the only child in the world who had temper tantrums, she was not the only mom in the world who has had to deal with them, and that most likely they would both live through this phase of childhood.

After a short pause, another mom said, "Well, I'm having trouble with potty-training. I've tried everything I know. Even the M&M's aren't working."

Once again, the room was a buzz with sagas of potty-training exploits, victories, and defeats.

For two hours, as busy hands collated, folded, stamped, and sealed, moms shared their struggles and were met with encouragement and hope. Whether the advice of fellow moms worked or not, the point was that the ladies had the chance to voice their frustrations and be encouraged by others who had similar feelings and experiences.

What I realized that night was that these women did not come together for the joy of collating, folding, stamping, and sealing. They came together because of the bond of friendship and the joy of fellowship. And that, my friend, is one of the keys to fostering a spirit of volunteerism! It's not about the job at hand. It is about the relationships of the people who are working together.

Do you want more women to volunteer? Pair them up two by two or gather them together in work groups. There's a lot we can learn from our ancestors who held quilting bees and canning sessions.

Volunteering in Areas of Giftedness

Many times a volunteer is simply used to fill a need, regardless of her spiritual gifts, passions, abilities, or personality. This is a formula for disaster. For example, if a woman who is a task-oriented introvert is asked to be a greeter or solicitor for door prizes, she will be very unhappy and most likely unsuccessful in her endeavor. While this task might drain her emotionally, working on brochures or registration might energize her.

In chapter 10 we took a brief look at various spiritual gifts. Consider having a potential volunteer complete a spiritual gifts assessment and then place her in a position that is most likely to set her up to succeed and find fulfillment. Discovering how God has equipped your volunteers for ministry will save them and you frustration and expedite fulfillment.

In *The Volunteer Revolution*, Bill Hybels suggests simply experimenting to discover where a volunteer would like to serve. Invite a woman to volunteer for a short time to see if her passion and giftedness line up with the job at hand. After a brief period (it could be as brief as once), ask them the following questions:

1. Did the work feel meaningful?

2. Was your emotional energy higher or lower after you served?

3. Did you enjoy the people with whom you served?

4. Does this serving opportunity fit into your schedule?[1]

Volunteering in Areas of Passion

There is no better volunteer than one who is motivated by the passions that stir her heart. No one can help a woman who is struggling with a wayward teenager better than one who has welcomed a prodigal home. No one can help a woman who is struggling with breast cancer like the woman who bears the same scar upon her chest. No one can help a woman struggling with infertility or miscarriage like the woman who knows the pain of empty arms. In the Bible Paul writes, "Praise be to the God and Father of our Lord Jesus Christ, the Father of compassion and the God of all comfort, who comforts us in all our troubles, so that we can comfort those in any trouble with the comfort we ourselves have received from God. For just as the sufferings of Christ flow over into our lives, so also through Christ our comfort overflows" (2 Corinthians 1:3-5). In other words, God doesn't comfort us simply to make us comfortable. God comforts us to make us comfort-able...able to comfort others.

Look for volunteers who have gone through particular struggles in their lives and who are ready to help others overcome similar struggles. Talk to women. Find out what they are passionate about. Discover their unique interests. Ask them what stirs their hearts and makes them want to get out of bed in the morning. Look around and see who has been greatly impacted by their relationship with Christ and who has a burning desire to give back to Him. These will be some of your best volunteers.

Volunteering in Proper Perspective

I have discovered that many people have a difficult time asking women to volunteer because they hold to a wrong perspective. Are we asking women to lend *us* a helping hand, or are we inviting women to *team up with God to change the world?* No offense, but I would rather team up with God than with an individual. Are we asking women to help fulfill our mission, or are we inviting women to see beyond the daily grind of life to impact the world for Christ? Are we presenting participation as something someone *has* to do or something someone *gets* to do?

Today's busy woman does not need another duty on her to-do list to check off. What she does need is to find fulfillment by participating in something bigger than herself—bigger than her little world. Bill Hybels explains the difference:

> Too many willing-hearted volunteers have been wounded "on the job." They've responded to an invitation to serve, only to end up in a volunteer position that was poorly conceived, resulting in tasks that few people would find fulfilling. Or they show up to serve and discover they have nothing to do; an unprepared volunteer coordinator has wasted their time, causing them to lose precious hours they had willingly carved out from their busy schedule.
>
> Some work hard on menial tasks without ever hearing how their efforts serve a grander cause; they're given plenty of work, but no vision. Others have felt overwhelmed by unreasonable demands for which they've not received proper training; rather than being set up to win, they get put on the express lane to frustration and failure.
>
> Many have been hurt when a coercive leader drafted them to "fill a slot" without considering their gifts or talents or what they love to do. Some have given hours—maybe even years—in voluntary service to an organization or church, without receiving a single thanks.[2]

In *The Volunteer Revolution,* Bill Hybels mentions Allan Luks, the author of *The Healing Power of Doing Good.* Luks explains that there are very real health benefits to serving others. He "makes it clear that when we persuade someone else to volunteer face-to-face, we are giving an enormous gift, much like a membership in a health club."[3] Helping others offers long-term health benefits, "including relief from back pain and headaches, lowered blood pressure and cholesterol, and curbed overeating and alcohol and drug abuse."[4] When someone volunteers and feels that they are helping others, there is a release of dopamine, the chemical that produces the pleasurable sensation activated by certain drugs and other addictive behaviors.[5]

For too many years we have looked at volunteers as people who are helping us. We need to look at volunteer opportunities as a way to help the person!

When inviting women to become volunteers, regardless of the program or event, keep the following points in mind. A happy volunteer is one who:

- Feels cared for

- Understands how her "job" helps impact the vision

- Receives the proper training for her "job"

- Knows that others see her time as valuable

- Feels that she is a vital part of a team

Ralph Waldo Emerson once said, "It is one of the most beautiful compensations of this life that no man can sincerely try to help another without helping himself." When we invite someone to help by serving, they will inevitably feel better about themselves. If they do not, we need to ask ourselves why.

- Did we thank them?

- Did we inadvertently set them up to fail?

- Did we give them enough responsibility?

- Did we ask them to serve in an area of their giftedness?

Volunteering in Response to an Invitation

As we have already seen in this manual, women love to be asked or invited to serve. It is very rare for a woman to come forward and tell a women's ministry director that she is interested in volunteering or that she is especially gifted at a particular task. I believe there are women in our churches who long to make an impact, but who are waiting for someone to simply ask. As I said earlier, Jesus didn't put up a sign-up sheet for potential disciples to sign up to be a part of His team. He invited the Twelve to join Him.

On the other hand, even though it is important to personally ask or invite volunteers to put on the towel of servanthood, it may be enough for some to consider themselves invited if they are simply made aware of the need. We can make our needs known by publishing them in the church bulletin or weekly newsletter, posting them on the website or weekly e-mail, making an announcement before the Sunday service, having a ministry opportunity fair in the fall and spring, or playing video clips of various ministries during Sunday morning worship service.

One survey reported these reasons people say yes to volunteer opportunities:

- It sounds like fun.
- I want to be where the action is.
- They really need and want me.
- It is a chance to learn new skills.
- It could help me with my personal life.
- I have received a lot of help. Now it is my turn to repay.
- It is a critical need. I have got to do my part.
- I will have a chance to really influence what happens.
- Service is a tradition in our family. It's expected.
- My best friend is asking me.
- I will make new friends.[6]

Regardless of which method you choose, you'll find that the personal invitation is always the best. And who better to do the inviting than someone who is already enjoying volunteering herself?

Let me tell you of one method that does not work: guilt. One of the fastest ways to turn off a congregation is to try and guilt them into serving. Phrases like, "If you don't care for these children, who will?" or "If we really cared about the lost, we would volunteer to go door-to-door on Wednesday nights." I have seen very few joyful volunteers who are serving out of guilt rather than out of a sense of passion and purpose.

When inviting someone to volunteer, it is all in how you ask. Examine these two "invitations."

Invite 1: "Hey, Mary, would you be willing to help me stuff 500 envelopes with invitations for the upcoming women's retreat? It's just grunt work and very boring, but somebody's got to do it."

Invite 2: "Hey, Mary, I'm helping with the women's retreat this year and next Wednesday I'm mailing out the invitations. This is going to be the best retreat ever and these invitations are the seeds we're sowing to draw women closer to Christ. I would love for you to join me so we can spend some time together. We're going to pray over each invitation as we stamp them. And of course, there will be chocolate!"

Here are some ways to invite that are hard to resist:

- ❧ "Barb, you always know how to make women feel loved and cared for, as though they are the most important person in the room. You would be perfect to be in charge of our greeters for the retreat. Could you minister to the ladies by helping them feel welcome?"

- ❧ "Beth, you have such a flair for decorating. Even your outfits are put together like a professional model. You would be the best person I know to head up the decorations for the banquet. Would you like to be in charge of making this a night to remember?"

∽ "Sue, you have a gift for taking us right to God's throne when you pray. I don't know of anyone who would be better for heading up the prayer committee for the retreat. Would you consider leading us?"

Volunteering in Light of Scripture

When it comes to volunteering, let's keep the following verses in mind:

∽ "Your Father, who sees what is done in secret, will reward you" (Matthew 6:4).

∽ "Be steadfast, immovable, always abounding in the work of the Lord, knowing that your work is not in vain" (1 Corinthians 15:58).

∽ "Let us not become weary in doing good, for at the proper time we will reap a harvest if we do not give up. Therefore, as we have opportunity, let us do good to all people" (Galatians 6:9-10).

∽ "And let us consider how we may spur one another on toward love and good deeds" (Hebrews 10:24).

∽ "For we are God's workmanship, created in Christ Jesus to do good works, which God prepared in advance for us to do" (Ephesians 2:10).

∽ "Encourage one another and build each other up, just as in fact you are doing" (1 Thessalonians 5:11).

—PART SIX—
Programs Designed for Outreach

*I*n Jesus' last words to His disciples, He gave them a charge: "But you will receive power when the Holy Spirit comes on you; and you will be my witnesses in Jerusalem, and in all Judea and Samaria, and to the ends of the earth" (Acts 1:8). We have looked at how to build an effective women's ministry with a sturdy foundation, walls and rooms, a protective roof, and the mortar of prayer holding it all together. But imagine what a house would be like without windows. Suppose each of us came in the front door, found our rooms, and never looked at the people on the outside of our neat and tidy home—some who may be curious and want to join us, some who are longing to know the truth, some who are shivering in the cold of this dark and dreary world.

In Acts 1:8, Jesus reminds us to include windows in our ministry plan. Let's turn our attention to installing windows to the world.

Viva la Difference

For centuries, churches had the idea that if you build it…they will come. But that is no longer the case in our modern society. Church is no longer the center of activity. It is no longer the only place where women and men can get their needs for fellowship, purpose, support, and belonging met. Today, we can choose the YMCA, book clubs, exercise groups, tennis teams, moms play groups, Bunko groups, and a multitude of support groups that address every malady imaginable. Purpose-driven churches and purpose-driven programs realize that in order to attract unchurched people, we have to understand the culture and adapt to draw them in. Paul was a master at being "seeker sensitive." For example, when he visited Athens, he observed the people before he spoke. His desire was to meet the people where they were and make his sermon culturally relevant. He said, "Men of Athens! I see that in every way you are very religious. For as I walked around and looked carefully at your objects of worship, I even found an altar with this inscription: TO AN UNKNOWN GOD. Now what you worship as something unknown I am going to proclaim to you" (Acts 17:22-23).

Paul adapted his message to those who were in his audience without compromising the truth. We can do the same. Listen to his words to the Corinthians:

Though I am free and belong to no man, I make myself a slave to everyone, to win as many as possible. To the Jews I became like a Jew, to win the Jews. To those under the law I became like one under the law (though I myself am not under the law), so as to win those under the law. To those not having the law I became like one not having the law (though I am not free from God's law but am under Christ's law), so as to win those not having the law. To the weak I became weak, to win the weak. I have become all things to all men so that by all possible means I might save some. I do all this for the sake of the gospel, that I may share in its blessings (1 Corinthians 9:19-23).

You only have to watch television for ten minutes to understand that our culture is very different from the Robert Young and Jane Wyatt days of *Father Knows Best*. And yet, many of our churches still function as if they are in the 1950s. Gary McIntosh, in his book *Three Generations: Riding the Waves of Change in Your Church*, says that our "failure to understand and respond to the changing generational influences in the United States may have negative impact on our churches and ministry."[1] McIntosh mentions five potential results of ignoring cultural changes:

1. A slow decline for many local churches and related denominations

2. Fewer recruits for missions, with a resulting loss of influence on unreached peoples

3. Less money with which to finance missions or other local church ministries

4. A continual trend toward the liberal agenda in the United States

5. An inability to fulfill our God-given purpose to "make disciples of all nations" (Matthews 28:19)[2]

McIntosh identifies three broad generations of people in the United States today: the Builder Generation (people born before 1946), the Boomer Generation (people born between 1946–1964), and the Buster Generation (people born between 1965–1983).

In general, *Builders* grew up during WW I and the Roaring Twenties. They survived the Great Depression and their formative years were shaped by a rural lifestyle. They experienced the advent of the automobile, radio, and television. Builders are hard workers, savers, patriotic, private, cautious, and respectful. They are stable and not quick to change. Spiritually, Builders are committed to the church, support foreign missions, enjoy Bible study, worship in reverence, and minister out of duty. They enjoy group activities, Sunday school, mission projects, and contact with other generations.

In general, *Boomers* grew up with television, rock 'n' roll, the civil rights movement, economic affluence, the Vietnam War, and the energy crisis. They are educated, media oriented, independent, cause oriented, fitness conscious, and question authority. Spiritually, Boomers are committed to relationships, want to belong, desire to live their faith, and tolerate differences well. They desire purpose, quality, multiple options, small groups, visual communication, local ministry, and short-term missions. Boomers are much more open to women in leadership positions and women's ministry in general.

Finally, *Busters* are shaped by Roe v. Wade, high-tech video games, television, music, a variable economy, the Persian Gulf War, and the advent of AIDS. They enjoy freedom, community causes, and practical education. Busters tend to postpone marriage, have short attention spans, reject Boomer values, and often feel lonely and neglected. Spiritually, Busters are committed to family, local causes, faith that meets a need. They want less structure, up-to-date options, and a clear ministry vision. They enjoy small groups, short-term service, need-based ministries, and contemporary worship services.

Keeping the differences between Builders, Boomers, and Busters in mind, the way we reach out to the unchurched in each generation will vary. For example, a Builder would be drawn to support groups, traditional activities, and intergenerational activities; a Boomer would be drawn to family-oriented activities, service opportunities, and community projects; and Busters would be drawn to "how to" messages, life skills, and large-group activities.

When you throw a pebble into a pond, concentric circles emanate from its point of entry. Jesus' penetrating power has the same rippling effect as He calls us to reach out to those around us, then a little farther out, and then even further still. Let's take a look at how we, as women in ministry, can open the curtains wide and have windows to the world.

Different Strokes for Different Folks

What makes a program that is intended for outreach different from one that is intended to encourage and equip believers?

- ∾ The program

- ∾ The presentation

- ∾ The people you invite

A program and presentation geared toward outreach will have specific characteristics. Here are some considerations to keep in mind:

- ∾ Avoid titles that are steeped in "Christianese."

- ∾ Avoid speakers that teach in-depth spiritual principles that are difficult for seekers to understand.

- ∾ Assume the audience has no Christian background or biblical knowledge.

- ∾ Make sure the women in the church understand that the event is an outreach and remind them to invite their unchurched acquaintances (rather than their Christian friends who already embrace Jesus Christ as Savior and Lord).

Now let's take a look at some specific examples of programs specifically designed for outreach.

Creative Connections

Women's ministry director Cheri Jimenez began to reach out to the unchurched women in her community with a program called Creative Connections. Let's take a look at the *who, what, where, why,* and *how* of the program she developed in order to spur your imagination to create similar programs in your church. Rather than me telling you about Creative Connections, we have the privilege of hearing it directly from Cheri.

Cheri Jimenez

Community evangelism should be a vital and strategic component of any flourishing ministry. Our call as leaders is to spiritually disciple our women so they can be equipped to influence their world for the sake of the kingdom. Jesus made this mandate clear in the Sermon of the Mount. He referred to the body of believers as a "city set on a hill" with the challenge of letting our light shine "in such a way" that unbelievers will witness our good works and will be drawn to the Savior (Matthew 5:14,16 NASB).

In the twenty-first century, however, letting our light shine "in such a way" that the lost are drawn to the church can be quite a challenge. In the past, church events have played dual purposes for the sake of necessity—wrapping fellowship and evangelism into one program or event. While this is not always the wrong approach, I believe we must be much more intentional about reaching the women in our community. We must use our creativity to make connections that are truly effective with lasting impressions.

From this challenge, Creative Connections was birthed. The goal of this ministry was to provide a creative outlet to make connections with friends and family members who might never darken the door of a church to hear a Christian speaker, but would be interested in attending a scrapbooking party, gardening seminar, or gourmet cooking class. These activity-driven events establish common bonds and shared interests in a nonthreatening setting, while giving numerous opportunities to share the love and light of Jesus Christ in an effective and compelling fashion.

First, we made sure to educate the women of the purpose of the Creative Connections events. We laid out the plan for creative evangelism and talked about the event we were planning for the spring. We had different sign-ups for helpers and volunteers to assist in putting on such an event. The women in the church really felt they were making a difference and being more intentional about evangelism. These events gave our churchwomen an avenue and a place to use their creative talents for the sake of evangelism.

We made the tickets affordable and encouraged each member to purchase two of them—one for themselves and one for an unchurched friend. We even offered to help cover the price of the second ticket if purchasing two tickets was cost prohibitive. Again, we emphasized that this was an outreach event and strongly discouraged members from bringing friends and family members who were already believers.

Creative Connections proved to be just the avenue needed to engage those who had previously not been open to church functions. The success of these events was found in heightening the awareness of evangelistic opportunities in the congregation and providing specific outlets for church members to share their faith in creative ways. The feedback we received was tremendous. Women tended to be much more open to attend other functions sponsored by the church after experiencing the love and fellowship of our church in a non-threatening way.

Spring Gardening Seminar

Our first Creative Connections event was a Spring Gardening Seminar. I had a contact that worked for a local gardening shop, and she agreed to give a short talk on seasonal ideas for potting containers. Again, we reminded ladies to invite their neighbors, coworkers, hairstylist, and manicurist—anyone in their sphere of influence who was not a Christian.

The speaker demonstrated various ways to pot plants and also shared how gardening had helped her grieve the loss of her husband. She also shared how God created the earth to give us pleasure and reflect His love for us. After the short seminar and demonstration, everyone who attended put together an English-garden container to take home.

The ladies were delighted to have a container ready to display. We served coffee and breakfast foods prepared by some of our ladies who felt called to share their gifts of hospitality, and the room was beautifully decorated with potted flowers donated by the sponsoring garden shop. The shop benefited from the publicity, and everyone who attended received a coupon.

Seminar Schedule

9:30–10:00	Register and view different assembled pots around the church (Samples were for sale after the event.) Coffee bar open
10:00–11:00	Gardening demonstration and devotion (inside)
11:00–12:00	Participants went through the different stations outside and put together their containers in the parking lot. (Ten women served as helpers.)

Over 100 women attended our first Creative Connections event and 50 women volunteered. If a member didn't know someone to invite, we encouraged her to come and help. This gave everyone an opportunity to participate in the outreach event and built a sense of teamwork and community among the members.

If your church decides to host a gardening outreach event, here are a few helpful hints:

- Contact a local nursery.

- Because you will be ordering a large quantity, ask for a bulk discount.

- Have the soil and other supplies delivered to the church the day before.

- Spread heavy plastic on the surface of the parking lot to collect the dirt during the potting.

- Have men available to unload the trucks.

- Set up centers in the parking lot to assist in the flow of the assembly line.

- Watch the demonstration inside the facility, and then move to the parking lot for assembly.

- Have several women serve as roving helpers to assist and troubleshoot.

- After the event, discard the plastic and blow the parking lot clean.

At the conclusion of the seminar, we auctioned all the containers that were used for demonstration to help underwrite the expense of the event. With a little bit of creativity and marketing skills, we were able to put on a first-class seminar that truly shared the love and light of Jesus Christ. The women walked away feeling pampered and encouraged by the fellowship of believers. At the conclusion of the seminar, we invited the attendees to pick up a women's ministry brochure listing Bible studies and upcoming events. A lot of interest was generated from this simple invitation.

Valentine Cooking Class

Another Creative Connections event we held was a Valentine Cooking Class titled, "Cooking for the One You Love." We advertised the event as a "class to learn how to prepare a Valentine's dinner for your special someone." We included instructions on everything from the table setting to the dessert. Several chefs from a popular restaurant taught the classes, which served as an instant draw. The head chef was a Christian, and he was excited to use his skills for an outreach event.

"Cooking for the One You Love" was held on a Saturday morning from 9:30–12:00. The following served as our schedule for the morning.

Cooking Class Schedule

9:30–10:00	Registration and table observation (Four women decorated tables with both formal and everyday dinnerware.) The ladies enjoyed gathering ideas as they looked at the various table settings.
10:00–10:50	Group A—salad/dessert class
	Group B—main course class
10:50–11:00	Break and switch groups
11:00–11:50	Group A—main course class
	Group B—salad/dessert class
11:50–12:00	Q & A

Because of the hands-on nature of the class and the size of the church kitchen, we limited the registration to 45 attendees. Each woman received a folder of handouts, recipes, and pad for note-taking. The menu was as follows:

■ ■ ■ ■ ■ ■ ■ ■ ■ ■ ■

Menu

Freshly prepared salad and dressing
(with various topping ideas)

Veal scallopini with pasta

Chocolate cake with chocolate icing
(with mint and raspberry presentation)

■ ■ ■ ■ ■ ■ ■ ■ ■ ■ ■

Here are some guidelines to consider as you begin to shape your own Creative Connections events:

❧ Pray for wisdom and discernment as you put together a team of women who have a passion for evangelism and discipleship.

❧ Assign a leader who has specifically identified her spiritual gift as evangelism—this will aid in special insight and direction in the planning of events.

❧ Choose events that make time for caring and developing intimate fellowship.

❧ Make the event a "first class" experience with special attention to detail—go the extra mile.

❧ Use seasonal ideas to plan your event (i.e., Spring Gardening Seminar, Valentine Cooking Class, Holiday Scrapbooking Party).

❧ Assign a marketing director who can use the resources of the church and community to help promote and underwrite the expense of the event.

❧ Educate the women in the church about the purpose of Creative Connections.

Ideas for Creative Connections Events:

- ❧ Spring or fall gardening seminar
- ❧ Holiday cooking class
- ❧ Christmas decorating and organization
- ❧ Vacation/summer scrapbooking
- ❧ Decorating your home seminar (Invite interior decorators in for a morning seminar to talk about simple window treatments, picture placement, and furniture refurbishing.)
- ❧ Pottery painting (Invite a local pottery shop to bring in plates, cups, and unusual pieces for the ladies to paint.)
- ❧ Jewelry-making class (Invite someone to teach a class on jewelry making and provide the necessary supplies to make various pieces to take home.)

Neighborhood Bible Studies

*W*indows to the world begin right in our very own neighborhoods. Where we live is no accident. The apostle Luke said, "From one man he made every nation of men, that they should inhabit the whole earth; and he determined the times set for them and the exact places where they should live" (Acts 17:26). God could have put you in any nation during any time. In accordance with His perfect plan, He chose for you to occupy this particular time in history and your particular address.

I love how Eugene Peterson paraphrases John 1:14: "The Word became flesh and blood, and moved into the neighborhood" (MSG). As soon as you moved into your particular neighborhood, Christ in you moved there too! We become His official representatives and an extension of our women's ministry right where we live.

One year I joined two of my neighbors who were members of my church to pray for what God would have us do to reach out to our neighborhood. We decided to prepare a Christmas tea to bring the women together. On the invitation we mentioned that a friend would share an inspiring message about Christmas. Forty-five women showed up. We ate Christmas goodies, connected with old friends, met some neighbors for the first time, and shared our favorite Christmas traditions. Then someone gave a brief devotional on what Christmas meant to her, which included a very nonthreatening presentation of the gospel. At the close of the tea, we extended an invitation to women to join us in a neighborhood Bible study. I'll never forget how one woman sheepishly asked, "I've never studied the Bible before. Is it all right if I come?" Of course, I couldn't say yes fast enough!

In the following years I watched relationships grow and mature. We've cried when children went away to college, prayed for each other during hard times, offered monetary gifts during financial crises, opened up our homes for shared meals, cared for each other's children, cooked dinners for those who were ill, and gathered for going-away parties.

Women's ministry doesn't end when we leave the church parking lot. It is only beginning.

Pattern for Neighborhood Bible Studies

Because neighborhood Bible studies take on a whole different flavor from Bible studies held at the church, I've separated them out into a chapter of their own. Neighborhood Bible studies are usually geared toward outreach; therefore, they will have a different focus. It is always best if there are at least two neighbors who are cohosting the study.

1. Extend an invitation to the women in your neighborhood. You never know with whom God has been working, so don't try to estimate who would and who would not be interested. Invite them all and let God handle the rest. You never want anyone to feel left out. If you have a very large neighborhood, start with three or four streets and then move on from there.

2. Explain the purpose of the meeting on the invitation. A friend of mine, Mary Ruth Diffy, wrote an invitation on a green piece of paper shaped like a piece of lettuce. She placed the invitation between two slices of bread along with a red piece of paper shaped like a slice of ham and an orange piece

of paper shaped like a slice of cheese, placed the "sandwich" in a plastic sandwich bag, and then wrote the person's name on the bag with a permanent marker. Mary Ruth then placed the lunch bags in her neighbors' newspaper boxes.

The invitation read:

> *Hungry for More?*
> *Come join Mary Ruth Diffy and Jo Ann Highfield*
> *as we explore the possibility of forming a neighborhood*
> *Bible study.*
> *Time: 9:30 A.M.*
> *Place: Mary Ruth's home, 725 York Street*
> *Phone: (add your number, if you choose)*

3. When the women gather, greet them with a hug and a smile, provide name tags, and serve light refreshments. It is important to remember that for many women, simply showing up at such an event is a huge leap of faith.

4. During the fellowship time, have the neighbors introduce themselves, tell how long they have lived in the neighborhood, where they live, and the makeup of who lives in their house (including pets).

5. After about 30 minutes of fellowship and a possible icebreaker, gather the women into one room and explain that your desire is to get to know one another and explore the Bible together. Assure them that this is not a study for experts but for those wanting to learn more about God and what the Bible has to say about life. Explain that this will not be a time of lecture, but a time for mutual sharing and learning together.

6. Show or tell about what the group will be studying.

7. Introduce the facilitator, or explain that you will take turns leading the group through the questions each week. Assure them that if they choose to act as the facilitator, they will have

the easiest role because the facilitator is simply the question asker and doesn't have to know the answers!

8. Explain the guidelines for the study:

    a. We will study only one passage at a time.

    b. We will avoid quoting individual pastors.

    c. We will stay away from denominational issues.

    d. We will look at what the passage has to say.

    e. We will look at what the passage means.

    f. We will look at what the passage means to me and how I can apply it to my life.

Creative Invitation Ideas: Here are some creative invitation ideas. Tie an invitation around or to:

- A bottle of water: *Need some refreshment in your life?*

- Bite-sized candies: *Treasures…We treasure your friendship. Hugs…Need some TLC?*

- Tea bag: *Come steep in God's Word with us!*

- A spoon: *Get the scoop on God.*

- Puzzle piece: *Come learn how we all fit into God's plan.*

- Lifesavers: *Drowning in busyness and stress? Grab a lifesaver and join us for a neighborhood Bible study!*

- Candle: *Need an extra bit of light in your life?*

The Facilitator: The purpose of the facilitator is to simply move the women through the Bible study questions. She should avoid giving answers every time or appearing as the teacher. She should let the participant's answer stand on its own, as though to say, her answer was enough. Also, it is important that the facilitator avoid the use of church words that the unchurched attendee might not understand. (For more on Fabulous Facilitators, see chapter 18.)

Time: As with any Bible study, a neighborhood Bible study should begin and end on time. Suggested time frames are 7:00–8:30 P.M., 7:30–9:00 P.M., or 10:00–11:30 A.M. Allow 15 minutes at the beginning of each gathering for refreshments and visiting.

Size: One of the best problems you could have with a neighborhood Bible study, as with every small-group function, is that it is too big! The ideal size for a small group is 8 to 12 participants. If the group has more than 12 members, some will feel as though they cannot share. If the group grows to consistently more than 12, you may want to consider breaking the discussion group up into two separate groups. This will allow for more discussion and also give someone else the opportunity to lead.

Seating: Seating in a circle or casually around a den or family room allows everyone to see each other's face. Some prefer the floor while some older neighbors may need a comfy chair. Rather than have a room with 12 chairs, bring in chairs as they are needed. This will avoid the feeling that you had less show up than you were expecting.

Neighborhood Bible studies serve as a wonderful tool for deepening friendships, introducing Jesus Christ, and building relationships. After all, that could very well be why God has placed us right where we live today.

Christmas Events

Christmas dinners or Christmas teas provide a wonderful opportunity for outreach and are traditionally the most highly attended special event of the year. Therefore, let's take a closer look at this type of gathering.

People are more open to hearing about the Christ child during the holidays, and those who would normally be offended with a discussion of Jesus almost expect it during the Christmas season. So take advantage of a time where hearts are more receptive to the gospel message.

Everything about a Christmas event should be festive and inviting. From the table decorations to the invitations to the ladies' bathroom, make this an occasion to remember. The purpose of a Christmas event is twofold: share the gospel of the Christ child with those who have not yet believed in Jesus as their Savior and help focus believers on the reason for the season. Because you have the potential of impacting the way many will celebrate the holidays, schedule the Christmas event in late November or early December. Remember to secure a speaker well in advance. Many professional speakers have special Christmas presentations.

When it comes to decorations for a Christmas event, the options are endless. Consider some of the following: poinsettias, Christmas trees, beautifully wrapped boxes, bowls filled with Christmas ornaments, white lights, colored lights, luminaries, garlands, miniature trees, and children's toys with big bows tied on them.

A festival of tables event is particularly beautiful for a Christmas event. Invite women to host tables they have decorated with their own Christmas china and linens.

Because Christmas is a time of the year when hearts are more open to hearing about Jesus, make sure to have a speaker who can share the gospel message in a nonthreatening and inviting manner. At the close, offer the women an opportunity to accept Christ as their Savior. This will be the best present you will give all season!

Birthday Party for Jesus

One fabulous outreach to children is to host a birthday party for Jesus. Chances are many children in your community are unclear about the true meaning of Christmas. Hosting a birthday party for Him will give you an opportunity to share about the Savior's birth and perhaps plant a few seeds into a child's heart. All children hold birthday parties in high esteem and will love to join the celebration.

Here are a few ideas from my book *Celebrating a Christ-Centered Christmas* to get you started:

- Create a party invitation that exudes excitement, activity, and fun.

- Ask each child to bring an inexpensive gender-neutral gift to exchange ($5 limit).

- Decorate the room as you would for any other birthday party: use streamers, balloons, confetti, and a birthday banner.

- During the party, play games with a Christmas twist: musical chairs with Christmas music, bingo using the word "angel" instead of "bingo," or pin the tail on the donkey (show a picture of Mary riding to Bethlehem on a donkey).

∾ Have each child make a simple Christmas craft as a take-home gift.

∾ Number the gifts each child brought. Write the numbers on a slip of paper. Then have the child pick a number to determine which gift he or she gets to keep. Explain that Jesus was the first Christmas gift. God gave His Son as a gift to take away our sins. And when we accept Him as our Savior, He comes to live in our hearts and we will live forever in heaven with Him. Now at Christmastime, we give gifts to each other to remind us of God's great gift to us.

∾ Of course, no birthday party is complete without a cake. Have a birthday cake with candles and sing "Happy Birthday" to Jesus.

∾ Read the Christmas story from Luke 2 and have the children act it out. Prepare some simple costumes ahead of time: sheets and rope belts for shepherds, Mary, and Joseph; halos and wings for angels; beautifully wrapped gift boxes and bathrobes for wise men; a baby doll as Jesus; a pillow for the hump in the camel's back; and a fuzzy white blanket for the sheep.

∾ After the "play," tell the rest of the story. Give a very simple presentation of the gospel and an opportunity for the children to accept Christ as their Savior.

∾ When the parents come to pick up their children, invite them in to see the performance. Read from Luke 2 again and let the children act it out. Not only will you be ministering to the precious children, but you will also be touching their parents' hearts as well.[1]

Lifestyle Evangelism

*A*s we read the pages of the New Testament, we see Jesus ministering to men and women as He walked along the road, enjoyed a cozy dinner, or celebrated at a wedding feast. Ministry wasn't something Jesus did 40 hours a week. It was something He lived 24 hours a day. Genia Rogers is a friend of mine who exemplifies lifestyle evangelism better than anyone I know. I've asked her to share in this chapter what she has learned through sharing her life with others.

Genia Rogers

Often the mere thought of sharing Christ with others floods our minds with thoughts of inadequacy, fear of rejection, and a repulsion of door-to-door salesmen. As God has developed my passion for sharing Christ with nonbelievers, I have realized that His greatest desire is that I simply be willing to lay aside my pride, my insecurities, my agenda, and my goals, and allow His love to flow through me.

Over the past ten years I have shared Christ while running on the treadmill, sharing a cup of coffee with a friend, sitting in an airplane, standing in a used car parking lot, and changing my daughter's diaper. Whether we realize it or not, each day God brings people into our lives who are in desperate need of His truth and grace. As you think about living a lifestyle of evangelism, ask Him to remind you of people He has specifically brought into your sphere of influence to see Christ through you.

The Benefits and Costs of Lifestyle Evangelism

There are benefits and costs to living a life dedicated to lifestyle evangelism. But I have discovered the joys of sharing Christ and seeing lives transformed before my very eyes far outweigh any emotional expense expended.

The Benefits

- ∽ *Exciting Adventure:* Our spiritual lives take on a sense of adventure as we enter into challenging conversations with others about Christ.

- ∽ *Divine Purpose:* We begin to face our daily tasks with a whole new sense of purpose. Our trip to the grocery store or coffee shop takes on the possibility of an eternity-altering experience.

- ∽ *Spiritual Maturity:* We experience spiritual growth and maturity in our own lives as we research the Bible for answers to questions, memorize Scripture, and experience fulfillment in knowing that we have been used by God.

- ∽ *Personal Purity:* We naturally focus on personal purity as we recognize that our lives are a walking testimony of God's love and the life He lives in us through Jesus Christ.

- ∽ *Biblical Assuredness:* We gain biblical assuredness and confidence in our beliefs as we study and communicate scriptural truths to others in new and unique ways.

The Costs

- ∽ *Investment of Time and Energy:* Developing relationships requires time and energy. Devoting your life to sharing Christ with others may mean interruptions in your schedule. It's inevitable that God will present an opportunity, and you will have laundry to do, dinner to cook, or a deadline to meet. The inconvenience may be annoying but the rewards will be eternal!

ᴥ *Risk of Rejection and Embarrassment:* Sharing your faith will bring the risk of rejection and embarrassment. You could even face persecution for your beliefs. The question is, Whom are you trying to please? Are you willing to live for an audience of one?

ᴥ *Exposure to Real-Life Hardships:* Walking alongside people will bring you face-to-face with real-life hardships. Whether you are in relationships with nonbelievers or believers, when you invest time into the lives of others long enough to uncover the truth of what they are going through, you may get a bird's-eye view of complicated, dysfunctional, and wounded lives.

Yes, there are costs, and I have wept over the devastation I've seen in the lives of others. Yet the joy of seeing spiritual eyes open and watching the fruit ripen on the tree of a newly yielded heart is far greater. The process of giving birth is always difficult, but the rewards of watching a child take her first breath and later take her first steps quickly melt away the pangs of childbirth.

Profile of a Nonbeliever

As I have led evangelistic-type Bible studies, spoken to nonbelieving audiences, discussed the Bible over coffee with nonbelieving friends, and read Christian material on evangelism, several common characteristics of the nonbeliever have emerged. Let's look at several profiles of a nonbeliever. Below are some common misbeliefs they have about Christian faith:

1. There are many paths that lead to God, and we are free to choose our own path.

2. We are all basically good and deserve to go to heaven. If God is a loving God, how could He not let me into heaven?

3. Jesus, whether He was a true historical figure or not, set a good example of how to be a good person. However, I do not see a need for a personal savior, nor do I think we have a sin nature.

4. Of course I am a Christian. I went to church with my family when I was little and still go on holidays. I am just too busy to go to church every weekend.

5. The church is full of hypocrites.

6. Religion is a crutch for the weak of heart.

As we study the life of Christ and look at how He approached lifestyle evangelism, we will see that He related to the culture of His day and made His message culturally relevant to the people He was talking to. By looking at Christ, we will be better equipped to meet the needs of others in our own culture.

Models and Commands of Christ

How would you describe Jesus' ministry? He met people where they were; He sought out intimate, close, authentic relationships; He often went against the religious rules or norms of His day; He spoke often of God's love; and He modeled God's love in profound and tangible ways. There are several principles to be learned as we summarize the manner in which Jesus interacted with nonbelievers.

Develop a Lifestyle Motivated by God's Love and Grace

In Philippians 2:7-8 we see that Jesus left heaven to not only become one of us, but also to take the very nature of a servant. Jesus modeled a life based on humility and was willing to lay aside His personal rights and desires to serve others. Following the example of Christ, we must be willing to lay aside our comfortable lifestyle, our control of our circumstances, and our own agendas. Unless we lay aside these things, it is unlikely we will ever be available to be a conduit for God's love and truths to flow through our lives to the lives of others.

Tailor the Gospel Message to Each Individual

Jesus took into account a person's life experiences, gender, spiritual background, cultural background, misunderstandings of God, and unique personality. Obviously, He had one paramount advantage to us—He was all-knowing. For example, with the woman at the well, He already knew she was living with a man who was not her husband and that she had been married five times before. We acquire these insights about a person's background as we develop authentic and mutually vulnerable relationships. I have found that people are willing to share when I have made myself vulnerable and intentionally fostered a nonjudgmental atmosphere in the relationship. There have been times when I have had to mask my shock at my nonbelieving friends' life experiences or belief systems. As John Wesley once said, "There, but by the grace of God, go I."

Provide Hope and Clearer Understanding of God, His Character, His Purposes, and His Ways

The message of the gospel has been significantly diluted in our society today. Many people in our postmodern world have grown up with false teaching—or the absence of any teaching—on the Christian faith. Many people refuse to see themselves as sinners in need of a savior or salvation, but base their eternal destiny on whether or not they are a "good" person who does "right" things. Others dedicate themselves to trying to earn their place in heaven by living under and abiding by certain laws. Sadly, many individuals focus on being religious while never experiencing the sweetness of a personal relationship with the living Christ.

Jesus repeatedly encountered religious sects and nonbelievers who had a misunderstanding of God, His character, His purposes, and His ways. He often used parables or stories to communicate spiritual truths. As you experience difficulties in your life, you will be able to communicate that the object of your hope is Christ Jesus, not "positive thinking" or reliance on your own ability to cope and persevere.

Effectively Communicating Christ

Let's consider how we can acquire the ability and skills needed to live a life conducive to sharing Christ with others. Bill Hybels has developed an excellent formula that packages the various aspects of living a life that presents the gospel each day. His formula, as depicted in *Becoming a Contagious Christian*, is as follows: MI = HP+CP+CC. Maximum Input equals High Potency plus Close Proximity plus Clear Communication.[1] Let's take a look at how that formula translates into building an effective women's ministry. We'll use the formula Maximum Impact = Influence + Involvement + Intercommunication.

Maximum Impact

Maximum impact is the ability to have the greatest spiritual influence possible on those around us. We need to have enough "white space" in our days, similar to that of the margins on this page, to meet the needs of nonbelieving friends. Are we so overcommitted with activities that we cannot spend extra time at the grocery store visiting with a neighbor who tears up after you ask how she is doing? Are we too busy to arrange a playdate with a friend who is going through a family crisis? If so, we need to get out the eraser and create wider margins for ministry.

Influence

High potency means that we have such a strong concentration of Christ's influence in our lives that His power and presence will be undeniable to others. In Matthew 5:13-14 we are reminded to be salt and light to the world. Before we can be influential in the lives of others, we must be empowered by God through spiritual disciplines such as:

- ∾ Meditating on biblical truths

- ∾ Spending time in prayer

- ∾ Fellowshipping with spiritually mature Christians

- ∾ Serving in a church

- ∾ Sharing our faith with others

Involvement

Involvement with nonbelievers requires that we develop close relationships with those who do not know Christ. It is very tempting to engage in a fortress mentality that sets out to protect our family and our lives from the evils of the world. We can send our kids to a Christian school and surround ourselves with Christian friends, doctors, plumbers, hairstylists, housekeepers, etc. Yet if we do this, we miss out on the adventure God has created and invited us to participate in with Him.

The notion of becoming involved in others' lives is built on the concept of fostering common ground with nonbelievers in our sphere of influence. Our sphere of influence includes coworkers; clients; our children, their teachers, and the parents of their friends; our neighbors; members of social, civic, or professional organizations we belong to; and any other person we come in contact with each day. Ask questions and learn about others' life stories, hopes, dreams, struggles, and worldviews. One of the basic needs of all humans is to know they are loved and appreciated. Entering into conversations with nonbelievers based on common ground is a springboard to discovering their reference point.

In targeting our message to the audience God has given us, we must first recognize that we can build on the common ground we have with nonbelievers. Common ground can take many forms. Here are a few to consider:

- ∾ *Similar Backgrounds:* growing up in certain geographical regions, going to the same college, being an only child, growing up in a large family

- ∾ *Similar Current Lifestyles:* mothers of young children, mothers of teenagers, empty nesters, people with similar professions, people who are widowed or divorced, wives who have husbands who travel, mothers who have kids with common interests or hobbies

- ∾ *Shared Interests or Hobbies:* walking, aerobics, gardening, sewing, antique shopping, reading, writing, cooking

- ∾ *Shared Life Experiences:* death of a child or spouse, a loved one with a specific disease, rape, abuse as a child, experience with a violent crime or accident

Intercommunication

Intercommunication involves clearly and attractively presenting God's truth to others. By relying on the Holy Spirit for wisdom and discernment, we are given the ability to recognize His timing. As you share and rely on the Holy Spirit, you will be amazed at the analogies, descriptive words, or stories the Holy Spirit allows to flow through your mouth as you address the questions and concerns of nonbelievers. When sharing, keep focused on major tenets of the Christian faith: why man needs a savior, the purpose of the cross, grace, God's loving nature, and His sovereignty. Another wonderful tool is labeled the big "S" and little "s" theory. We are able to share the big story of Jesus and the cross through the little story of our own life. Recount past experiences while correlating Scripture that God used to help you gain a better understanding through the experience.

We have all had life experiences, faced difficult choices, and experienced great joy or unbearable heartache. Ask God to reveal His truths through you to others as you engage in authentic relationships.

Relationship-Building Skills

In an attempt to live a lifestyle conducive to engaging nonbelievers, many Christians have experienced frustrations, bruised egos, disgust at their pride, judgmental attitudes, and personal rejection. I hope the following will save you a few bumps and bruises.

1. *Learn to Wait on God's Timing:* Your job is to point them to the Savior, not to be their savior.

2. *Set Boundaries:* Many people are suffering and in great need of support and encouragement. It is very important to learn how to act responsibly without feeling responsible for their problems.

3. *Cover Your Relationships with Prayer:* Pray specifically that God would give you words, analogies, and stories to communicate His truths in nonthreatening ways.

4. *Maintain a Nonjudgmental Approach:* Remember, it is the Holy Spirit's job to clean up the life of a new believer, but you can be a source of Scripture references and encouragement as the person makes difficult changes in their life.

5. *Continually Seek Out Common Ground in Your Relationships:* Be willing to help your friend paint her kitchen, pick out a new piece of furniture, begin an exercise program or diet, plan a vacation, or try to repair a broken relationship. Let your actions earn you the right to be heard.

6. *Look for Ways to Learn Something New from Others:* Many nonbelieving friends are better mothers or wives than I am at times, more well-versed in classical plays and music, have traveled more extensively, and definitely know more about gardening and cooking. My non-Christian friends have often

humbled me by their gracious gifts and cards, baby showers in my honor, and willingness to be there for moral support during difficult times.

7. *Be Authentic:* Simply be yourself. Allow your friends to see your highs and lows and the times when you cling to God's promises.

8. *Learn the Art of Asking Thought-Provoking Questions:* When someone raises a strong opposition to God or the Bible, try to explore the events that led them to where they are today. Often they have had a bad experience with a hypocritical Christian or a church in the past. Some thought-provoking questions that can be effective are:

    ∾ If you could write your own epitaph, what would it say?
    ∾ How does your life now match up with the epitaph?
    ∾ Where do you find the most joy in your life?
    ∾ If you could change one thing in your life, what would it be?
    ∾ What would you change about yourself?

9. *Seek Out Ways to Bring the Scripture Alive:* During an interview on the *Today* show, Jimmy Carter cleverly avoided Katie Couric's snare as she tried to get him to say that only Christians would go to heaven. Knowing that a direct answer would seriously jeopardize the incredible ways in which God had used him to negotiate peace treaties in war-torn countries, President Carter simply told a fabulous story. The story revealed Jesus' passionate love for the people He came in contact with. If anyone didn't already know Jesus, they were very likely intrigued to learn more! When conversations turn into debates, it's time to back off. Try a softer approach by sending encouraging or thank-you notes that include a Scripture. Look for ways to tell them about new understanding you have

gained that day while reading the Scriptures or through an experience.

10. ***Build a Library of Resources That You Can Loan Out:*** Tapes on marriage, parenting, leadership, finances, and testimonies of speakers are a wonderful way to allow your friends to listen to a Christian perspective in a nonthreatening way. Often Bibles directed toward children or teenagers are a great option.

Go Change Your World!

In *My Utmost for His Highest,* Oswald Chambers includes an entry that spurs us to set out to live a life conducive to sharing Christ with others. It is based on 1 Corinthians 9:22: "I have become all things to all men so that by all possible means I might save some." Chambers challenges us with these words:

> Never make this plea—If only I were somewhere else! All God's men were ordinary men made extraordinary by the matter He has given them...
>
> "I have chosen you." Keep that note of greatness in your creed. It is not that you have got God but that God has got you...God is at work, bending, breaking, moulding, doing just as He chooses...He is doing it for one purpose only—that He may be able to say, This is My Man, My Woman. We have to be in God's hand so that He can plant men on the Rock as He has planted us.[2]

What "matter" has God already built into your life? Is He currently filling you with His "matter" in the form of overflowing blessings or a time in the desert? Our prayer is that you would go forward embracing the "matter" He has filled you with. We join you as you set out to be recognized as His woman of faith, passionate about sharing Him and willing to weave your life story into relationships with others.

PART SEVEN
Hurdles and Hindrances

One of the joys of working in women's ministry is the incredible bonds of friendship that are forged along the way. Glynnis Whitwer is one of God's priceless gifts to me. We have faced many hindrances and jumped many hurdles together. I have asked Glynnis to join me in this section of *Building an Effective Women's Ministry*. It is only fitting, as we talk about hurdles and hindrances, that the two of us grab hands and jump the hurdles together. Our hope is that you will grab a hand with us...jump the hurdles and throw off the hindrances! Let the race begin! We'll start with Glynnis.

Leadership *Hurdles*

Glynnis Whitwer

I watched the 100-meter Olympic hurdle race in stunned amazement. How could this happen? The favorite to win the race, and world's top-ranked woman hurdler, fell heavily upon the ground after tripping over the first hurdle. Her pain was evident with frustration showing in every inch of her body.

This Canadian runner who had trained for years and won countless other races was in prime physical condition. This was the race of her life and the first hurdle eliminated her chance of winning...or even finishing. In an instant, her dreams of a gold medal died.

Her accident alone was devastating. But as the Canadian runner lost her balance, she bumped into the Russian Olympian in the next lane, bringing her down as well. Two runners knocked out of the race because of a millimeter misstep.

My heart ached for those two women, who had devoted their lives to the sport. They were focused, competent, highly trained, and they had sacrificed much to get to the pinnacle of amateur track and field. Yet one mistake, one misjudgment, one miscalculation ended their chances of winning.

The similarities between a racer and a woman in ministry are striking. In fact, the writer of Hebrews speaks of the Christian life in

303

terms of a race: "Therefore, since we are surrounded by such a great cloud of witnesses, let us throw off everything that hinders and the sin that so easily entangles, and let us run with perseverance the race marked out for us" (Hebrews 12:1). We, like Paul, are involved in a race of eternal importance.

Throughout the Bible God tells us that He has a plan and a purpose for us in this great race of life. In order for us to fulfill our purpose and finish the race well, we'll need to utilize the gifts He has given us and develop our abilities to their fullest potential. While we were still being knit together in our mothers' wombs, God formed and shaped our physical and emotional traits with a specific purpose in mind. As we grow in spiritual maturity, it's as though we're in training. We are pursuing and developing the character, knowledge, and skills it will take to live a God-pleasing life.

Sprints, Cross-Country, or Hurdles?

Since God is preparing us to run a race and accomplish our purpose in the process, what type of race will it be? When I picture a sprinter's race, I immediately think of the smooth surface of a high school or college track. It's the perfect environment for speed. The bleachers or walls of a stadium block the wind, volunteers remove obstacles from the lanes, and the track is well marked and level. When you finish, someone hands you a cold drink and an encouraging slap on the back. Those who have been Christians for more than 24 hours know that life is seldom that predictable.

Then there's a cross-country race. Runners brave the elements, dodge rocks, mount hills, and balance the dips. In contrast to the circular track, the cross-country trail can be difficult to follow. The races can be lonely at times, as you run far from the cheering crowd. Now that's sounding a bit more like the Christian life I know.

However, I believe for Christians in ministry, life is more like a cross-country hurdle race. Not only do we need to brave possible storms, search for the correct path, keep our balance on uneven ground, and be in top condition to complete the race, we need to jump hurdles along the way. Whether you face one hurdle or ten, to stay in ministry...to stay in the race...you need to know how to get over the hurdles.

The Nature of Spiritual Hurdles

A woman can be well prepared, spiritually fit, and abundantly gifted—but if she isn't careful, one obstacle can trip her up and knock her out of the race. Unlike a normal hurdle race where the barricade-like structures are specifically placed and obvious, hurdles in ministry pop up in the most surprising places and catch us off guard.

Hebrews 12:1 mentions two types of hurdles that affect how well we run our race of the Christian life: things that hinder and sin that entangles. The word "hinder" is a noun meaning any kind of weight. This could include extra weight on the runner or things keeping the racer from putting forth her best effort.

The other type of hurdle is sin. The pervasiveness of sin works into almost every area of life. I imagine a vine creeping up a trellis, its tendrils reaching out and wrapping around all the posts. Like a vine, sin can start as a small shoot but grow, wrap itself around our hearts, and entangle our souls to the point of ineffectiveness.

The Way to Soar over Hurdles

The good news is that the hurdles we face are no surprise to God. He's not wringing His hands wondering how we're going to get over the current challenge or finish our race. In fact, He already has the solution to every challenge we'll face, and He even sent us a trainer to show us how to do it.

> Let us fix our eyes on Jesus, the author and perfecter of our faith, who for the joy set before him endured the cross, scorning its shame, and sat down at the right hand of the throne of God. Consider him who endured such opposition from sinful men, so that you will not grow weary and lose heart (Hebrews 12:2-3).

To finish our race well, we need to cast off every weight and sin that hinders us from completely following God's call on our lives.

Identifying the Hurdles in Ministry

Conquering hurdles in ministry is tiring. At times we wonder, *Is it really worth it? Is it worth the fear I feel each time I get up to teach? Is it worth listening to others complain? Can I handle one more day of emptiness?* Some women answer no and move away from ministry. Some answer yes and watch God do more than they could have ever imagined.

Overcoming hurdles and hindrances in ministry has eternal significance. Nothing of value is ever easy or cheap. When I wonder if women's ministry is worth the cost, I remember that Jesus told me *I* was worth the cost, and then I'm ready to face whatever hurdles come my way.

By identifying the most common hurdles in ministry, keeping our eyes on Jesus, and seeking biblical solutions, I believe we can grow spiritually and increase our effectiveness. There is a harvest waiting to be reaped, and God is looking for women who are willing to face the challenges, overcome the hurdles, and rise when they fall to try again.

Burnout

Sharon Jaynes

Leadership burnout is not a new concept. In the Bible we see many leaders who experienced times of burnout. After Jonah's miraculous delivery from the big fish and prophetic announcement to the people of Nineveh, he sank into a depression and wanted to die (Jonah 4:3). After Elijah called down fire from heaven that miraculously burned up the sacrifices of Baal, defeated the 850 false prophets, and successfully prayed for God to end a three-and-a-half year drought, he ran away from Jezebel and hid under a tree in despair (1 Kings 18–19). Elijah prayed, "I have had enough, LORD. Take my life" (1 Kings 19:4). Both of these are extreme cases, but basically, the men wanted to quit.

How do we avoid those same feelings of emptiness and despair when working in ministry? The first step is to realize that it can happen and does happen to the best of us.

Burnout is defined as "a state of mental and/or physical exhaustion caused by excessive and prolonged stress."[1] It is a gradual process that seems to occur in three stages.

Initial Stress Response: Stress may initially manifest itself with physiological symptoms (stomach problems, insomnia, headaches, heart palpitations, high blood pressure) and psychological symptoms (crying, irritability, forgetfulness, and inability to concentrate).

Compensation Response: Under stress, a person may attempt to compensate and adapt to the stress. If the attempts to adapt fail, behavior might include procrastination, excessive lateness, persistent fatigue, social withdrawal from family and friends, and apathy.

Exhaustion: It is during this third stage that most people admit that something might be wrong. Symptoms include chronic sadness or depression, chronic stomach or bowel problems, chronic mental and/or physical fatigue, chronic headaches, thoughts of suicide, and withdrawal from people and events that used to bring pleasure and fulfillment.[2]

We can see the above progression of burnout in the prophet Elijah. What was God's response to Elijah? Take a look at 1 Kings 19.

- ∾ He allowed Elijah to sleep (19:5)—rest

- ∾ He sent an angel to provide food for him to eat (19:5)—refreshment

- ∾ He allowed Elijah to sleep again (19:6)—more rest

- ∾ He sent an angel to provide food for him to eat again (19:7)—more refreshment

- ∾ He caused Elijah to ponder what he was doing. "What are you doing here?" (19:9)—reflection

- ∾ He spoke to Elijah personally (19:11)—response

- ∾ He again caused Elijah to ponder what he was doing. "What are you doing here?" (19:13)—more reflection

- ∾ He told Elijah what to do next (19:15)—redirection

- ∾ He showed Elijah whom He had appointed to help him (19:16)—reinforcement

Self-Assessment Exercise

Below is a self-assessment exercise to see if you are headed for burnout. Choose the most appropriate answer for each of the following ten statements.

How often do you

    a. almost always
    b. often
    c. seldom
    d. almost never

_____ 1. Find yourself with insufficient time to do things you really enjoy?

_____ 2. Wish you had more support/assistance?

_____ 3. Have insufficient time to complete your work most effectively?

_____ 4. Have difficulty falling asleep because you had too much on your mind?

_____ 5. Feel people simply expect too much from you?

_____ 6. Feel overwhelmed?

_____ 7. Find yourself becoming forgetful or indecisive because you have too much on your mind?

_____ 8. Consider yourself to be in high-pressure situation?

_____ 9. Feel you have too much responsibility for one person?

_____ 10. Feel exhausted at the end of the day?

Calculate your total score as follows:

    (a) = 4 points, (b) = 3 points, (c) = 2 points, (d) = 1 point

            Total =_____ points

This exercise was designed to assess your level of stress due to overload. Overload, or overstimulation, refers to the state in which the demands around you exceed your capacity to meet them. Some aspect(s) of your life are placing excessive demands on you. When these demands exceed your ability to comply with them, you experience distress.

The four major factors in overload are (1) time pressures, (2) excessive reponsibility or accountability, (3) lack of support, and (4) excessive expectations from yourself and those around you. Any one or a combination of these factors can result in stress from overload.

Your total number of points on this exercise will help you assess how stressed you are by overload. A total of 25-40 points indicates a high stress level, one that could by psychologically and physiologically debilitating.[3]

The most effective way to avoid burnout is to be in constant communion with God. Author and teacher Henry Blackaby notes:

God has a plan for each person that is uniquely suited to that individual. Unlike people, God never piles on more than someone can handle. God never overbooks people. God never drives his servants to the point of breakdown. God never burns people out. God never gives people tasks that are beyond the strength or ability he provides.

If this is true, why do so many people struggle with too much to do? Why are Christian leaders burning out from overwork and exhaustion? Is God responsible? No. When people become overwhelmed by their commitments and responsibilities, they are operating on their own agenda. Ministers of religion [and women in ministry] are particularly susceptible to assuming responsibility for things they should not. They do this because their work is never completed. There is always another phone call to make, a

Scripture passage to study, a person who needs visiting, a prayer to be offered. The key for overworked leaders is to examine each of their current responsibilities to determine whether they have inadvertently assumed ownership for things God has not intended them to carry.[4]

To recap—how do we, as ministry leaders, avoid burnout?

- ∾ Rest often. (God rested on the seventh day.)

- ∾ Refresh with proper diet.

- ∾ Reevaluate priorities and responsibilities on a regular basis (monthly).

- ∾ Relegate and delegate.

- ∾ Review commitments regularly (monthly).

- ∾ Resist saying yes to demands and requests that do not line up with what God has called us to do.

- ∾ Resist being ruled by our schedules and allow for divine appointments from God that may not be on our schedules.

- ∾ Remove superfluous activities that interfere with or choke out God's agenda.

- ∾ Refocus on what God called us to do rather than what others would like for us to do.

- ∾ Remain in close and constant communion with God.

40

*B*alance

Glynnis

*B*alancing the needs of our families, jobs, homes, and ministry seems a never-ending task. There's always someone who needs our help, an assignment that needs to be finished, laundry that needs to be washed. And there are never enough hours in the day to do it all.

Finding balance is one of the top hurdles women face in ministry and in life. It's as though we're those Gumby and Pokey dolls, whose arms, legs, and heads could stretch in multiple directions. Although those rubber dolls didn't break, sometimes women do break from the strain of demanding responsibilities.

Women discover their relationships strained, health exhausted, homes disorganized, and work and ministry performance compromised. I believe this is also one reason why depression is a growing problem among women.

I attended a Weight Watcher's meeting where the leader asked this question: "If you had a free Saturday morning, what would you do?" Three-quarters of the group yelled, "Sleep!" Women are tired of trying to have it all and do it all.

Jesus knew He couldn't do it all. He knew He only had enough time to do the will of His Father. Jesus lived a focused life, but not a hectic life. He clearly knew His priorities, how to balance His responsibilities, and when to stop and rest.

313

There are three keys that have enabled me to serve God more effectively, meet my family's needs efficiently, and keep my sanity.

Key One: Know Your Priorities

Here's a challenge. List the most important areas of your life in order. This list might include your relationship with Christ, your marriage, your children, your friends, ministries, and your job. Now allocate the number of hours each week you devote to each one. How does it balance out? Unfortunately, sometimes the things we value most receive the least amount of time, energy, and enthusiasm.

A balanced life starts with clearly defined priorities. If you aren't sure about your priorities, ask yourself these questions:

1. What can only I do? (Only I can be me, my husband's wife, and my three sons' mother.)

2. What has God entrusted to me? (God has entrusted me with the care of a home, the care of children, my health, and the management of my time and money, to name a few.)

3. Am I a good steward of what I already have? (Do I manage money well? Do I care for my home? Do I love my husband and children the way I should?)

4. What passion has God put in my heart? (I have a passion for helping children and youth come to love Jesus, and for women to draw closer to God and align their lives with His will.)

5. What has God asked me to do that I haven't done yet? (For years I knew God was calling me to write, but I did nothing about it.)

When you answer these questions, you'll have the foundation for the top priorities in your life. A woman with a balanced life has clearly defined priorities. She realizes she can't do it all and do it all effectively.

Key Two: Live According to Your Priorities

Once we have identified our priorities, then we determine if we need to make changes in our lives to increase our effectiveness in these areas. Sacrifice and pruning are part of the process.

Rick Warren said, "If you want your life to have impact, focus it! Stop dabbling. Stop trying to do it all. Do less. Prune away even good activities and do only that which matters most."[1]

My friend Lynda was a teacher. She loved being a teacher and the schedule worked well with her two daughters. But one day Lynda became a single mother, and she realized she was giving the best of her time and energy to other people's children. Lynda decided that her own daughters needed to be her priority. While still working, she began a home-based business. When she was able to replace her income, she quit her teaching job, continued her business, and homeschooled her two daughters. It was a difficult decision to make, but one that yielded great rewards.

What responsibilities in your life, even good things, keep you from being effective in the best things? The answer will guide you to what needs pruning in your life and what needs fertilizing for maximum growth.

My husband and I had children eight years into our marriage. That was a lot of time to delve into ministry at church. After we had our first son, the second two arrived within the next few years. I loved our ministry at church and hardly skipped a beat as I continued my hectic pace while dragging around three little boys. The problems arose when I started seeing my children as obstacles to my ministry.

In the midst of my madness, God picked up my family and moved us 2000 miles from home. While in my enforced ministry hiatus, I read a book called *Living Life on Purpose* by Lysa TerKeurst. Lysa challenges readers to consider their ministry and ask, "Where am I to serve?" She listed her primary areas of ministry and one of them was her family and home. This was a new concept to me. I had always considered ministry as what happens outside my home. But God was showing me that my responsibilities at home were my primary ministry at that point in my life. He had given me my husband, my children, and my home, and I was shortchanging my primary responsibilities to serve elsewhere. I had to start pruning activities outside my home and focus on ministering to the one man and three little men God had placed in my life.

This may not always be the case for me, nor is it true for every woman. The point is to identify your priorities, prune the responsibilities that hinder you from fulfilling your purpose in those areas, and then learn to say no when good activities affect your priorities.

Key Three: Prayerfully Consider New Ministry Opportunities

When you have identified your priorities and made changes in your life, then jealously guard your time. When an opportunity for ministry arises, prayerfully consider how it will affect your existing commitments.

Make a habit of praying about new opportunities before giving an answer. Even if it's something you can easily do, ask God to confirm it in your heart. If you are married, discuss it with your husband and ask his opinion.

Many women feel guilty saying no when asked to help in a ministry at church. Consequently, they say yes to many good things. However, good things aren't always God's best. When you are making decisions according to your priorities, there is a magnificent freedom to say no.

Finding balance in your life might take time. Some things you can prune immediately, while others may take time while you fulfill your commitment. Some things might look impossible to prune, like a full-time job. But God won't call you to something He can't work out.

Confidence

Sharon

I hope the mere fact that this hurdle is included in *Building an Effective Women's Ministry* gives you some assurance. Most women who feel called to minister to others feel somewhat inadequate for the task and insecure in taking on the role of "leader." If someone is totally confident in her own abilities, I daresay she may not be the person for the job.

I can still remember the panic I felt when God called me to work in a leadership role. "Lord," I complained, "You know I don't like speaking in front of people. I can't run an international ministry. Why, I'm just a homemaker." After I reminded God of several of my other shortcomings, He took me on a spiritual treasure hunt to discover the type of men and women He chooses to carry out His plans.

God's Chosen Leaders

Moses was one of history's great leaders. After being raised in Pharaoh's household as his adopted grandson, he reached 40 years of age and decided he was ready to save the Israelite nation from slavery. He planned a work and then began working the plan—which failed miserably. Then Moses ran away and took care of sheep in the desert for the next 40 years. He was so insecure that he developed a speech impediment and preferred the company of smelly sheep to people. It was then, at Moses' lowest point in life, that God decided he was ready for leadership. God appeared to Moses in a burning bush and called him to lead the Israelite nation out of Egypt.

Moses argued fervently with God, "You've got the wrong person! I can't even speak without stuttering. Have you considered my brother, Aaron?" Four times Moses said, "What if this happens…" And each time God answered, "I will do it for you."

That is the same answer God gives us today. See, when Moses thought he was ready at age 40, he wasn't. When he thought he wasn't ready at age 80, he was. When are we ready to do the impossible for God? We are ready when He calls us and when we know that we cannot do anything in our own strength but only by the power of God working in us. Once Moses believed God would do the leading, he had the confidence to move forward.

Gideon is another mighty warrior who argued with God's call. When God came to Gideon to appoint him the next leader of the Israelite army, he was busy in a winepress threshing wheat. Now, ladies, you don't usually thresh wheat in a winepress. You thresh wheat by throwing it up in the air in an open field and letting the wind blow away the chaff while the grain falls to the ground. So what was he doing in the winepress? Gideon was so terrified of his enemies that he was hiding. And yet, when the angel of the Lord came to him, he addressed Gideon as "O valiant warrior!" (Judges 6:12 NASB). Can't you just see Gideon looking around and saying, "You talkin' to me?"

Yet God called him "valiant warrior" because He knew what Gideon could be if he trusted in God's power to work through him.

Then there's one of the most powerful leaders of all time—King David. When the prophet Samuel went to Jesse's house to anoint the next king of Israel, he asked to see each of Jesse's sons. One by one the strapping young men paraded before Samuel for inspection, but God rejected them all. Confused, Samuel asked Jesse, "Is that it? Do you have any more sons?"

Jesse thought a moment and replied, "Oh, I forgot. I do have one more son. Little David is out in the field taking care of the sheep." David was so insignificant to his family that his father had forgotten all about him.

When Samuel saw this young lad, and God gave him the thumbs-up, even he doubted God's choice. Samuel thought David's tall, dark, and handsome brother Eliab looked much more like king material than little David. But God answered Samuel's objection when He refused Eliab with, "Do not consider his appearance or his height, for...man looks at the outward appearance, but the LORD looks at the heart" (1 Samuel 16:7).

What about women in the Bible? If you were God and were going to list only five women in the lineage of Jesus, whom would you choose? I'd perhaps select Mrs. Noah, Mrs. Moses, or the lovely Mrs. Abraham. But God had a different idea. In Matthew 1, along with Mary, the mother of Jesus, He listed Tamar, who had an incestuous encounter with her father-in-law; Rahab, who had been a prostitute; Ruth, who was a foreigner from a cursed land; and Bathsheba, who had an affair with King David. These are perhaps not whom we would choose, but it is a wonderful example of 1 Corinthians 1:26-31, which says that God deliberately seeks out the weak things and the despised things because it is from them that He can receive the greatest glory.

God's Extraordinary Work Through Ordinary People

If you feel weak, ordinary, and even a bit fearful, then you are exactly the type of leader God is looking for! God chooses to do extraordinary work through ordinary people who will bring glory to His name.

I remember when Anne Graham Lotz, Billy Graham's daughter, first began her ministry. She was taken to a soccer stadium in South India that was filled with thousands of expectant people and asked to give an evangelistic message like her daddy. Although Anne told her hosts that she was not a preacher, she stepped into the pulpit and preached. She said, "I was sitting there thinking, 'I'm an American housewife. I don't belong here.' But I stepped aside and let God take over. And it's amazing what He can do."[1]

Once we take those first steps of obedience, it is crucial to remember that it is God who will bring the results. I love the account of one of the most famous preachers in the nineteenth century, Charles Spurgeon.

> In late nineteenth-century England, Charles Spurgeon was by all accounts the greatest preacher in the capital of the most powerful nation on earth. Huge throngs, including the wealthy and powerful, came to London's cavernous Metropolitan Tabernacle to hear him preach the gospel.
>
> Spurgeon held himself to towering standards, always feeling his best wasn't good enough. One day, his worst fears were realized when he preached an awful sermon. He was so traumatized by his poor work that he rushed home and fell to his knees. "O Lord, I'm so feeble and You're so powerful!" he prayed. "Only You can make something of such a ghastly sermon. Please use it and bless it."
>
> You or I might have told him to put his failure behind him and move on, but Spurgeon kept praying all week for God to use this terrible sermon. Meanwhile, he set about to do better the following Sunday. And he did. At the conclusion of that sermon, the audience of thousands all but carried him out on their shoulders.
>
> But Spurgeon was not to be fooled. He decided to keep careful records of the result of the two sermons. Within a few months that outcome was clear. The "ghastly" sermon had led forty-one people to know Christ; his masterpiece had led to no observable results at all.

Spurgeon knew or suspected what most forget: Our success in ministry is never about ability in the first place, but about God's power and our dependence on it. Spurgeon leaned on God in his weakness and God blessed his flawed efforts.[2]

As you begin your journey in women's ministry, always remember that it is God who is at work in you. Nothing takes the place of preparation. God does not bless laziness. But the results are in His hands. That should give you great confidence.

God is able to do exceedingly abundantly more than we could ask or think (Ephesians 3:20 NKJV). How amazing that He chooses to do it through us.

I want you to take a little quiz based on the wisdom of Charles Schulz:

1. Name the five wealthiest people in the world.

2. Name the last five Heisman Trophy winners.

3. Name the last five winners of the Miss America contest.

4. Name the last five Academy Award winners for best actor and actress.

5. Name five people who have won the Nobel or Pulitzer prize.

How did you do?

Now I have five more questions for you:

1. List five teachers who aided your journey through school.

2. Name five friends who have helped you through a difficult time.

3. Name five people who have taught you something worthwhile.

4. Name five people who have made you feel appreciated and special.

5. Name five people whose stories have inspired you.

"The point is, none of us remember the headliners of yesterday. These are no second-rate achievers. They are the best in their fields. But the applause dies. Awards tarnish. Achievements are forgotten. Accolades and certificates are buried with their owners. The people who make a difference in your life are not the ones with the most credentials, the most money, or the most awards. They are the ones that care."—Charles Schultz.[3]

Criticism

Glynnis

When I was a junior in high school, I had a particularly hard teacher. On the first test that I took in her class, I received a C. I was an A student, so I went to the teacher to ask how I could do better on my next test. I'll never forget her snippy words. "You aren't an A student, are you?" While it was not a direct assault, the subtle nature of her question left no doubt about her purpose—to put me in my place. I knew she believed I wasn't capable of above average work.

Criticism can take many forms—from subtle jabs to direct insults. Either way, criticism can set a woman on the sidelines of life faster than anything, which is exactly where the devil wants you. He wants you out of the race and out of God's service.

As a semi-perfectionist and recovering people-pleaser, I loathe criticism. I would love a world where everyone's happy and every conversation ends with a hug. As a result, I find criticism particularly hard to deal with. My natural tendency is to react with anger or tears, but when I keep my eyes on Jesus and follow His example, I am able to handle criticism with grace. Let's take a look at three biblical responses to criticism we will surely face in women's ministry.

Key One: Respond in Truth

Jesus said, "I am the way and the truth and the life" (John 14:6). He is truth and He knows all things. However, because of our limited ability combined with a sinful nature, we aren't able to always see the true motives behind our critics. If we have been deeply hurt in the past, we may perceive criticism as rejection rather than constructive advice. In order to view criticism in a proper perspective, consider the following:

- ∽ *Consider the Source:* Is the person supplying negative feedback someone you trust? If the answer is yes, then look for the truth in the message. Sometimes well-meaning people offer important feedback in an inappropriate way.

  If the person providing the feedback has a history of unfounded negative attacks, then you might not place as much weight in their comments.

- ∽ *Consider Personal Opinions:* Sometimes people just disagree on the details. For instance, if you are planning an event in August and you decide to use yellow napkins, someone could say that yellow is a horrible color for August, and that it should only be used with autumn colors. This is just a matter of opinion and shouldn't be taken personally.

  God made each of us delightfully different. When we are given a responsibility in ministry, we should trust that God cares about our opinion. We should do our best to be better informed and get wise counsel, but in the end, your personal opinion matters.

  As an editor of a national Christian women's magazine, I make a lot of decisions every month. I make decisions on the selection of articles, on how to edit, on photos, and on books to offer for sale. While I care deeply about the opinions of my ministry team members, I know that God has placed me in this position because my opinions and decisions have value to Him.

  This doesn't mean I have perfect judgment. I have made decisions I won't repeat. This doesn't mean I disregard everyone's opinion. God has also placed my partners in ministry because their opinion matters too. But it does mean that I can be confident in making a decision that someone else might handle differently.

∽ ***Consider Our Own Sin:*** This issue may be harder to identify as we are often blinded to our own sin. The sin of pride is one that many leaders struggle with but can overlook. While we may miss it in our own lives, you can be sure that the women who serve with you won't.

When you are criticized, humbly approach the Lord in prayer and ask Him to reveal any sin in your life. We can pray as David prayed: "Search me, O God, and know my heart; test me and know my anxious thoughts. See if there is any offensive way in me, and lead me in the way everlasting" (Psalm 139:23-24).

If God does reveal any sin, confess it immediately. If you have hurt anyone as a result of this sin, go and ask forgiveness directly from that person. This will not weaken your leadership position. On the contrary, a leader with a teachable heart, who is willing to be humbled, is a leader God can use.

Key Two: Respond in Love

The children's ministry director at my church often has to make difficult decisions. Approximately 1000 children attend each weekend, and you can imagine how many particular and protective parents that makes. I've watched Jody deal with a multitude of negative opinions and noticed how she consistently responds to her critics with love. She lives out Proverbs 15:1: "A gentle answers turns away wrath." Jody is spiritually mature enough to look past the angry demeanor or the frustrated tone of voice and see the hurting and sometimes scared parent underneath.

To be able to respond in love to critics means that you have to prepare in advance for it to happen. Jesus said, "Blessed are you when people insult you, persecute you and falsely say all kinds of evil against you because of me" (Matthew 5:11). Notice that Jesus didn't say blessed are you *if* people insult you, but *when.*

If there are 100 women in a room, we need to expect that at least ten of them will not be happy with something. Before you make any decision, seek to have the heart of Jesus for your detractors.

Here's how Jody handles the issue of making decisions that can incite negative opinions:

> Knowing that some people will be thrilled with my decisions while others will be upset can weigh heavily on a peaceful phlegmatic personality! The way that God helps me face this challenge is through prayer, seeking Him, and learning to trust that I will hear His voice.

Key Three: Respond with Confidence

Even those who love us and support our ministry might criticize what we do or how we do it. It happened when Peter rebuked Jesus for talking about His death. Peter loved Jesus and desired with all his heart to follow God, but he didn't like Jesus being obedient unto death. Jesus saw that the criticism wasn't truly coming from Peter, and responded by saying, "Get behind me, Satan! You are a stumbling block to me; you do not have in mind the things of God, but the things of men" (Matthew 16:23).

When you feel tempted to abandon God's call on your life due to criticism, remember that Satan will use others to dissuade you from your conviction. But you can remain confident that God, who called you, will equip you.

My church offers a contemporary style of worship and only occasionally does the band include a hymn, and then it usually has a beat. The church makes no apologies because this is what God has called them to do. I'm always amazed when someone complains that the band is too loud, has too much of a beat, doesn't play enough hymns, should have an organ, and so on. If our worship pastor responded to every negative comment, our band would be running in circles. Instead, they know their calling and can respond with confidence.

Life is too short, and our calling is too great, to be sidetracked by critics. After all, Jesus received much criticism and, as Scripture reminds us, a servant is not above his master.

> Blessed are you when people insult you, persecute you and falsely say all kinds of evil against you because of me. *Rejoice and be glad, because great is your reward in heaven,* for in the same way they persecuted the prophets who were before you (Matthew 5:11-12, emphasis added).

Theodore Roosevelt said:

> It is not the critic who counts, nor the man who points out how the strong man stumbles or where the doer of deeds could have done better. The credit belongs to the man who is actually in the arena, whose face is marred by dust and sweat and blood, who strives valiantly, who errs and comes up short again and again, because there is no effort without error or shortcoming, but who knows the great enthusiasms, the great devotions, who spends himself for a worthy cause; who, at the best, knows, in the end, the triumph of high achievement, and who, at the worst, if he fails, at least he fails while daring greatly, so that his place shall never be with those cold and timid souls who knew neither victory nor defeat.[1]

43

Competition

Sharon

It was a phone call that took me completely off guard. A friend had read an article in our ministry magazine, *P-31 Woman*, about a home-based business.

"I can't believe you would print an article in your magazine by and about that woman who has the same business I have," the caller complained. "You know good and well she's my competition! We do the same type of training, and now you've given her free advertising by publishing her article."

"Claire," I responded, "Proverbs 31 Ministries is not about competition or promoting one person over another. I have written a book on parenting, but we still offer other books on parenting. Lysa TerKeurst [my ministry partner] has written books on marriage, but we still offer other books on marriage. We aren't about competition. We're helping women develop an intimate relationship with Jesus Christ and build strong families."

"Well, I can't believe you would print something by my competition. I'm withdrawing all financial support to your ministry. I think I need to give my money elsewhere."

Click.

My husband, sitting within earshot in the next room, called out, "What was that all about?"

"You don't even want to know," I said, sighing.

It was not my first brush with the anger and frustration competition can bring out in people, and as long as God continues to use
imperfect people to be His hands and feet, it would not be my last.

Competition is older than the Garden of Eden. Satan's very
downfall was ignited by his burning passion to surpass and capture
God's position. The prophet Isaiah described, "How you have fallen
from heaven, O morning star, son of the dawn!... You said in your
heart, 'I will ascend to heaven...I will make myself like the Most
High' " (Isaiah 14:12-14). But instead of becoming like the Most
High, he lost his position as "anointed cherub" and was "thrown out
of heaven." Then he proceeded to sow seeds of competition and jealousy into the hearts and minds of men and women throughout the
earth.

Satan started with Eve in the garden by tempting her to compete
with God's wisdom. "When you eat of it [the forbidden fruit] your
eyes will be opened, and you will be like God, knowing good and
evil" (Genesis 3:5). Then he moved on to her son Cain. God saw the
rivalry Cain felt toward his brother, Abel, and warned Cain about the
seed of jealousy that was taking root in his heart. He cautioned Cain,
"Sin is crouching at your door; it desires to have you, but you must
master it" (Genesis 4:17). Cain didn't master it; it mastered him. His
jealousy led him to kill Abel and leave him dead in a field.

Competition among Christians in ministry is much like the lion
crouching at the door. We have a choice to let it in and allow it to
master us, or we can grab the whip and tame it into submission.

Jesus also dealt with competition among His disciples. One day
He walked in while they were arguing about who was the greatest.
When Jesus asked what they were discussing, they hung their heads
and quieted their quarrel. He met their silent reply with, "If anyone
wants to be first, he must be the very last, and the servant of all"
(Mark 9:35). Later, Jesus showed them a portrait of servant leadership as He placed a towel around His waist, filled a basin with water,
and knelt to wash and dry their dusty feet (John 13:1-5).

Paul addressed competition in the early church with strong words.

> Brothers, I could not address you as spiritual but as worldly—mere infants in Christ. I gave you milk, not solid food, for you were not yet ready for it. Indeed, you are still not ready. You are still worldly. For since there is jealousy and quarreling among you, are you not worldly? Are you not acting like mere men? For when one says, "I follow Paul," and another, "I follow Apollos," are you not mere men? What, after all, is Apollos? And what is Paul? Only servants, through whom you came to believe—as the Lord has assigned to each his task. I planted the seed, Apollos watered it, but God made it grow. *So neither he who plants nor he who waters is anything, but only God who makes things grow.* The man who plants and the man who waters have one purpose, and each will be rewarded according to his own labor. For we are God's fellow workers; you are God's field, God's building (1 Corinthians 3:1-7, emphasis added).

In contrast to the telephone call I mentioned earlier, I received an e-mail that showed the power of various ministries working in tandem. Sylvia wrote to thank me for the work of Proverbs 31 Ministries. Her husband had attended a Promise Keepers event and picked up one of our ministry books. In the book, we recommended the late Larry Burkett's Crown Financial Ministry to those seeking to change their spending habits and develop a budget. Sylvia wrote to say that she and her husband had contacted Crown, implemented their principles, cut living expenses, and established a lifestyle that allowed them to fulfill one of their hearts' desires—spend more time with their children. What a joy to see how three ministries dovetailed to affect one family. One planted; one watered; and God gave the increase.

So where does competition fit in the body of Christ? I think when unhealthy competition is staring at us in the mirror, we need to ask a few tough questions:

- ∾ Why are we in ministry?
- ∾ Whom are we competing against?
- ∾ What do we hope to gain by competing?
- ∾ Is God limited in His blessings that He can only bless a few?

Paul, the writer of Colossians, leaves us with some wonderful advice: "Whatever you do, work at it with all your heart, as working for the Lord, not for men, since you know that you will receive an inheritance from the Lord as a reward. It is the Lord Christ you are serving" (Colossians 3:23-24).

PART EIGHT
Growing Pains

*M*ary and John just completed building their first home. Just as the last touches of paint dry on the trim and the final curtain is hung, Mary discovers that she is pregnant! While they are overjoyed with the unexpected news, their minds begin to reel with new ideas for their home. This expansion will require baby locks on the cabinets, covers on the outlets, and a nursery with stars on the ceiling and a painted mural of Noah's ark on the wall. Over the next few months, the previously decorated guest room is transformed into a nursery fit for the new little prince or princess.

But lo and behold, six months later, the ultrasound reveals that there will be both a little prince and a princess! Once again, the plans are changed and adapted to include two cribs, two rocking chairs, and two changing tables. Just when the babies are settling in to their cradles, Mary learns that her grandfather has passed away and the couple decides to invite her grandmother to move in with them. Once again, their plans change. They hire a builder to add on a room to the back of the house complete with a small kitchen and bath, so that Grandma can have a bit of privacy.

Life happens. Plans change. People adapt.

With the growth of any women's ministry, much like the growth of a family, there will be change, and with change comes growing pains. In this next section, let's take a look at several common growing pains women in ministry face.

ॐ ॐ ॐ

44

Dividing
and Multiplying

*T*he hope of any small group is that it will continue to grow and multiply, bringing more and more people into community with other believers. But dividing can be painful for those who have grown comfortable with their group, and dividing can cause some groups to take a few steps backward rather than moving forward.

The best way to alleviate the anxiousness of multiplying and dividing a small group is to state at the very beginning that the hope is expansion. During the course of the small-group time, keep an eye out for potential leaders. When you sense that someone might be a good small-group leader, give her small responsibilities and observe how she follows through. Also, ask a potential leader to help you with some of the administrative and teaching duties in order to spread her wings. This way you will be mentoring the potential leader.

When the group grows to about 15 consistent members, it is time to divide and multiply. Ideally, you have spotted a leader from among the group. Perhaps you have spotted two. Ask one or two ladies if they would consider leaving the group and starting another one. Also, ask for one or two mature Christians in the group to go along with the new leader as support and encouragement.

Before the members of the group leave to begin a new group, have a time of celebration. Make the last meeting together special.

Consider praying over the ones who will be leaving, giving them a special bon voyage gift or having each person remaining tell one thing they really appreciate about each individual.

As a caution, if the group is reluctant to multiply and divide, and the group grows too large, participation tends to decline. Small groups are called small for a reason. When the group becomes too large, members tend to stop sharing as openly, begin to lose interest, and the intimacy level of the group declines.

The following is a model of how Mary Ann Ruff divided and multiplied her Mornings for Mothers small groups.

Year One

Mary Ann

8 members (including Vicki and Lynn)

Year Two

Mary Ann	Vicki	Lynn
8 members	8 members	8 members

Year Three

Mary Ann	Sharon	Lisa	Vicki	Barb	Becky	Lynn	Lisa	Sarah
8	8	8	8	8	8	8	8	8

Year Four

Each group leader began two new groups: 9 x 2 = 18

Year Five

Each group leader began two new groups: 18 x 2 = 36

By the fifth year, what began as *one* group had divided and multiplied to *36* groups.

With an average of *eight* women per group, after five years, *248* women were attending the Mornings for Mothers small-group ministry.

Simply reading through the book of Acts, we see the beauty of dividing and multiplying small groups to provide a nurturing environment that fosters spiritual growth and development.

45

Recognizing Stages in the Life of a Small Group

*M*ost small groups progress in stages. While the following is not the road that all small groups travel, it is a good idea to note common road signs so you won't be surprised along the way.

Stage One—The Dating Stage: Just as two people put their best foot forward during the early dating days, the members are on their best behavior. There is a lot of excitement and a sense of mystery and anticipation.

Stage Two—The Honeymoon Stage: The group members are still very excited about their newly formed relationships, and there are very few bumps in the road.

Stage Three—The Disillusionment Stage: Reality begins to set in that the group members are indeed human. Someone is disappointed with a response, upset with a comment, or let down because her expectations were not met.

Stage Four—The Commitment Stage: Even though the honeymoon is over, an atmosphere of trust and acceptance develops and the group becomes committed to one another.

Stage Five—The Maturity Stage: This is a time of spiritual growth and development.

Stage Six—Closure: The group grows restless and there is a sense of stagnation. During this stage, it is evident that it is time for the group to celebrate what God has done and move on. It is a mistake to continue a group when there is a sense that it is time for the group to end.

Small-Group Covenant

One of my favorite words seems to be going by the wayside these days: commitment. Restaurants rarely take reservations any longer, doctors hire receptionists for the sole purpose of confirming appointments and filling broken ones, and now you can even "rent" engagement rings. Everything from home appliances to relationships are not made to last. With the divorce rate at more than 50 percent, it is apparent "commitment" to anything is a struggle in our throwaway society.

So what about small groups? What can we do to help build community that will last...at least for one year? If you have been in ministry for very long, you have experienced the dwindle effect on small groups. We start out with high attendance, and then after the excitement wanes, the numbers begin to wane as well.

One idea is to establish a group covenant. A group covenant brings a sense of commitment to the group members, but also sets up clear boundaries and expectations and helps with disillusionment as the group moves through the anticipated life stages.

A small-group covenant answers the following questions:

- ∞ Why do we want to have a small group?

- ∞ What do we expect to get out of this group?

- ∞ What goals do we want to accomplish in this small group?

- ∞ What do we want to see happen in and through us as a result of our involvement in this group?

- ∞ What ingredients do we want to include in our small group? (Prayer, Bible study, recreation, etc.)

∾ What do we *not* want to do in this group? (Give advice, hold counseling sessions, debate nonessentials, etc.)

∾ What needs to happen before we consider this group a success?

∾ What do we hope to see happen in our time together?

∾ What are the ground rules? (No advice giving, attend whenever possible, do the homework for each session before you arrive, everything shared in the group must remain confidential, etc.)

∾ When will we meet and how often?

∾ What is the duration of this group? (One year, from September to May.)

Sample Small-Group Statement of Commitment

I pledge myself to the following disciplines for my own spiritual growth, and to participate in the spiritual growth of the members of this group.

To *attend* every week unless I am out of town or ill, and to be on time

To *study* and be prepared by completing the assignment each week

To *share* as I am honestly able to within the group

To *love* by being sensitive to the feelings of others

To *pray* on a regular basis for the members of the group

To keep *confidential* things shared within the group

To be held *accountable* to members of the group

To hold others in the group accountable

Name_____ (sign and date)

Stagnation

At some point during the life of a small group or during the life of a women's ministry program, stagnation may occur. There is no growth to speak of, and there might even be a dwindling effect that resembles a slow leak. Perhaps it is time for a checkup. Consider the following:

- ∾ Ask women who came at one time why they stopped coming. Make sure they feel safe in answering the question and not intimidated. Above all, ask in such a way so that they do not feel guilty for not coming.

- ∾ Examine the environment of the gathering. Is it too crowded, too cold, too warm, too noisy, too many babies? Does the hostess have an annoying pet?

- ∾ Consider the take-home value of the meeting. Do women feel that the time spent is worth their investment?

- ∾ If women say that they are "too busy," consider that a red flag. Women make time for what they feel is important and valuable in their lives.

- ∾ Has the program become centered on an individual rather than on the group as a whole?

- ∾ Has the program become a clique that makes some feel uncomfortable?

- ∾ Is the program or group respectful of others' time? Does it start and end on time?

- ∾ Have the women had changes in their lives that prevent them from coming? Have women had babies and now need child care? Have the attendees joined the workforce and are unable to attend meetings during the day?

- ∾ Are attendees spending too much time discussing personal issues and not biblical principles?

- ∾ Ask yourself, "Would I come to this program or group if I were not the leader?"

- ∾ Finally, has the program or group served its purpose? Is it time to end? If so, celebrate and end well.*

---

* See chapter 47 for details on finishing well.

*D*ealing with *C*onflict

I haven't read this verse in the Bible anywhere, but I think it still holds true: "Where two or more are gathered, there will be conflict." Part of working with people is learning how to deal with conflict. We have already touched on how to deal with difficult personalities in a small group setting, and now we will turn our attention to dealing with conflict among the members of the ministry team.

During Jesus' last days on earth before He faced the cross, He stressed the importance of unity among the team He was leaving behind. Jesus prayed,

> My prayer is not for them alone. I pray also for those who will believe in me through their message, that all of them may *be one,* Father, just as you are in me and I am in you. May they also be in us so that the world may believe that you have sent me. I have given them the glory that you gave me, that they *may be one as we are one:* I in them and you in me. May they be brought to *complete unity* to let the world know that you sent me and have loved them even as you have loved me (John 17:20-23, emphasis added).

Jesus prayed for unity among the believers. Why? Because He knew that unity would be imperative for an effective ministry team, and unity would be difficult among people with their own ideas, idiosyncrasies, and insecurities. Jesus said, "Any kingdom divided against itself will be ruined, and a house divided against itself will fall" (Luke 11:17). The same principle that applies to building a kingdom applies to building a women's ministry. So let's take a look at how to deal with conflict and maintain a spirit of unity.

When Conflict Is the Result of an Offense

We all like for someone to take our side on an issue. Perhaps that is why we have a tendency to tell someone else about a conflict we have had with another person rather than going to that person who we feel has wronged us in some way. We love to hear the words "you are right and she is wrong." However, the Bible gives us the following instruction on how to deal with conflict.

> If your brother sins against you, go and show him his fault, just between the two of you. If he listens to you, you have won your brother [or sister] over. But if he will not listen, take one or two others along, so that every matter may be established by the testimony of two or three witnesses. If he [she] refuses to listen to them, tell it to the church; and if he [she] refuses to listen to even the church, treat him [her] as you would a pagan or a tax collector (Matthew 18:15-17).

For example, if someone has said something unkind about you, go to the person directly and lovingly confront her. "Susan, I need to talk to you about something. I have heard that you are having a problem with the way I lead the discussion groups on Tuesday. Can we talk about that?"

At that time, ask Susan to come directly to you with any concerns she may have about your leadership style, rather than going to someone else. If she continues to cause dissension by talking about you behind your back, take someone else along and confront her again.

Below are the steps outlined in Matthew 18:15-17:

1. Go directly to the person who has offended you and try to iron out your differences.

2. If she does not listen to you and continues in the offense, take someone else along for a second confrontation.

3. If she continues in the offensive behavior, bring the issue before the leadership team and make a decision as to whether the person needs to be relieved of her duties.

Consider the following from John Maxwell's book, *Developing the Leaders Around You:*

- ∾ Separate the person from the wrong action. Address the harmful action and confront it, not the person.

- ∾ Confront only what the person can change. If we ask a person to change something she can't, she will become frustrated and it will strain your relationship.

- ∾ Give the person the benefit of the doubt. Always try to start with the assumption that a person's motives were right.

- ∾ Be specific. The person being confronted can only address and change what is specifically identified. If you can't identify specifics, there may be further misunderstanding.

- ∾ Avoid sarcasm because it indicates anger with people, not their actions.

- ∾ Avoid saying things like "You always" and "I never."

- ∾ Affirm her as a person and a friend. Prepare to confront in the same way you fix a sandwich. Put the confrontation in the middle, between affirmation and encouragement.[1]

When Conflict Is Due to Sinful Lifestyle

Let's say that you have a wonderful team of ladies working with you in women's ministry. Betsy is one of those women. She's a talented woman who has the gifts and abilities to run a major corporation, and yet she has chosen to give her time to the women's ministry of your church. There's just this one little problem—you have just discovered that Betsy has moved in with her boyfriend. What do you do?

Because of the nature of our society and the continuing decay of our moral fiber, I fear scenarios, like the one with Betsy, will become all too frequent in our churches today. How do we handle such situations? Do we turn a blind eye? Do we simply say "We're all sinners?" Or do we lovingly confront? Let's go back and look at a couple of biblical examples of people in similar situations.

We are all familiar with the account of Joshua and his men taking the city of Jericho as they moved into the Promised Land. When the walls fell with a shout, and the army moved in, Joshua commanded the men not to take any of the "devoted things" for themselves, but to destroy everything in the camp except for the silver and gold that was to be given in the Lord's treasury. However, one man, Achan, disobeyed God's command and hid some of the spoils for himself. Some days later, the Israelites went into battle once again, but this time the Lord did not bless their efforts and they were routed.

Joshua was devastated at their defeat and cried out to the Lord. God answered Joshua and told him that the reason He had removed His hand from them was because of one man's sin. The next day Joshua confronted the people and discovered Achan's sin. Once they dealt with Achan and his sin, then God's favor was once again on the people of Israel (Joshua 6–7).

Some parts of this story may seem harsh, but the point remains—one person's sin can affect an entire group. While Betsy may be a wonderful worker, her sin will affect the effectiveness of the entire ministry.

Remember Jonah? Again, one man's sin of running from God affected an entire crew. Jonah's shipmates just about lost their lives because of Jonah's disobedience to God (Jonah 1). And when Moses' sister, Miriam, gossiped and spread rumors about her brother Moses, the progress of the entire nation was halted for seven days while she recovered from God-inflicted leprosy (Numbers 12).

Because of the nature of this type of confrontation, I suggest two people rather than one person meeting with Betsy. This keeps everyone accountable and makes sure that if anything is repeated or recounted later, the facts will be correct.

In a situation such as this, the women's ministry leadership has a wonderful opportunity to mentor and help a woman understand biblical principles more clearly. It is not a time to condemn. It is a time to lovingly correct.

When the church leaders brought a woman caught in the act of adultery before Jesus, He did not condemn her. He forgave her and then told her, "Go now and leave your life of sin" (John 8:11). We should confront Betsy with her sin, and then give her the opportunity to remedy the situation. If she refuses, then we ask her to step down from leadership. It is difficult, but the results of turning a blind eye can be devastating.

A Constructive Strategy for Conflict Resolution

Judy Huckaby has dealt with more conflict than I care to imagine. She is a licensed professional counselor and serves as a counseling advisor for a 3000-member church in North Carolina. Below is a pattern Judy uses when resolving conflict and one we can use as well.

Judy Huckaby

1. Begin by acknowledging the conflict or disagreement that exists between those involved, and commit to each other to seek understanding and resolution.

2. Read Proverbs 18:13, "He who gives an answer before he hears, it is folly and shame to him" (NASB). There are certainly other Scriptures (Ephesians 4:25-29; James 1:19-20; 3:1-12) that can be used to remind of godly perspectives. Then pray

together; consciously acknowledge the need for God's help to genuinely seek understanding.

3. Invite the other person to tell you her perspective. Give her full opportunity to express herself. Work at disciplining your mind to listen well, trying to grasp both the content and the emotions. At the end, ask clarifying questions. Some examples are:

> ∞ "Help me understand what you mean by
> _____."

> ∞ "I'm not sure I understand what you were saying when you said something about _____."

> ∞ "Tell me what _____ would look like to you."

> ∞ "Clarify for me how you see _____."

> ∞ "What is the bottom line of what you would want me to understand and see?"

Then you tell your perspective.

4. Express to each other your new understanding of the other's perspective. At this point, you are only attempting to see as they see, not refute anything. Then ask the other to make any clarifying corrections. You might say something like, "After hearing me tell you my understanding of your perspective, do you think anything needs your further clarification?"

5. At this point, give your feedback to each other about the other's perspective and discuss.

> ∞ I agree with you about...

> ∞ I think you have some inaccurate information about...

> ∞ I disagree with you about...

> ∞ I am (hurt, angry, offended) about...

> ∞ I am (encouraged, hopeful) about...

6. Discuss constructive steps for moving forward.

ᦉ Can anything be resolved?

ᦉ Is there a need to confess offenses and ask for forgiveness? Extend forgiveness?

ᦉ Are there any action steps that could be taken?

ᦉ Can you agree on any outcome of good progress?

7. Close by praying for one another.

An effective women's ministry will experience growing pains that require women to work through differing perspectives, preferences, and convictions. These challenges have the potential to make the team stronger, if individuals go through them in a constructive manner. Ultimately, our minds, hearts, and strategies need to be aligned by the gospel. Paul's words to the Ephesians serves as excellent counsel for conflict resolution:

Therefore I, the prisoner of the Lord, implore you to walk in a manner worthy of the calling with which you have been called, with all humility and gentleness, with patience, showing tolerance for one another in love, being diligent to preserve the unity of the Spirit...just as also you were called in one hope of your calling; one Lord, one faith, one baptism, one God and Father of all who is over all and through all and in all (Ephesians 4:1-6 NASB).

Finishing Well

As we come to the end of our building project, I'd like to take us back to where we started. We began by looking at Nehemiah's reconstruction of the walls of Jerusalem—he began with prayer, continued with prayer, and ended with prayer. In between he presented his plan to the correct authorities, surveyed what needed to be done, collected his supplies, rallied the volunteers, and kept the workers motivated. When the project was complete, he celebrated!

The book of Nehemiah is 13 chapters long, and the project was complete at the beginning of the seventh chapter. So what did Nehemiah write about for the next seven chapters? For the most part, he wrote about how the people celebrated. He called all the "committees and volunteers" together, built a platform to honor the "team leaders," led a worship service, and hosted a big banquet! "Go and enjoy choice food and sweet drinks, and send some to those who have nothing prepared. This day is sacred to our Lord. Do not grieve, for the joy of the LORD is your strength" (Nehemiah 8:10). Nehemiah also recognized each family that had participated in the building project, prayed a blessing over them, and sprinkled in reminders to remember all that God had done.

What a wonderful example for us to follow as we consider how to finish well.

What do I mean by finish? Is the work of women's ministry *ever* complete? Yes and no. When Jesus issued the Great Commission, He didn't put a time frame on it. So that's the no part. But for everything there is a season and a purpose under heaven (Ecclesiastes 3:1).

Someone once asked Michelangelo, "When is a painting finished?" He replied, "When it fulfills the intent of the artist."[1] When is it time for a program to end? When it fulfills the intent of God.

As we implement various programs with specific purposes in the context of women's ministry, there will come a time when the purpose is complete—when the program has served its purpose. We've all seen how the initiation of a program has caused great excitement and synergism. Then after several years, the enthusiasm begins to wane. There could be several reasons for the decline: lack of leadership, loss of the vision, laissez-faire attitude toward prayer, etc. But it could be simply that it is time to end. If that is the case, it is much healthier for the life of the church to stop and celebrate than to let the program dwindle down to a few who are "going down with the ship."

Celebration is very much a part of ministry. Jesus' last days on earth before His death and resurrection were spent in celebration. He rode into town on a donkey with the crowd waving palm branches and chanting, "Hosanna, Hosanna" (Matthew 21:9). He prepared a meal for His beloved disciples and honored them by washing their feet and praying a blessing over them. After His resurrection, He was with them once again, and even left them with an amazing parting gift—the Holy Spirit.

So how do we finish well? We celebrate.

Let's say that you have been having women's ministry dinners for five years. The attendance has been consistently high the whole time. But then during the sixth year you notice a trend that the attendance begins to drop off. After a while, the focus of the planning sessions turns to how to boost attendance rather than how to minister effectively. By the end of the year, the enthusiasm for the event is at an all-time low. At this point, you have several choices. You can continue on in hopes that the attendance will pick up, you can stop and evaluate to see if you need to adjust because the needs of the women have changed, or you can accept that the purpose of the dinners has been completed and it is time to stop.

If you decide it is time to discontinue a program, let me encourage you to finish well by celebrating rather than discontinuing the program with a sense of sadness.

- ∞ Send out an invitation to all the women who have participated in the planning and orchestration of the program or event.

- ∞ Host a luncheon or dinner for the team.

- ∞ Recount the past successes: how many women came to Christ, how many began attending Bible studies, how many became leaders in the church, etc.

- ∞ Have someone give a testimony about how their life was impacted through the program or event.

- ∞ Honor and thank specific women for their contributions.

- ∞ Pray a blessing over the team members.

- ∞ Give them a gift of appreciation.

Think about the impact of celebration! Those who are celebrated, rather than leaving with a sense of sadness and disappointment, leave with a sense of accomplishment and joy. Most likely, these same women will be enthused about serving again.

48

Getting Started

One day during the Civil War, General Stonewall Jackson's Confederate troops found their progress blocked by a small river. Jackson ordered his engineers to design and build a bridge, explaining to his wagon master that it was imperative that the wagon train cross the river as soon as possible.

Several men were soon enlisted to gather logs, rocks, fence rails, and whatever else might be fashioned into a makeshift bridge. Shortly before dusk, the wagon master proudly reported that the wagons and artillery had crossed the river. Jackson expressed his appreciation and asked where the engineers might be found. The engineers, the wagon master replied, were still in their tent—drawing up plans for a bridge.[1]

You may not feel that you have every team member in place functioning in their exact areas of giftedness, every jot and tittle on the yearly proposed budget calculated, or each team member scoring high in leadership skills and abilities. You may feel that you aren't quite ready to take the leap and begin. But I encourage you. Just begin!

Let me close with a story from my book *Dreams of a Woman: God's Plans for Fulfilling Your Dreams:*

I was sitting on the balcony of a condominium at the beach listening to the excited squeals and splashes as children played in the water. One particular little girl caught my attention. She appeared to be about six years old and wore bright yellow water wings wrapped around her arms like blood pressure cuffs. As she stood on the side of the pool nervously flapping her arms, her daddy was poised in waist-deep water with his arms outstretched.

"Come on, honey, you can do it," he coached. "Go ahead and jump. I'm right here."

"But I'm scared," she whined and flapped.

"Don't be afraid. I'm right here," he assured her.

This bantering went on for at least fifteen minutes. I was amazed at the father's patience. Finally, she jumped! By the end of the morning, the little girl was making her way across the once seemingly treacherous waters.

God spoke to my heart through this scenario. Sometimes I'm that little girl standing on the side of the pool.

"Come on and jump in," my heavenly Father calls.

"But I'm scared," I cry.

"Don't be afraid, My child. I'm right here."

So I've learned, like Peter, to jump in with both feet, but never let go of His hand.[2]

Let me encourage you to take the leap and jump into women's ministry. Women need you. God will empower you. I will cheer for you. "Things which eye has not seen and ear has not heard, and which have not entered the heart of man, all that God has prepared for those who love Him" (1 Corinthians 2:9 NASB).

$\mathcal{A}$ppendix
Resources

Leadership

- ❧ *Leading Women to the Heart of God* by Lysa TerKeurst
- ❧ *Leading Life-Changing Small Groups* by Bill Donahue
- ❧ *The Volunteer Revolution* by Bill Hybels
- ❧ *Courageous Leadership* by Bill Hybels
- ❧ *Spiritual Leadership* by Henry and Richard Blackaby

Balance

- ❧ *A Woman's Secret to a Balanced Life* by Sharon Jaynes and Lysa TerKeurst
- ❧ *Margin: Restoring Emotional, Physical, Financial, and Time Reserves to Overloaded Lives* by Richard A. Swenson, M.D.
- ❧ *Boundaries* by Dr. Henry Cloud and Dr. John Townsend
- ❧ *Living Life on Purpose* by Lysa TerKeurst

Bible Studies by Sharon Jaynes

- ❧ *Becoming a Woman Who Listens to God*
- ❧ *Dreams of a Woman: God's Plans for Fulfilling Your Dreams*
- ❧ *Being a Great Mom, Raising Great Kids*
- ❧ *Becoming the Woman of His Dreams* (marriage)

- *Ultimate Makeover: Becoming Spiritually Beautiful in Christ*
- *A Woman's Secret to a Balanced Life*

Mentoring

- *Woman to Woman Mentoring: How to Start, Grow, and Maintain a Mentoring Ministry* by Janet Thompson
- *Apples of Gold: A Six-Week Nurturing Program for Women* by Betty Huizenga
- *Finding a Mentor, Being a Mentor* by Donna Otto
- *Women Mentoring Women: Ways to Start, Maintain, and Expand a Biblical Women's Ministry* by Vickie Kraft and Gwynne Johnson
- *A Garden Path to Mentoring: Planting Your Life in Another and Releasing the Fragrance of Christ* by Esther Burroughs
- *Spiritual Mothering: A Titus 2 Model for Women Mentoring Women* by Susan Hunt

Women in the Workplace

- *How to Thrive from 9 to 5* by Mary Welchel
- *The Snooze-Alarm Syndrome* by Mary Welchel
- Priority Associates: Reaching Young Professionals— Developing Leaders from the Inside Out
  797 North Orange Avenue
  Orlando, Florida 32801
  407-843-3294
  www.priorityassociates.org
  www.workplaceministrytraining.com
- Holiday Brochure Set for sharing faith in the workplace during 20 holiday seasons. Available through Priority Associates.
- www.christianworkingwoman.org

Personalities

- ❧ *Personality Plus* by Florence Littauer and Marita Littauer

- ❧ *Getting Along with Almost Anybody* by Florence Littauer and Marita Littauer

- ❧ *Your Spiritual Personality* by Marita Littauer

- ❧ Personality Profiles can be ordered from CLASS, PO Box 66810, Albuquerque, NM 87193. Call 800-433-6633 or visit www.classervices.com.

Spiritual Gifts

- ❧ *19 Gifts of the Spirit: Which Do You Have? Are You Using Them?* by Leslie Flynn

- ❧ *Your Spiritual Gifts Can Help Your Church Grow* by Charles Peter Wagner.

Icebreaker Ideas

- ❧ *Good Things Come in Small Groups* by Steve Barker and Ron Nichols

- ❧ *201 Great Questions* by Jerry Jones

Retreats

- ❧ *Women's Retreats: A Creative Planning Guide* by Sue Edwards, Kelley Mathews, and Linda Robinson

Speakers and Writers Conferences

- ❧ She Speaks
  www.proverbs31.org
  877-731-4663

- ❧ CLASS
  P. O. Box 66810
  Albuquerque, NM 87193

800-433-6633
info@classervices.com
www.classervices.com

co Speak UP with Confidence
www.speakupspeakerservices.com

Speakers Bureaus (to obtain speakers)

co Proverbs 31 Ministries, Inc.
www.proverbs31.org
877-731-4663

co CLASS (Christian Leaders, Authors and Speakers Services)
www.classervices.com
800-433-6633

co Milk 'n' Honey Speakers Services
888-547-2879

Infertility

co **The Hannah's Heart Network:** A nonprofit organization under the National Heritage Foundations established to serve women and churches. They are available to assist in organizing infertility ministries throughout the world. For more information about The Hannah's Heart Network, visit www.hannahsheartnetwork.org.

Newcomers Ministry

co **N.E.W. Ministries:** N.E.W. Ministries is committed to the spiritual and emotional well-being of women who are going through the transition and adjustment of moving. Visit www.justmoved.org.

Notes

Chapter 1—Why Do We Need Women's Ministry?

1. Adapted from Charles R. Swindoll, *Come Before Winter and Share My Hope* (Grand Rapids, MI: Zondervan Publishing House, 1985), pp. 224-26. This rendition appeared in *Insights* newsletter, vol. 8, no. 11, November 1998.

2. Miriam Neff and Debra Klingsporn, *Shattering Our Assumptions* (Minneapolis, MN: Bethany House, 1996), pp. 194-95.

3. Elizabeth Baker, *How to Hang Loose in an Uptight World* (Gretna, LA: Pelican, 2002), p. 17.

4. Ibid., p. 101.

5. Charles R. Swindoll, *Encourage Me* (Grand Rapids, MI: Zondervan Publishing House, 1982), pp. 18-19.

6. Bill Hybels, *Courageous Leadership* (Grand Rapids, MI: Zondervan Publishing House, 2002), p. 23.

Chapter 2—What Is the Purpose of Women's Ministry?

1. Adapted from Sharon Jaynes, *Being a Great Mom, Raising Great Kids* (Chicago, IL: Moody Publishers, 2000), p. 73. Used by permission.

2. Excerpt from a letter written by John Sittema. Used by permission.

3. Swindoll, *Encourage Me,* p. 90.

Chapter 4—Mission Statement: Defining Your Purpose

1. Hybels, *Courageous Leadership,* p. 48.

Chapter 5—Program Options: Devising Your Plan

1. U.S. Department of Health and Human Services [www.cnn.com/SPECIALS/2001/working.moms/stories/mainstory.html].

2. Ibid.

Chapter 8—Proposal Presentation: Obtaining Approval from Church Leadership

1. Lysa TerKeurst, *Leading Women to the Heart of God* (Chicago, IL: Moody Publishing, 2002), p. 102.

2. Ibid., pp. 104-05.

3. James Dobson, *Solid Answers* (Wheaton, IL: Tyndale House Publishers, 1997), p. 398.

4. Bill and Pam Farrel, *Men Are Like Waffles—Women Are Like Spaghetti* (Eugene, OR: Harvest House Publishers, 2001), p. 13.

Part Three—Leadership Development

1. Warren Bennis and Burt Nanus, *Leaders: Strategies for Taking Charge* (New York, NY: HarperCollins, 1997), p. 4.

2. Henry Blackaby and Richard Blackaby, *Spiritual Leadership* (Nashville, TN: Broadman and Holman Publishers, 2001), p. 20.

Chapter 10—Spiritual Gifts: Utilizing God-Given Abilities

1. Charles R. Swindoll, *The Tale of the Tardy Oxcart* (Nashville, TN: Word Publishing, 1998), p. 1.

2. This material is published by Purpose Driven® Publishing. Used by permission. You can find more information about the resources available from Rick Warren from [www.purposedriven.com].

3. Leslie B. Flynn, "Nineteen Gifts of the Spirit" as quoted in James S. Hewett, general editor, *Illustrations Unlimited* (Wheaton, IL: Tyndale House Publishers, 1988), p. 231.

Chapter 11—The Call to Leadership: Developing the Team

1. Hybels, *Courageous Leadership*, p. 81.

2. Ibid., p. 85.

Chapter 13—Team Building: Unifying the Members

1. J. David Branon, "Sharing the Load," *Our Daily Bread*, June 1992, no. 3.

Chapter 14—Leadership Training: Equipping the Team

1. Charles R. Swindoll, *Leadership* (Waco, TX: Word Books, 1985), pp. 19-20.

2. Hybels, *Courageous Leadership*, p. 132.

Chapter 15—Leadership Support: Encouraging the Team

1. Zig Ziglar, *Raising Positive Kids in a Negative World* (New York, NY: Ballantine, 1989), p. 54.

2. Blackaby, *Spiritual Leadership*, pp. 138-39.

Chapter 16—Leadership Retreats: Deepening Relationships

1. Henry Blackaby and Richard Blackaby, *Experiencing God Day-by-Day* (Nashville, TN: Broadman and Holman Publishers, 1997), p. 276.

Chapter 17—A Leader's Personal Faith Walk: Growing in Intimacy with God

1. Dietrich Bonhoeffer, *Life Together* (San Francisco, CA: Harper and Row Publishers, Inc., 1954).

Chapter 18—Fabulous Facilitators

1. As quoted in Oletta Wald, *The Joys of Discovery* (Minneapolis, MN: Augsburg Publishing House, 1975), p. 8.

2. Charles R. Swindoll, *The Grace Awakening* (Dallas, TX: Word, 1990), pp. 5-6.

Chapter 19—The Power of a Question

1. Adapted from Jaynes, *Being a Great Mom, Raising Great Kids,* p. 52.

2. Deena Davis, *Discipleship Journal's 101 Best Small-Group Ideas* (Colorado Springs, CO: NavPress, 1996), p. 22.

3. Robert C. Crosby, *Now We're Talking!* (Colorado Spring, CO: Focus on the Family, 1996), p. xiii.

Chapter 20—The Art of Listening

1. Mark Price, "Get a Life," *Charlotte Observer,* November 1, 1998.

2. Dennis Rainey, *Staying Close* (Dallas, TX: Word, 1989), p. 216.

Chapter 21—Personality Puzzle

1. The Personality Profile and concepts on Personalities used in this chapter were developed by Fred and Florence Littauer and are used by permission. CLASServices, Inc. may be contacted at P.O. Box 66810, Albuquerque, NM 87193, 505-899-4283, and at [www.classervices.com].

Chapter 24—Creative Ways to Lead Prayer

1. Adapted from Evelyn Christenson, *What Happens When Women Pray* (Colorado Springs, CO: Victor Books, 1991), pp. 50-62.

Chapter 28—Retreats and Getaways

1. Sue Edwards, Kelley Mathews, Linda Robinson, *Women's Retreats: A Creative Planning Guide* (Grand Rapids, MI: Kregel Publications, 2004), p. 15.

2. Adapted from Edwards, et al., *Women's Retreats,* pp. 17-20.

Chapter 30—Mentoring

1. Win Couchman, "Cross-Generational Relationships," speaking at Women for Christ conference, 1983.

2. Susan Hunt, *Spiritual Mothering* (Franklin, TN: Legacy Communications, 1992), p. 67.

3. Ibid., p.12.

4. Janet Thompson, *Woman to Woman Mentoring* (Nashville, TN: Lifeway Press, 2000), p. 231.

5. Ibid., p. 15.

6. Ibid., p. 46.

7. Ibid., p. 106.

8. Ibid., p. 15.

Chapter 32—Gathering Volunteers

1. Bill Hybels, *The Volunteer Revolution* (Grand Rapids, MI: Zondervan Publishing House, 2004), pp. 74-75.

2. Ibid., p. 25.

3. Ibid., p. 56.

4. Ibid., p. 34.

5. Ibid., p. 36.

6. Charles Willis, "Volunteer Enlistment Critical to Meet Ministry Needs," *Indiana Baptist,* August 30, 1994, p. 6.

Chapter 33—Viva la Difference

1. Gary McIntosh, *Three Generations: Riding the Waves of Change in Your Church* (Grand Rapids, MI: Fleming H. Revell, 1995).

2. Ibid., pp. 19-21.

Chapter 36—Christmas Events

1. Sharon Jaynes, *Celebrating a Christ-Centered Christmas* (Chicago, IL: Moody Publishers, 2001).

Chapter 37—Lifestyle Evangelism

1. Bill Hybels and Mark Mittelberg, *Becoming a Contagious Christian* (Grand Rapids, MI: Zondervan Publishing House, 1994).

2. Oswald Chambers, *My Utmost for His Highest* (Grand Rapids, MI: Discovery House, 1992), October 25.

Chapter 39—Burnout

1. Daniel A. Girdano, Dorothy E. Dusek, and George S. Everly Jr., *Controlling Stress and Tension* (Boston, MA: Allyn & Bacon, 1996). Adapted from "Burnout," an article posted by the Texas Medical Association at [www.texmed.org/cme/phn/psb/burnout.asp].

2. Ibid.

3. First published by Texas Medical Association 2001. Reprinted with permission [www.texmed.org/cme/phn/psb/exercise.asp].

4. Blackaby, *Spiritual Leadership,* pp. 202-03.

Chapter 40—Balance

1. Rick Warren, *The Purpose-Driven Life* (Grand Rapids, MI: Zondervan Publishing House, 2002), p. 32.

Chapter 41—Confidence

1. Gustav Neibuhr and Laurie Goodstein, "Who Will Be the Next Billy Graham?" *Charlotte Observer,* January 2, 1999, section A, p. 15.

2. Bruce Wilkinson, *Prayer of Jabez Devotional* (Sisters, OR: Multnomah, 2001), pp. 62-63.

3. [www.exchangedlife.com/humor/moral/schultz_philosophy.shtml].

Chapter 42—Criticism

1. Theodore Roosevelt, "Citizenship in a Republic," from a speech given at the Sorbonne, Paris, April 23, 1910.

Chapter 46—Dealing with Conflict

1. John Maxwell, *Developing the Leaders Around You* (Nashville, TN: Thomas Nelson Publishers, 1995), pp. 126-27.

Chapter 47—Finishing Well

1. Nell W. Mohney, *From Eve to Esther* (Nashville, TN: Dimensions for Living, 2001), p. 43.

Chapter 48—Getting Started

1. [www.bible.org/illus.asp?topic-id=1701].

2. Sharon Jaynes, *Dreams of a Woman: God's Plan for Fulfilling Your Dreams* (Wheaton, IL: Tyndale House Publishers, Inc, 2004), p. 240.

Acknowledgments

Just as one person cannot build a house alone, I could not have constructed this book without the help of a dedicated crew.

Mary Ann Ruff: Thank you for sharing your vast wisdom gleaned from years of working in women's ministry. The lives you have touched and the women you have impacted will echo through generations to come.

Van Walton: Thank you, my sanguine friend, for helping us to understand how God has given each of us unique personalities for specific purposes.

Glynnis Whitwer: Thank you for all the years you have dedicated to women's ministry, not only through the local church, but also as editor of the *P31 Woman* magazine.

Dan Southerland: Thank you for your wise counsel through Church Transitions, Inc. and for sharing your wife, Mary, with us here at Proverbs 31 Ministries.

Mary Reitano: Thank you for your heart for the woman in the workplace and for helping us to see the vast mission field right in our own backyards.

Amanda Bailey: Thank you for establishing The Hannah's Heart Network and for your passion to comfort women experiencing the pain of empty arms.

Cheri Jimenez: Thank you for sharing your creative ideas on ways to reach out to the community through Creative Connections and Mentoring. The lives you have touched will in turn continue to touch others for years to come.

Judy Huckaby: Thank you for helping us learn how to live and love as children of the King in community with one another.

Genia Rogers: Thank you for being a living example of lifestyle evangelism and challenging us to live a lifestyle of ministry.

This book would not be possible without the support of the staff and volunteers of Proverbs 31 Ministries: Lysa TerKeurst, Lara Guretzky, Mary Southerland, LeAnn Rice, Marie Ogram, Barb Spenser, Renee Swope, Glynnis Whitwer, Jill Tracey, and Bonnie Schulte.

Also, a special thanks to the team at Harvest House: Carolyn McCready, LaRae Weikert, Terry Glaspey, Kim Moore, Betty Fletcher, Teresa Evenson, and Barb Sherrill.

And to the man who has learned more about building an effective women's ministry than he ever thought possible…my precious husband, Steve. Thank you for editing and reediting every page.

"Unless the LORD builds the house, its builders labor in vain" (Psalm 127:1). Most of all, I thank God for giving me creative ideas and solid solutions. I am honored and amazed that He has given me the privilege to minister to His most fabulous creation—women.

How to Contact
the Author

Sharon Jaynes is vice president of Proverbs 31 Ministries Radio and cohost for their international daily radio program. She is the author of several books, including *Ultimate Makeover: Becoming Spiritually Beautiful in Christ; Being a Great Mom, Raising Great Kids; Dreams of a Woman; Becoming a Woman Who Listens to God;* and *Becoming the Woman of His Dreams.* Sharon is also a popular speaker at women's events from coast to coast and lives in North Carolina with her husband, Steve, and son, Steven.

To learn more about Proverbs 31 Ministries or information on having Sharon speak at your event, visit www.sharonjaynes.com or contact Proverbs 31 Ministries at 877-731-4663.